CUSTER'S FALL

Also by David Humphreys Miller

GHOST DANCE
BB 943

CUSTER'S FALL

The Indian Side of the Story

DAVID HUMPHREYS MILLER

Illustrated by the author

UNIVERSITY OF NEBRASKA PRESS
LINCOLN AND LONDON

First Bison Book printing: 1985
Most recent printing indicated by the first digit below:
      4   5   6   7   8   9   10

Library of Congress Cataloging in Publication Data
Miller, David Humphreys.
  Custer's Fall.
  "Bison books."
  Reprint. Originally published: New York, Duell,
Sloan and Pearce, 1957.
  1. Little Big Horn, Battle of the, 1876. I. Title.
E83.876.M6 1985   973.8'2   85-5874
ISBN 0-8032-3098-2 (cloth)
ISBN 0-8032-8129-3 (paper)

The map on page 40 is reproduced from *Custer Battlefield National Monument—Montana,* by Edward S. and Evelyn S. Luce, published by the National Park Service.

Reprinted by arrangement with E. P. Dutton, Inc.

Second cloth printing: 1986

This book is for Jan—

Wica-cante-yuha-winyan—

Captures-Everybody's-Heart-Woman

Preface

THIS BOOK is about a day and a battle and the people who fought in it. Most of the combatants were American Indians and the story of the battle from their viewpoint has never before been told. That is the purpose of this book.

It is a true story—completely factual from the soldiers' killing of the Indian boy at dawn to the discovery of Captain Keogh's horse, Comanche, in the final chapter. Fiction no longer has a place in the reconstruction of the bloodiest twenty-four hours in the history of the American frontier. Although set down here in English, rather than the native Indian language spoken at the time, the words said by the Indians throughout these pages are direct quotations as remembered and recounted to me by Indian witnesses. No guesswork or poetic license has colored these statements.

No other single event in American history ever captured the public imagination more completely than "Custer's Last Stand." It came to symbolize all the chivalrous grit and determination that went into the winning of the West. Even today, most Americans are familiar with the fact that our Army once went down to devastating defeat at the hands of wild Indians. Beyond that, little is actually known about Custer's debacle by the average citizen.

There have been good reasons for this lack of knowledge. Few facilities existed in 1876 for the accurate reporting of historical events as they occurred. A newspaper reporter accompanied Custer's cavalry, but was killed during the battle. Had he survived and written about the campaign, days—possibly weeks—would have passed before his firsthand account could have reached the public. The fighting took place in what was then rough remote country, the untamed wilderness of south central Montana—a vast region known only a decade earlier as The Great American Desert. No means then existed whereby news could be sent back to civilization other than by mounted courier, under conditions of extreme peril.

In a day and age when impartial news-gathering agencies, such as our modern wire services, were unheard of, current news was invariably slanted or garbled to suit the editorial policies of the newspaper publishers. Such was the bias of the times that, when word of the Custer fight finally appeared in print, the facts were misconstrued to the extent that Custer and his troops had been massacred. To this day, the Battle of the Little Big Horn is known to many as "The Custer Massacre," although it was in no sense a massacre of unarmed noncombatants as the term implies, but a pitched battle between armed antagonists—*after* Custer had attacked the Indians.

Adding private interpretations to early accounts of the battle, the War Department of 1876 did much to confuse the issues and details of Custer's campaign. Today, it is virtually impossible to get a clear, concise reconstruction of the Little Big Horn fight from existing military annals. A handful of present-day writers—most notably Colonel W. A. Graham and Edgar I. Stewart—have done much to clarify the military viewpoint of the battle. However, a great portion of the story has remained shrouded in mystery for

over eighty years. With other sources of information exhausted, only one untapped lead has remained: the Indians
who fought Custer.

As a friend and adopted son of the Sioux and a lifelong
student of Indian ways, I became interested some twenty-two
years ago in learning their version of various battles with
white men. Somehow, the American history textbooks I had
studied in high school and college never seemed to ring true
when it came to the Indian wars. Knowing the Indians intimately, I soon realized their side of the story had been glossed
over or ignored completely by historians. Thus, my mission
became clear: it was up to me to uncover information hitherto
unknown to any white man.

Work began in the summer of 1935. Finding out the truth
about the Battle of the Little Big Horn presented the most
challenging opportunity, for much of it could be told only
by the Sioux and Cheyennes who had taken part in the fight.
No white man had survived to tell of Custer's final hour.

My first interview was with Chief One Bull of the Hunkpapa Sioux, then near ninety years of age. He was a nephew
of Sitting Bull, and had been the Indian leader's bodyguard
and lieutenant during the Little Big Horn fight. We became
good friends and I had many further discussions with One
Bull before his death in 1947. From him I learned much about
early phases of the battle—particularly the Sioux counterattack against Reno, led by One Bull himself. One Bull's
elder brother, Chief White Bull of the Minneconjou Sioux,
was prominent among the warriors fighting Custer. I knew
him quite well and interviewed him often concerning that
phase of the battle.

Of all Indians who participated in the Custer fight my

closest friend was Black Elk, famed Ogalala Sioux medicine man, who adopted me as his son in 1939. Associated with me in producing Indian pageants and ceremonials, he often talked to me by the hour about that far-off day in 1876 when the Little Big Horn ran crimson with white men's blood. In later years another survivor, Iron Hail—known to whites as Dewey Beard—also adopted me as a son. He was the very last of the warriors who had fought Custer. I interviewed him on a number of occasions, the last of which was the summer before his death in November, 1955. He was ninety-eight.

In all, I interviewed seventy-one aged Indians who had actually participated in the Battle of the Little Big Horn. Copious notes were made on their statements, and when possible I arranged joint conferences with a number of survivors, who provided reminders and check-points for each other. A breakdown of the Indian informants is as follows: fifty-four were Sioux, sixteen were Cheyennes, one was Arapaho. All were in their eighties or nineties when interviewed. Conversation with them was carried on in their language, as none of them spoke or understood English. This resulted in my learning to talk fluent Sioux and Plains Indian sign language. I sketched or painted life portraits of every one of these old warriors.

The last of Custer's Crow Indian scouts, White-Man-Runs-Him, died shortly before I began my investigation. However, relatives and associates of the scouts provided me with much information concerning Custer's own actions and words the day of the battle. Particularly helpful were Little Nest, a brother-in-law of Crow interpreter Mitch Bouyer, and Pretty Shield, aged widow of scout Goes Ahead.

It should be understood that among the tribes involved a

considerable tradition has grown up around the endless details of the Battle of the Little Big Horn. Although the Indians never set down these facts in writing—since they had no written language until recent years—they have handed them down by word of mouth from generation to generation. If the Custer fight has carried much symbolical significance through the years to the white man, it has meant even more to the Indian. For the Sioux and the Cheyenne, that day on the Little Big Horn was a true milestone—the high-water mark of their entire history. Though doomed to suffer cultural death throes during the Ghost Dance outbreak a scant fourteen years later, the Sioux and their Cheyenne allies were at peak strength the summer of 1876. Never before had they gathered in such numbers. Never before were they more fiercely determined to follow their age-old way of life.

The Custer tragedy had no earth-shaking consequences for the majority of white Americans at the time. Militarily, the engagement was comparatively unimportant. But as an ugly interruption to the gala centennial celebration in Philadelphia, it soon assumed outsize importance. A full-scale military campaign was stepped up against the Sioux and Cheyennes, putting an early end to their wanderings.

After Little Big Horn the tribes dispersed and never again were victorious over the white invader. At last the power of the hoop—the sacred circle of the universe that mythically bound the Sioux Nation and their allies together—was forever broken. While the glory of their victory over Long Hair, as they called Custer, never diminished, the Sioux were finally a vanquished people.

Indians of that day kept no track of time, and one of the difficult problems in writing this book has been the accurate correlation of events according to the time of day they occurred. Many incidents have been pinpointed by relating them to the position of the sun in the sky at some particular moment. Time lapse has also been a complicated factor. My informants agreed, for example, that the action against Custer's command occupied the time it took for the sun to travel the width of the shadow of a tepee pole across the ground. By actual measurement this turned out to be almost exactly twenty minutes.

Although the Indians' own story of the Custer fight is true and complete, it seemed somewhat out of context without the added background of the chapter called "White Man's World." The summer of 1876 was memorable in many ways, perhaps; yet obviously, for both Indian and white man, the Battle of the Little Big Horn finally overshadowed all else.

DAVID HUMPHREYS MILLER

Los Angeles, California

Contents

In Appreciation

This is the Indians' own story. Had they not passed long-remembered facts on to me, this book would never have been possible. For valuable data aside from that provided by Indians who took part in the battle, I am much indebted to Chief Ben American Horse and Chief Howard Bad Bear, both of Pine Ridge Reservation in South Dakota. Last but by no means least I wish to express my unending thanks to my mother and father and my wife, Jan, for their constant faith in a long-term project.

CURLEY'S LOOKOUT

CUSTER BATTLEFIELD

MEDICINE TAIL COULEE

KEOGH'S BTN.

BATTLE RIDGE YATES'

"PRESENT MONUMENT
RETREAT & END OF
CUSTER'S COMMAND (4:15-4:40 PM)

BTN.

I

L

F

C

E

CROW SCOUTS FI
ON VILLAGE

LITTLE BIG HORN RIVER

FORD

LOW RIDGE

SANSARCS

BRULES

CHEYENNES

MINNECONJOUS

HUN

OGALALAS

BLACKFEET

BENCH

1/4   1/2   0   1 MILE

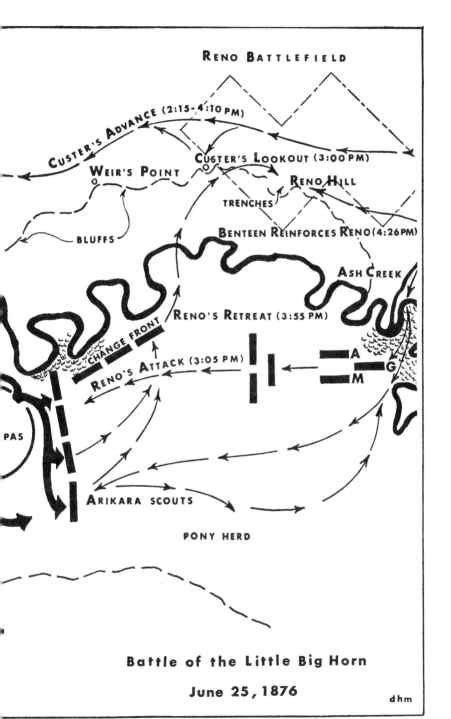

Battle of the Little Big Horn

June 25, 1876

dhm

Sunup

THE DAY broke hot and cloudless as morning sunlight flooded the valley of the Little Big Horn. Scarcely a breeze stirred anywhere. The weather had been dry for some time, and the trails were thick with dust.

With a moccasined toe, Deeds kicked at clumps of buffalo grass near the Lodgepole Trail, scattering grasshoppers in all directions. Then his foot came against something solid. Looking down, he saw a drab square box—a container unlike anything used by his people back in the great camp by the river. Such a rare find called for a closer look. The boy hunkered down beside the box.

Deeds was barely ten years old. His whole life had been spent deep in the Hunkpapa hunting grounds, far from the white men's spreading settlements. Sparked by a growing boy's naïve curiosity, he had not yet learned a warrior's caution.

The box had dropped in such a way that the lid had been loosened, yet needed prying to reveal the contents. From the hide sheath hanging against his slim brown flank Deeds took the old skinning knife with the bone handle and went to work. As he pried at the lid, he glanced around, hoping to catch sight of his older brother. Brown Back was still somewhere up the divide, rounding up their grandfather's ponies.

As soon as Brown Back came along with the herd, Deeds

3

would pick out a favorite mount and help his brother drive the animals down to the camp. Then their grandfather Four Horns would give away the ponies and all the personal belongings of their grandmother.

Deeds still could not believe his grandmother was dead. She had died before dawn that morning, while the drums of the all-night scalp dance still throbbed. It was hard to imagine any camp without his grandmother fleshing hides nearby or carrying in a load of kindling wood or wild turnips, as she had done almost every day as far back as he could remember.

Adding to the mystery of death were the solemn words of Deeds's uncle, Sitting Bull, who spoke to the family as they all gathered around the old woman's deathbed.

"Her passing means a great event is about to take place," Sitting Bull had announced gravely. "Perhaps my vision of our enemies falling into camp may soon be fulfilled!"

The grownups, including the sobbing old Four Horns, had nodded knowingly, while Deeds mutely looked down at all that remained of his grandmother. A little later Brown Back had called him away to help bring in the ponies.

The lid came free at last. Inside the box were crumbling slabs of hardtack bread. The boy brought a flake to his nostrils and sniffed. The aroma was not at all like that of the fry bread made by Sioux women. He bit into it, knowing instinctively he was tasting white man's bread for the first time.

At the sudden clatter of hoofs on the broken trail, Deeds looked up, expecting to see Brown Back riding toward him with the herd. Still munching hardtack, he turned quickly, realizing the hoofbeats came from behind him.

Three white soldiers were riding down on him at a fast gallop, firing their carbines.

4

"He's got the box!" one of them yelled, as shots crashed through the lazy morning stillness.

The boy Deeds munching hardtack as soldiers approached on trail.

Before Deeds could cry out or run away, a trooper's bullet caught him full in the chest and brought him down. Still afoot, Brown Back came running at the crack of gunfire. An Ogalala youth named Drags-the-Rope followed at his heels. His ponies, too, had strayed up the divide during the long night graze. Now he lent a helping hand to his young Hunkpapa cousins. At a glance he saw he was too late.

Deeds lay dead, an ugly wound through his lungs. Without dismounting, the soldiers fired at the older boys as they ran forward. One trooper with stripes on his sleeves seemed to be giving orders to the other two. Dodging the deadly carbine fire, Drags-the-Rope found temporary cover and drew on his training as a warrior's apprentice for a fast decision. Snaking through the grass to where Brown Back crouched cowering

5

and uncertain, he told the Hunkpapa boy to make a run for the village and spread the alarm.

"I'll hold off the soldiers until you get away!" Drags-the-Rope shouted.

And Brown Back leaped and dodged down the slope like a prongbuck. Once the boy was safely away, Drags-the-Rope pulled at his long nose and grinned. A little victory yell started deep in his throat. His thought now was to recover Deeds's body—if he could. But with the soldiers reloading and firing continuously, there was no chance of reaching the dead boy.

Drags-the-Rope waited until Brown Back was safely out of range, then sprang to his feet and ran a fast zigzag course downhill. If he could reach the distant clump of box elders that marked the head of Medicine Tail Coulee off to the northwest, he could follow the dry wash down to the river and cross directly over into camp. Later, he might guide a small war party back and show them where to find Deeds's body.

Ready for anything, he expected at every step to hear the thunder of hoofs behind him. An old Sioux war cry kept echoing in his mind: "This is a good day to die!"

But the blue-clad soldiers did not ride him down. And he felt no impact of bullet against his flesh as he ran. Once he was out of range, they stopped firing. He glanced over his shoulder to see all three of them riding on down the Lodgepole Trail, the old Indian route across the Wolf Mountain divide from Rosebud Creek to the Greasy Grass—as the Sioux called the Little Big Horn. If they kept going, they would run head-on into the south end of the great village—the end where the Hunkpapas were camped. Sensing that more soldiers lurked up on the divide, Drags-the-Rope somehow knew at

6

that moment that these troopers had just fired the first shots of what was destined to be a great battle for Indian and white man alike.

From the Crow's Nest, a rocky promontory high in the Wolf Mountain divide, an unseen enemy stealthily watched the retreat of the two young Sioux.

The Wolf or Little Chetish Mountains, lying between the valleys of the Rosebud and Little Big Horn Rivers in southeast Montana, are not properly mountains but rough broken country gullied and cut by the erosion of wind and water and time. From precipitous hills and deep narrow gulches in the divide, the Little Big Horn follows a tortuous course northwest across undulating prairie to the Big Horn River, some forty miles away. A rapid stream twenty to forty yards wide, the Little Big Horn has a pebbled bottom, but soft abrupt banks. Depending on the width of the channel, the water at normal stages is from two to five feet deep, shallower at several natural fords. Rolling grassland gives way here and there to scattered groves of cottonwood and box elder. Like the wide sky above it, the valley is broad and open.

An old tribal lookout afforded three Crow Indian scouts a sweeping view of the entire Little Big Horn basin. Members of a tribe numerically weak, several Crows had teamed up with the white soldier-chief, Custer, to deliver what they hoped might be a mortal blow to their hated foe, the Sioux. The sun was just up when Hairy Moccasin, lean and wiry and sharp-eyed, first sighted the pall of smoke that hung above the great enemy camp twelve or fifteen miles away. Then Goes Ahead, handsome with his hawk nose and high pompadour, spotted the Sioux pony herds grazing on hills south of the big village. At this distance the milling horses looked like tiny maggots crawling on a fresh-killed buffalo robe pegged out for scraping. Finally, White-Man-Runs-Him, oldest and tallest of the three, suggested that Son-of-the-Morning-Star—as the Crows called Custer—should see the enemy camp for himself.

"More Sioux are in that village than all of Son-of-the-Morning-Star's soldiers have bullets!" he said, getting up from where the three Crows had crouched through the dawn hours, and moving down into the pocket of ground where the other scouts dozed.

Lieutenant Varnum, Custer's Chief of Scouts, had been napping fitfully for forty-five minutes. He came awake instantly at White-Man-Runs-Him's touch. With his prominent nose and bristling mustache, Varnum looked more than ever like a sleepy old bear. After the Crow had told him in signs that the Sioux camp had been sighted, the Chief of Scouts indicated that he should rouse the other scouts. White-Man-Runs-Him first awakened the other three Crows, then the Arikaras.*

As the Arikaras awoke, they stood up and started to sing in unison one of their war songs. White-Man-Runs-Him signed to them all to keep silent. These Arikaras were brave enough, he decided, except when it came to fighting the Sioux. Then they went to pieces, making a lot of unnecessary noise just to keep up their courage. Compared to other Plains tribes they seemed small and wiry and dark-skinned. They were dirty and careless in their personal habits, and White-Man-Runs-Him failed to understand why Custer had nearly

* Also called Arikarees or Rees.

8

forty of them guiding him west from Dakota Territory when he could have used Crows entirely. Even Custer's favorite scout was the Arikara Bloody Knife, who was half Sioux and had a great weakness for the bottle, like other Indians who associated freely with white men.

An older Arikara named Crooked Horn came up with his nephew, Red Star. Talking in sign, White-Man-Runs-Him told them the Sioux camp had been sighted. The tall Crow smiled wryly to see them hurry off, leading the other Arikaras to high ground from which they could look for signs of the enemy. Once the routine scouting was done, the Arikaras were quick to take advantage and gain the credit. Even now Lieutenant Varnum was ordering Crooked Horn to have someone ready to ride the ten miles or so back up the trail to where Custer and his horse soldiers waited. Naturally an Arikara would be picked to go.

Crooked Horn squinted out across the valley.

"Look sharp, my boy," he told Red Star. "You have better eyes than I."

Red Star gazed for quite a while until he saw a light blur that could be smoke rising above the village. The tepees were hidden by an intervening ridge, but smoke was drawing out and up. Beyond the blur Red Star saw some dark specks he thought were ponies.

The famous white scout "Lonesome Charley" Reynolds— called Lucky Man by the Indians—joined them presently and looked in the direction of the camp a long time. He took field glasses from a scarred leather case hung around his neck and looked again. Finally he put the glasses down and nodded silently. Reynolds seldom spoke to anybody, then only a word or so at a time. It was because of a woman, the

9

other white scouts said, a Mexican woman far to the south in the Spanish town of Sante Fe. But nobody knew much more than that. Reynolds took out a notebook and scribbled something on a page. Then he tore out the page and folded it and handed it to Crooked Horn, who in turn passed it on to Red Star.

"Saddle up your pony, boy," Crooked Horn ordered, then singled out another Arikara youth. "Bull, saddle your pony, too. Both of you will take the talking paper to Long Hair Custer."

They started off downhill, Red Star carrying the note and feeling his special importance. He paid little attention to Bull, who was poorly mounted on a runty little horse and had trouble keeping up. Red Star rode at a steady lope, glancing back only occasionally to make sure Bull was following.

Riding up out of a hollow high in the divide a while later, Red Star was hailed by blue-clad sentries guarding the soldiers' breakfast fires. He quickly gave the low owl-hoot signal—although the Sioux and Cheyennes also used the same call. Then he began turning his horse zigzag, back and forth, as a sign he had sighted the enemy. Finally he got down and tied up his pony's tail in a knot, according to the Arikara custom of preparing for battle. Recognizing him as a scout, the sentries let him through.

Bob-tailed Bull, Bloody Knife, and Stabbed—the Arikara leaders—were gathered around a pot of coffee with Long Hair Custer and Girard, the white man who had raised chickens for officers' wives at the fort back in Dakota Territory but now acted as interpreter for the Arikaras. Stabbed got up and came over to Red Star.

10

"My son," he said, "this is no small thing you have done."

It was a great honor, among the Arikaras at least, to have carried such an important message. Stabbed called out to the whole column, "Why do you all sleep? Red Star has come back!"

It was poetic license; no one slept, nor had anyone more than napped briefly the whole long night. Bob-tailed Bull, his gaudy uniform with the gold epaulets still resplendent though soiled and dusty, stood up, and Red Star caught the trace of a proud smile on his lips. Bloody Knife even left Custer's side to stride over and ask Red Star what he had seen.

"We have found the camp," Red Star announced, trying to keep his voice calm.

Translating for Custer's benefit, Girard handed Red Star a cup of coffee. Red Star squatted down by the fire and sipped the coffee slowly. It was up to Custer to ask him what he wanted to know, so he volunteered nothing. But before anything more was said, in word or sign, Red Star was aware of a strange light dancing in Long Hair's eyes. Mounted bareback on Vic, his white-stockinged blaze-faced sorrel, Custer had been riding around camp telling his officers what to do. Without finishing his morning meal, he had left the officers' breakfast fire as soon as Red Star had signaled the sentries. Even to those who knew Custer best, his manner now had a rare excitement.

George Armstrong Custer was thirty-six years old. Celebrated among whites as the Civil War's "Boy General," later famed as the West's most noted Indian fighter, he was rapidly gaining a wide reputation among the red men of the Plains. The Crows called him Son-of-the-Morning-Star. Less poetically, the friendly Arikaras knew him by his cultivated trademark: flowing untrimmed locks worn shoulder length after the fashion of old-time plainsmen. Even some of the enemy Sioux and Cheyennes had heard of the long-haired soldier-chief. In each of their tongues he was called Long Hair.

Today, however, as it had been for several weeks, his thinning blond hair was close-cropped by the clippers of Lieutenant Varnum. Always vain, he wore the usual broad-brimmed whitish gray hat to hide his increasing baldness. As though to compensate for his shorn locks, his mustache was left full and drooping picturesquely over his thin tight lips.

He was dressed this morning in a plain blue-gray flannel shirt, open at the throat and bare of insignia, and fringed buckskin trousers stuck into high jack boots, their spit-and-polish luster dulled by days of trail dust. In spite of the informality of the moment, every member of his command aside from Indian scouts referred to and addressed him as General—although his present rank was actually that of lieutenant colonel.

One of his brothers tagged along with him. Captain Tom Custer was a younger, paler edition of the General—down to fringed buckskins and flowing mustache. Moody and preoccupied, he lacked Long Hair's verve. Red Star scarcely wasted a glance on him, although he watched Long Hair attentively over the rim of his tin coffee cup.

Long Hair signed to Red Star, asking if he had sighted the Sioux. The Arikara promptly signed that he had, then reached inside his tattered shirt for Charley Reynolds's note which he handed to Custer.

The General slowly read the note and nodded. Grinning, he indicated his solemn-faced brother and signed to Bloody

Knife: "Our brother is frightened. His heart flutters in fear of the enemy. His eyes roll in fright at this news of the Sioux. Maybe only after we have beaten the Sioux will he become a man."

Through Girard, Long Hair told Red Star to saddle up.

"We are going back to where the other scouts watch," he said.

Red Star quickly set down his half-filled coffee cup, kicking it over in his excitement as he got up. Flinching at the resemblance of the spilled coffee to dark blood in the dust, he hurried on to his pony and saddled up. By the time he was ready Bloody Knife, Bob-tailed Bull, Stabbed, and Girard were all mounted and waiting. Custer was swinging up from the stirrup, his orderly having just tightened up the cinch strap of his McClellan saddle.

They left the camp at a medium pace, the Indian ponies trotting to keep up with the fast-walking Vic. Red Star heard a bugle as they passed the outflung sentries. Once along the way they slowed to rest the horses a little. With Girard interpreting, Custer was talking to Bloody Knife and Bob-tailed Bull:

"If we beat the Sioux, I will be President of the United States—the Grandfather. If you Arikaras do as I tell you and kill enough Sioux for me and capture many Sioux ponies, I will take care of you all when I come into power!"

Red Star thought, Surely this Long Hair must be a great chief among the whites. Red Star's own important function in letting Custer know the enemy camp had been found would surely not be forgotten when Long Hair became President.

Presently they came to the footpath leading up to the Crow's Nest and Red Star signed this was the place. They all

13

dismounted, leaving Stabbed to watch the horses, and climbed the butte until they came to the scouts. Charley Reynolds walked over and led Custer away to the lookout.

Reynolds indicated where Long Hair was to look, but Custer saw only the chalk buttes of the ridge that cut off a full view of the enemy camp. He shook his head. "You're imagining things, Charley. No sign of a hostile camp that I can see."

Watching from a few paces away, Girard spoke quietly to the Arikaras in their own tongue, "Long Hair does not believe a camp is there."

Reynolds handed Custer his field glasses and again pointed out the location of the camp. Long Hair looked once more, finally nodded slowly. "It's possible. You may be right at that."

White-Man-Runs-Him had waited patiently for a word with Custer. Up to now, the Arikaras had gotten full credit for discovering the camp. The tall Crow wanted to let Custer know that it was he and his brother "wolves" (scouts) who had first sighted the Sioux. Bringing stocky Mitch Bouyer along to interpret for him, White-Man-Runs-Him squatted down behind Custer. Known to the Indians as Two Bodies, Bouyer was part French, part Sioux, but long ago had married into the Crow tribe and now served double duty as scout and Crow interpreter.

"This Indian here wants to know what you think of the enemy camp," Bouyer began without ceremony.

"If there is an enemy camp out there, they haven't seen our army," Custer answered. "None of their scouts have seen us."

Hearing the meaning of Custer's words, White-Man-Runs-

14

Him said, "You say we have not been seen. We saw two young Sioux a while ago, going fast toward the camp. They were close enough to see the smoke of your army's breakfast fires."

This was not at all what Custer wanted to hear. "I say again we haven't been seen," he snapped angrily. "That camp has not sighted us. I'm going ahead to carry out my original plan. We'll wait until dark and then march. We'll surround the camp and hit it from all sides."

"That plan is no good," said White-Man-Runs-Him. "The Sioux may already have spotted your soldiers, and will report your coming to the camp."

Custer glared contemptuously at the tall Crow. "I've already said what I propose to do. I'll wait until dark, then go ahead with my plan."

Standing, White-Man-Runs-Him said no more. After a moment or so he silently strode away to join the other Crows.

As he sat listening to Girard's piecemeal translation of all that was going on, Red Star thought Long Hair's plan was good and that the Sioux would surely be caught by surprise. The tall Crow scout apparently did not realize how important and wise a leader Long Hair was. Still, like the other Arikaras, Red Star had a strange presentiment of defeat. Too many signs pointed that way, and even the Arikaras knew that the "medicine" (power) of the Sioux Chief Sitting Bull was great.

Only a few days had passed since the Arikara scouts had found the abandoned Sioux sun-dance camp on the Rosebud. Here, in one of the sweat lodges, lay a long ridge of sand in which pictures had been drawn. Red Star remembered one drawing of hoofprints, indicating Custer's horse soldiers on one side and Sioux warriors on the other; between the two forces were dead soldiers with their heads toward the Sioux.

The Arikaras at once understood this to mean that the Sioux medicine was too strong for the soldiers and that the whites would surely be defeated. Beside the drawings were three stones in a row, all painted red. In sign language this meant that the Great Spirit would give the Sioux a great victory. Tobacco offerings tied to painted sticks and other signs showed the Arikaras that the Sioux were sure of winning. Even if Long Hair caught the Sioux off-guard, Red Star wondered if the soldiers could beat them.

A rider on a fast horse clattered to a standstill on the trail below. A moment later Captain Tom Custer came panting up the footpath, looking for Long Hair. Red Star pointed toward the lookout. Long Hair was just coming out and met his brother in the pocket of ground where all the scouts now waited. Tom Custer gasped out words.

"They've spotted us! The Sioux know we're marching against them!"

Long Hair blinked, then frowned. "I don't believe it. You're getting as jumpy as the Crows."

"No doubt about it, General. Captain Yates found a loose pack on one of the mules. A box of hardtack was missing from the pack. Looks like our fine civilian packers had let it go with a lick and a promise."

"This is no time for joshing!" Long Hair said harshly. "If this is some kind of prank — "

"I'm not joshing. Yates sent Sergeant Curtis and two men from F Troop back up the trail to recover the box. They found it all right—with an Indian kid sitting on it eating hardtack. Curtis shot the boy, thinking he was alone. Just then two Sioux bucks ran up over a hill, but they were a little far for carbines. When Curtis saw they were getting away, he rode back on the double and reported to Yates. Yates told Keogh, and Keogh told me. We sent Herendeen back up the trail to see how bad it was. I thought you ought to know at once, so I came on here. Reno's right behind me, bringing up the column."

They all heard the clopping of hoofs and the din of voices as the regiment clattered down the trail. Long Hair snorted, his irritation mounting. "They're making enough noise to alert every hostile in the territory! Well, I knew the Indians would have scouts out ahead of us, but I never dreamed others could trail after us and pick up stuff dropped by our careless packers!"

At a loss for words, Tom Custer stood silent. Most of the scouts kept at a safe distance from Long Hair for the moment, finding suddenly that their weapons and gun belts required close scrutiny. Lonesome Charley Reynolds opened his rawhide war bag, and began handing out personal mementos and other belongings to his Arikara friends. Those out of earshot took up a murmur of alarm. It looked as though Lonesome Charley did not expect to get through the coming battle alive.

Hairy Moccasin had remained in the lookout. Now he came down into the pocket and signaled Mitch Bouyer to come quick. Back on the promontory the Crow pointed out half a dozen Indian horsemen crossing the prairie less than a mile away. Hairy Moccasin drew a forefinger across his Adam's apple, making the sign for the cutthroat Sioux.

"*Lakota,*" he whispered. It was the word for the Sioux that both the Crow and the Sioux themselves used.

Bouyer grunted when one of the Sioux began riding his pony in a tight circle. "He signals he has sighted us," Bouyer muttered.

Hairy Moccasin signed no. "Not us. They see the dust made by the white men—the horse soldiers coming up."

Bouyer nodded, then left the lookout and found Custer. "A little bunch of Sioux is out there," he told Long Hair. "Only five or six warriors. The way one is circling his horse, it looks like they've spotted the soldiers coming."

Custer moved halfway up to the promontory and looked out across the valley. The Sioux riders had vanished over a grassy rise. Following Long Hair, Bouyer said excitedly, "They've started back! Word'll get to that camp in no time at all. The Sioux will scatter to the four winds. Don't wait 'til they all get away—attack now!"

Long Hair's pale blue eyes flashed a cold warning. "You do the scouting, and I'll attend to the fighting."

Rebuffed by Custer's manner, as much as his words, Bouyer turned away to join the Crow scouts who were huddled up in a little group apart from the others.

A white man in buckskins came up the footpath and stepped into the pocket. It was Scout George Herendeen. Seeing him, Tom Custer led him over to Long Hair. Herendeen moved fast, but talked slow.

"Well, don't just stand there, man!" snapped Long Hair. "What have you got to report?"

Herendeen was unruffled. "War party, General, way it looks. Fresh sign—and plenty of it."

"Did you get a look at them?" Custer wanted to know.

"I only seen one—an outridin' scout on a ridge a mile off."

But back up the trail, near where the bread box had been dropped, Herendeen had found plenty of fresh pony tracks in a ravine off to one side. Less than an hour old, the tracks

18

obviously had been made after Sergeant Curtis had caught the Sioux boy eating hardtack.

"If you ask me, General," Herendeen offered, "we got Sioux all around us. They're watching every move we make."

"Maybe they're getting set to launch an attack on us," put in Tom Custer.

Long Hair toyed with the idea, then shook his head. "Hardly. What's worse, they're likely to slip away from us entirely. Once they scatter, we're in trouble. Tom, run down and tell Cooke I want an officers' call as soon as the regiment comes up. And tell him all members of the command will stand weapons' inspection without delay. We won't wait for dark. This means a change of plan: we'll push on today and strike the hostiles as soon as we can find them!"

As Tom Custer hurried down the footpath, Long Hair called Lieutenant Varnum over. "Your scouts may see action long before nightfall, Lieutenant. Have them ready."

Varnum saluted and turned away to find his interpreters. Long Hair stood alone on the rim of the pocket—a vainglorious conqueror looking out across the land toward a rendezvous with destiny, well sensing the drama of the moment, knowing that here might well be a day to go down in history. Now the die was cast, his sudden decision firm and irrevocable. There could be no turning back. It was a reckless gamble against unknown odds, a quixotic tilting at the windmills of chance. But Long Hair Custer was a desperate man.

Behind him the scouts stirred with renewed activity. Girard had already called the Arikaras around him and was relaying Long Hair's message. At once the Arikaras began preparing for battle, shedding their dirty garments, stripping down to breechclouts and moccasins, daubing at their faces and arms and chests with smears of powdered war paint wetted with spit.

Long Hair Custer looking out over Little Big Horn valley as scouts prepared for battle.

Young Hawk had a handful of loose eagle feathers, carefully saved for such an emergency as this. Unbraiding his hair, he methodically tied the feathers into looping hair strands. As he worked he sang a little low-voiced war song. Like the other Arikaras, he expected to be killed and scalped by the Sioux. At least he would go to his death accoutered for war.

The Crow scouts quickly gathered what was going on. They heard Herendeen's story of the pony tracks, then Mitch Bouyer's translation of Custer's words. Quietly they made ready for battle. Goes Ahead tied some breath feathers into his scalp braid. White-Man-Runs-Him painted sacred white-clay stripes down his face. Half Yellow Face, who "carried the pipe" for the Crows (led them), made a tobacco offering to the four winds. Seeing the little Crow ceremony, Long Hair strode over.

"Why are you doing all this?" he asked.

With Mitch Bouyer interpreting, Half Yellow Face respectfully got to his feet and answered solemnly, "Because you and I are going home today—by a trail that is strange to both of us."

Long Hair Custer's face drained of color at this mention of death. Saying no more, he turned on his heel and walked slowly back to the rim of the pocket where he stood again for a long time, looking out across the valley.

White Man's World

I T WAS Sunday, June 25, 1876.

Almost a full century had passed since the signing of the Declaration of Independence, and the nation was feeling its oats. While the great Indian camp on the Little Big Horn still slumbered, whites across the land were awakening jubilant and tense with excitement over the coming centennial celebration now less than ten days away. Cheerfully, citizens sidestepped the toils of economic depression left over from the panic of '73, and proudly rose to the occasion of a grand once-in-a-lifetime jubilee.

A rare elation gripped Philadelphia, normally staid City of Brotherly Love, as the Centennial Exposition set the pace for all future world fairs. Occupying vast acreage in Fairmount Park, the fair had gotten off to an auspicious start on May 10, when President Grant, accompanied by the Emperor of Brazil, pulled the switch on the gigantic Corliss engine which operated all the machinery of the exposition. Nearly five hundred acres of mechanical exhibits displayed everything from a mowing machine with an unheard-of differential gear to such novelties as a typewriter and an automatic device for turning out "tailor-made" cigarettes. Alexander Graham Bell's improved telephone was featured prominently as the instrument over which were heard the "first intelligible words ever spoken through a wire." On the floor of Machinery Hall was also demonstrated an odd duplicating contraption, called a mimeograph by its young inventor, Thomas Alva Edison.

Such gadgetry would have been completely wasted on the Indians camped by the Little Big Horn. Living as they did in a stone-age culture, they could not have cared less about happenings in the outside world.

The exposition's most popular exhibit, however, was one which displayed a minimum of technological achievement. The Pacific Railroad's replica of a hunter's camp in the Colorado Rockies drew the largest crowds and the most favorable comment. The nation's pulse may have quickened in the gala atmosphere of Philadelphia, but her eyes were dreamily focused on the West. Perhaps the expansive yearnings of the populace were a holdover from the era of Manifest Destiny in the forties and fifties, when people were seized with a determination "to overspread and to possess the whole of the Continent which Providence has given us for the experiment of liberty." In any case, westward expansion and the consolidation of a preserved Union—nearly sundered by civil war a decade earlier—took the national spotlight.

A veritable snowstorm of publicity attended the continental crossing of a passenger train called the *Lightning Express*. Normally, such a trip required seven days or more. It was the audacious plan of Henry Jarrett, co-manager of Booth Theatre in New York City, to take a company of players to San Francisco by rail in a mere four days. The public breathlessly read progress bulletins issued by Jarrett at Chicago, Omaha, and Reno. Setting a record for many years to come, the *Lightning Express* achieved the impossible and made the cross-country jaunt in just eighty-four hours—twelve hours less than advertised. The nation was a long time recovering

23

from what was, until the Battle of the Little Big Horn, the year's major excitement.

Only a handful of Sioux and Cheyenne warriors had ever seen an "iron horse"—as they called the awesome locomotive that thundered across the prairie, belching smoke and hissing steam. Even wagons were still a novelty to the Plains Indians. They continued to rely on such time-tested transportation as half-broken mustangs and pony-drawn travois.

Finished early in the year, the steamer *Grand Republic* with its fastidious Victorian *décor,* miles of Turkish carpet, and ornate gingerbread woodwork was the last word in river-boat luxury. One of the last of the floating palaces in the great fleet of packets plying the Mississippi, Missouri, and other navigable rivers, she featured currently popular high-pressure engines in spite of competitors' warnings that her boilers might explode. An added inducement to a discriminating clientele was the fact that her staterooms were accessible only from the public grand salon, thus minimizing the opportunity for illicit amour among her passengers.

With no reference at all to skin color, white men were first known to Indians of the upper Missouri and Yellowstone by their habitual travel on the big rivers. The fact that early white trappers came by canoe, and traders and settlers followed later on larger craft, characterized the white race for some time.

Even histrionics took a western turn. Theater audiences were still talking about Buffalo Bill Cody's smash stage hit, *Scouts of the Prairie,* closed in April at the death of the star's only son, little Kit Carson Cody, in Rochester. Rumor now had it that the distraught scout-and-buffalo-hunter-turned-actor had deserted his wife, Louisa, and two small daughters for parts unknown. As it happened, on the morning of June 25, Cody was far from the footlights, guiding the Fifth Cavalry up the Dry Fork of Cheyenne River in northwest Nebraska. Yellow Hand's Cheyennes had "jumped the reservation," having suddenly left Red Cloud Agency to join Sitting Bull on the Little Big Horn. The Fifth was riding hard to head them off.

Cody's friend and short-time co-star, James Butler Hickok —better known as "Wild Bill"—had also left the stage under a cloud. After publicly trouncing an overcharging cabbie in front of his theater, Hickok had mistaken the enthusiasm of his New York audience for ridicule and had hurled his six-shooter at a gallery spotlight, smashing it to bits and promptly ending an ill-fated performance. It was reliably reported that he had caught the first train West. On that memorable Sunday, Wild Bill was leisurely strolling up the dusty main drag of Deadwood, the Dakota boomtown where later in the summer he was shot in the back of the head by a cocky little gun slick named Jack McCall.

Though happily married to a circus performer, Hickok had ridden into Deadwood a few days earlier with a hard-shooting mannish pony-express rider named Martha Jane Canary. Her sobriquet "Calamity Jane" would thereafter be linked romantically with Wild Bill's own name. On the morning of June 25, Calamity Jane lay in a Deadwood bagnio, recovering from illness brought on by exposure during one of her wild rides. Two years before she had guided Custer's Black Hills Gold Discovery Expedition, which had opened up western Dakota to prospecting and settlement. Now she was cursing her luck for having missed out on serving Custer as a scout against Indians on the Little Big Horn.

Throughout the West, citizens were striving vigorously to live down a reputation for being roughshod and uncultured. Betterment of self and community through education was a primary issue. Coinciding with the opening of Baltimore's Johns Hopkins University back east, the University of Oregon was set up at Eugene. Countless other institutions of higher learning sprang up in city after city across the land.

In 1876 Indians had no place in current educational programs. Three full years would pass before the establishment of the Carlisle Indian School in Pennsylvania—the first opportunity for education ever offered to the red man.

A wave of public morality swept across the West as more and more women asserted their vague yearnings for power and equality with men. Two ladies in Nevada—pioneers in the struggle for women's suffrage—Hannah Clapp and Ella Babcock calmly announced the unheard-of founding of a *coeducational* college.

Sioux and Cheyenne women in the Little Big Horn camp might well have laughed at their white sisters' clamor for recognition in matters with which females were not normally concerned. Never their husbands' chattel as commonly supposed, Indian women exerted tremendous influence within their own sphere of activities. An age-old division of labor kept both sexes happily occupied and without the white man's restless urge to reform that which was already long established by tribal custom.

Like lightning, the new morality struck at Marysville, California, when the city fathers—prompted by their womenfolk—loaded an entire bawdyhouse full of prostitutes on a dray, and reluctantly dragged the building and its protesting occupants beyond the town limits.

White Man's World

By instinct and ancient tradition, the Sioux and Cheyennes were among the world's most moral people. Violations of the old accepted pattern were rare simply because they were unthinkably impractical. Infrequent breaches of the unwritten code were dealt with harshly and promptly. Promiscuity or adultery was usually punished by banishment—or, occasionally, by cutting off the nose of the guilty woman.

Reflecting the trend, popular music had a certain forced sentimentality that marked it for all time. People the country over were humming and whistling "I'll Take You Home Again, Kathleen" or "Silver Threads Among the Gold." A familiar barroom melody, "How Dry I Am," actually began as an often-heard hymn, "O Happy Day," whose author providentially died before learning of its unholy fate. The westward look showed up in the plaintive "Home on the Range" and the risqué ballad, "Frankie and Johnnie."

While the valley of the Little Big Horn still resounded with the steady throb of rawhide drums, the minds of drowsy scalp dancers echoed simple words: "You may go on the warpath; when you return among the victors, I will marry you."

The summer social season was highlighted by the opening of the Grand Union Hotel at Saratoga Springs. With fitting aplomb, city dwellers flocked to fashionable resorts "where the days moved in a pleasant round of billiards, sherry cobblers, and a little gentle exercise such as the schottische." Socialites were still talking about the wide swathe cut the preceding winter in New York City by George and Elizabeth Custer. Although comparative strangers to Eastern society, they had been sponsored by no less a personage than the prominent publisher, James Gordon Bennett, whose son had just created a considerable stir at Newport by introducing from India the remarkable game of polo. Lawn tennis was considered a far more proper recreation, as prim young ladies rustled across grassy courts in heavy bustles and skirts to "return their escorts' well-mannered shots." Or, of a Sunday morning, one might spend a "refreshing hour or so touring the park in one's most elegant equipage and costume."

Indians always enjoyed visiting the old Sioux camping place on the Little Big Horn, where there was plenty of good water, lots of good grass for the pony herds, and plenty of wood. It was a fine spot for fishing or, if the water ran high, for swimming. The tribes always had fun there, racing their ponies and rolling willow hoops and playing hide-a-stick games.

East and West, it was an era of unchanneled free enterprise. Widely advertised for American homes were such diverse items as Rogers' Statuary (at $10 a grouping) and a better mousetrap which ingeniously caught mice alive and theoretically lured other mice to their doom. A concoction called Sozodont was guaranteed to eliminate "impure breath arising from catarrh or the use of liquor and tobacco." Mustache cups and elixirs enjoyed wide popularity among hirsute gentlemen—of whom there were many. Mrs. J. A. Drollinger of La Porte, Indiana, advertised a sure cure for the opium habit, with a "trial bottle absolutely free." The "best, cheapest, safest fireworks in the country" were offered for the coming Fourth of July Giant Centennial Celebration by E. I. Horsman of New York City.

One could buy Sharps's breech-loading rifles or Winchester '73s for as little as ten dollars in Eastern cities. Colt's seven-shot revolvers sold for five dollars, while lesser brands could be purchased for three-fifty.

28

Indians on the Little Big Horn would have given a lot for a chance to get arms and ammunition for hunting purposes. Few warriors had firearms. Most of them had to rely on old-fashioned bows and arrows to bring down game. Only a dozen or so men in the entire camp had repeating rifles—Winchesters or Spencer carbines. A few others owned single-shot Sharps and Henrys. Muzzle-loaders, even old-time flintlocks, were actually preferred because ammunition was so scarce. Some warriors carried cap-and-ball six-shooters and kept bullet molds and caps and powder horns. Cartridge cases were carefully saved and reloaded. Phosphorus was soaked off match heads and used to rebuild rimfire shells. There was no substitute for makeshift methods. The nearest trading post was hundreds of miles away.

It was an election year and a convention summer. With few clearcut issues before it other than widespread dissatisfaction with the Grant administration, the electorate saw the formation of a number of splinter parties and factions. Encouraged by the recent proposal in the House for a prohibition amendment to the Constitution, the Prohibition party had met in Cleveland late in May. General Green Clay Smith of Kentucky was nominated for President. The first convention of the new Greenback party was held in Indianapolis, nominating New York's Peter Cooper for the chief executive's post.

The Republicans convened early in June at Cincinnati. With three or four strong candidates to choose from, the delegates were at loggerheads until Ohio's dark horse, Rutherford B. Hayes, was finally nominated for President. W. A. Wheeler was named as his running mate.

The Democrats' convention was not slated until July, but by early summer their candidate-to-be, Samuel T. Tilden of

New York, was regarded as a shoo-in favorite for the fall election. Republicans conceded Tilden would be tough opposition, although no one dreamed the contest would prove to be the closest presidential race in history—with Hayes nosing out Tilden by just *one* electoral vote.

On no political platform was the Indian problem regarded as a campaign issue. No Indians were permitted to vote and, in light of the Army's get-tough policy with recalcitrant red men, President Grant's once inspired administration of Indian affairs by peaceful Quakers had proved immensely unpopular. An almost violent anti-Indian sentiment swept across the land.

Among best sellers of the day, one greeted with unexpected enthusiasm for its identification with the American scene, Mark Twain's classic *Tom Sawyer,* cast a mixed-blood Indian as its villain. Whites everywhere were outraged by bloodcurdling tales of Indian barbarity, both fictional and factual.

A New Mexican rancher named Frank Cody (no kin to Buffalo Bill) was reported to have been cooked to death on his own cabin stove by savage Mescalero Apaches. An unnamed officer, member of the garrison at Fort Selden, New Mexico Territory, was said to have been bitten to death by a rattlesnake presented to him in a box by a spurned Indian maiden who claimed, unjustifiably, of course, that he had seduced her. A wandering evangelist called Preacher Smith was found brutally slain by a Sioux war party in Dakota's Black Hills.

Out of long-standing fear of the red men grew hatred and contempt. In reprisal for sporadic raiding by other Apache bands, the Chiricahuas were moved summarily from their native Arizona mountains to dank marshlands near San Carlos

Agency, a mass death sentence for the tribe. When its friendly chief, Cochise, gave up the ghost late in June, whites in the territory sniffed "good riddance."

In Oregon a Wallowa Valley Nez Percé Indian was fatally shot by an encroaching white settler in a trivial dispute over a fence. Chief Joseph's protest at his tribesman's murder was greeted with cold disdain by his future antagonist, Bible-carrying, one-armed General Oliver Otis Howard.

"I'll listen to no more of your drivel," snapped Howard. "The Government says your tribe shall give up its claim to lands in Oregon and move to the Lapwai Reservation in Idaho. Yet you persist in defying the Government. If you don't move your people away, I'll take the matter into my own hands and make you suffer for your disobedience."

Other high Army officials were expressing similar contempt for Indians. Red men had degenerated from a full-scale menace to a mere nuisance. General of the Army William Tecumseh Sherman stated that the only protection needed by settlers against hostile Indians was whisky.

"Kills them like flies," Sherman added.

Reflecting the nation's pulse, Lieutenant General Phil Sheridan in Chicago airily coined the phrase: "The only good Indian is a dead one!" He had already well implemented his motto by clamoring in the press for wholesale destruction of the millions of buffalo that roamed the Plains. By early summer most of the great Southern herd had been ruthlessly slaughtered by hide hunters, who were already beginning to look North to the still intact Northern herd.

"Destroy the Indian's commissary, and you'll destroy him," Sheridan insisted. The hide hunters were doing their best to oblige.

31

With hide hunting now centered in the Texas Panhandle, western Kansas—previous headquarters for the industry—was doing a land-office business in bones. Buffalo bones were shipped East to button factories, while Indian skulls, used in making fancy combs, brought as high as $1.25 each in Dodge City. Local merchants found that arm and leg bones, properly cleaned and polished, made knife handles "beautiful to behold." More than one thrifty farmer, taking advantage of the opening up of five million acres of wheatland by the Kansas Pacific Railroad, made enough on Indian bones alone to tide him through the winter. After two years of drought and grasshoppers—"In God we trusted, in Kansas we busted"—plowing for old bones paid better than plowing for wheat.

While watching with satisfaction the passing of the buffalo—and, consequently, the Indian—from the Southern plains, homesteaders cast a greedy eye north to the sparsely settled grasslands of Dakota and Montana. Here lay a vast region virtually untouched, inhabited only by roving Indian bands until Custer's discovery of gold in the Black Hills in 1874. Miners and prospectors were swarming into scattered gold towns such as Deadwood, but the prairies were wide open. Land was free for the taking if one conveniently overlooked treaties with the Indians.

At first, the Army made half-hearted attempts to keep the whites out of Indian lands. But officers like Sheridan, who commanded the Missouri Department in which the disputed area lay, strongly urged a punitive expedition against the Indians to open up the country to white settlement. Public opinion was too biased to be ignored. Plans for a campaign against the Sioux and Northern Cheyennes, main fighting tribes of the region, were soon under way.

The Interior Department, which had nominal jurisdiction over the Indians, preferred to settle the issues involved without resorting to a shooting war. Military preparations were held up during the winter of 1875-76 while the Commissioner of Indian Affairs, acting on orders from the Secretary of Interior, ordered Indian agents in the Sioux country to notify all Indians in the territory that they were expected to come in to their respective agencies before January 31, 1876. Red men who failed to comply with this directive would automatically be considered hostile to the Government and appropriate action would be taken against them by the War Department.

In a word, the old free life of the Plains Indian was at an end. The Sioux and Cheyennes would hereafter "walk the white man's road" and "be lodged on reservations, where they would be maintained at Government expense." Messages were sent by indifferent agents to various chiefs in the dead of winter. Ill-timed and ill-advised from the start, the directive reached few, if any, Indian leaders in the Montana wilderness. Those chiefs who did hear of it paid little heed to such nonsense. By age-old practice and tradition, they felt they had every right to roam unmolested in their ancient hunting grounds. Furthermore, their right to do so had been guaranteed by formal treaty with the white man's Government. The Fort Laramie Treaty of 1868 defined their permanent territory as all the land from the Platte River north to the Canadian border and west of the Missouri to the Big Horn Mountains. This area was to belong to the tribes "as long as the grass shall grow." In the naïve Indian mind this meant forever.

On the morning of June 25, Ulysses Simpson Grant, eighteenth President of the United States, got up from the family breakfast table in the White House and slouched away toward the front of the executive mansion.

"I'll be along in a few minutes, Ulys," his wife Julia called after him, then launched into her usual Sunday-morning altercation about food with the official steward. "Beckley, don't you think we might have a little change of menu? Something a little more fancy?"

A wry smile tugged at the President's bearded lips. He had just finished his favorite morning meal of breakfast bacon and fried apples, washed down with strong coffee. The steward, he noted, gave his usual urbane answer.

"Madam, we are living at the absolute pinnacle now."

Grant took an after-breakfast cigàr from his vest pocket and licked one end preparatory to lighting up. He found that as he moved away the sound of Julia's voice receded until he was standing by one of the tall front windows looking out on Pennsylvania Avenue. The wide street lacked its usual weekday bustle, although several carriages and pedestrians passed on their way to early church services.

These were dark days for Grant. Even his fragrant Havana reminded him of trouble. The recent capture by Cubans of the American ship, *Virginius,* and the savage murder of her passengers and crew had brought the nation to the brink of war.

Here at home, in spite of the President's soothing, Julia was in a perpetual fret about their daughter Nellie's marriage to an Englishman. Mrs. Grant remained unreconciled to the fact that young Sartoris was a foreigner—even though he did happen to be the nephew of famed actress Fanny Kemble.

Far more serious was the domestic political situation. The Republican party seemed doomed to certain defeat in the coming November elections. A hostile Democratic House of

Representatives, angered by Grant's stubborn insistence on a humane policy toward the Indians among other things, had already passed an anti-third-term resolution aimed pointedly at the President, while Democrats everywhere were out for blood in their attempts to discredit his administration.

As a climax to numerous Reconstruction difficulties in the South, armed rioting had broken out in South Carolina with open conflict between whites and Negroes. Grant had been forced to resort to an unpopular expedient—sending in Federal troops to restore order. As it was, five Negroes had been killed.

Of considerable embarrassment to the administration was a drawn-out House investigation of alleged favors received while in office by former Speaker James G. Blaine from the Union Pacific Railroad. Matters were not improved when, in early June, Blaine had insisted on making an ultra-dramatic speech in his own defense on the floor of the House, and had succeeded only in further incriminating himself.

Far worse was the impending impeachment against former Secretary of War William W. Belknap for malfeasance in office. Leaks of vast corruption in the War Department had begun the previous winter with a series of vicious editorial diatribes against Belknap in the *New York Herald*. Grant was used to unfriendliness on the part of the press, which usually pictured him in an alcoholic stupor although he had not taken a drink since coming into office. But the *Herald's* attacks indicated that some undisclosed official source was providing Publisher James Gordon Bennett with classified information —ammunition that obviously sparked the Congressional investigation and impeachment proceedings against Belknap.

Most damaging of all to Grant personally was a *Herald*

35

feature article, "Belknap's Anaconda," published March 31, in which the President's own brother, Orville Grant, was implicated in the War Department scandals. The article reported that Orville Grant and Mrs. Belknap, covering up for her husband, were systematically dividing the proceeds from the illicit sale of Army supplies intended for military outposts and Indian reservations. With public attention focused increasingly on the West, this was political dynamite.

Grant was forced to drop Belknap like a hot potato. In May he had appointed Ohio's capable Alphonso Taft to fill the cabinet vacancy. It was too little too late, however, to appease the critics of the administration. But during the hubbub of the spring hearings, Grant had uncovered the author of "Belknap's Anaconda," the unscrupulous master mind behind nearly all of the *Herald*'s allegations. The President was a little shocked to find that the arch enemy of his family, as well as his administration, was a former brash Civil War subordinate, George Armstrong Custer. Grant remembered Custer mainly from the grand review in Washington in June, 1865, after the war. While the victorious Union Army was passing its commander, Grant, Custer's horse bolted past the reviewing stand without giving its rider an opportunity to salute. Grant had never forgotten the obviously intended slight to his own authority.

On leave in New York City during the winter of 1875-76, Custer and his wife Elizabeth enjoyed a gala holiday, attending all the plays and hobnobbing with hero-worshiping socialites. Highlights of the visit included seeing a revival of Shakespeare's *The Tempest,* and watching Joe Jefferson do his perennial title role in *Rip Van Winkle.* Not the least of their social coups was Custer's meeting with powerful James

Gordon Bennett. Among other great and influential admirers, the publisher quickly saw the "Boy General with Golden Locks" as presidential timber, and soon had Custer aspiring openly for the Democratic nomination in place of Tilden. Bennett felt he had a fine chance. It was high time the Democrats swept into office. But success depended on something more spectacular than skillful press-agentry or unethical revelations of War Department secrets. Bennett and Custer agreed that a golden opportunity lay in the long-promised campaign against the Sioux and Cheyennes in the West. A showy victory over hostile Indians would make Custer a national hero overnight. With public acclaim and a powerful press to back him, the Boy General might—in spite of his youth—make the coming Democratic convention in July sit up and take notice.

During the spring hearings in the House, Custer was called in to Washington to testify from his post as commander of Fort Abraham Lincoln, Dakota Territory. It was an order he did not want to obey. Operations against the hostile tribes were slated to begin as soon as weather permitted, and Custer was preparing to take the field as leader of the expedition. He telegraphed Congressman Clymer, chairman of the House investigating committee, requesting that he be permitted to answer questions by deposition. The committee was after big game, however, and too hot on the trail to permit such laxity. Custer reluctantly came to Washington and appeared as an unwilling witness at the hearings.

Fuming to return to his post, Custer testified that post traders on Indian reservations were paying tremendous kickbacks out of their fabulous earnings to a man named Hedrick —a brother-in-law of Secretary Belknap. With Belknap's

37

sanction, Custer charged, these traders were supplying liquor to Indians in violation of established treaties. Furthermore, Army garrisons, including his own command at Fort Abraham Lincoln, were being shorted on rations and other vital necessities presumably diverted to Belknap's various commercial enterprises. Deeply involved in these nefarious operations, he repeated, was the President's brother, Orville Grant.

These rash disclosures very nearly cost Custer his commission. He soon discovered that his influence in Washington had evaporated into thin air. Finally realizing his predicament, he attempted to secure an audience with the President, "in order to correct certain unjust impressions" about himself. Grant flatly refused to see him, letting him cool his heels in a White House anteroom until Custer at last decided to leave the capital.

The journey back to Fort Abraham Lincoln was far from smooth. By order of the President, Custer was arrested in Chicago. It seemed he had departed from Washington without taking proper leave from the War Department. Only through the prompt intercession of Custer's personal friend, Phil Sheridan, was he permitted to continue on to Dakota Territory.

Back at Fort Abraham Lincoln, he found that General Alfred H. Terry had been put in charge of the coming Sioux campaign. Custer was expressly forbidden to accompany the expedition. Terry, however, was inexperienced in Indian warfare and wanted Custer along. In 1868 Custer had destroyed Black Kettle's village of Southern Cheyennes on the Washita River, Indian Territory, thus earning himself quite a name as an Indian fighter. Fame as a frontiersman and explorer followed in 1874, when he led the Black Hills Gold Discovery Expedition into Sioux lands in Dakota.

After eating humble pie in a series of pleading letters to Grant, and securing further intercession from Sheridan and Sherman, Custer was at last permitted to accompany the Dakota column commanded personally by Terry. But he would go in the minor capacity of acting commander of his old regiment, the Seventh Cavalry—whose commanding officer, old Colonel Sturgis, was conveniently placed on detached service.

In violation of Sheridan's specific orders, Custer wheedled Terry into letting a newspaper correspondent accompany the expedition. Picked to cover the campaign for the press was young Mark Kellogg, an employee of C. A. Lounsberry, editor of the *Bismarck Tribune* and special correspondent for James Gordon Bennett of the *New York Herald*. Neither Bennett nor Custer was taking any chances that history-in-the-making might go unrecorded.

All through the winter and spring restless Indian bands were blazing trails across the prairie to join Sitting Bull in Montana. Almost constantly on the move, they pushed west out of Dakota and Nebraska with eyes fixed on the distant "Shining Mountains" (Big Horns) at the base of which their endless roaming might find surcease. From the Missouri and the Platte and the Cheyenne, from the Grand and the White and the Cannonball, they fitfully kept streaming westward— crossing the Belle Fourche and the Powder and the Tongue and the Rosebud. Between them and the mountains now lay only the river they called the Greasy Grass—that white men named the Little Big Horn.

Grand strategy for the campaign was mapped out by General Sheridan at his Chicago headquarters. A three-pronged attack was to converge on the Indians where they

39

were thought to be massed near the mouth of the Little Big Horn River. Terry was to strike west from Fort Abraham Lincoln. General Crook was to push north from Fort Fetterman, Wyoming. General Gibbon was to move southeast from Fort Ellis in Montana. All resistance on the part of the Indians was to be crushed, and the combined military forces were to escort the red men back to their re-defined reservations. On paper the plan looked perfect, a soldier's dream.

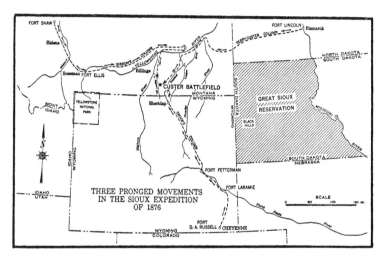

By the middle of June, the commands of Terry and Gibbon had trudged across the wild plains from their respective bases to establish contact at the confluence of the Yellowstone and Rosebud Rivers. Neither general then knew that the third arm of the triple attack, under General Crook, had been chased back into Wyoming with heavy losses after a sharp engagement on the Rosebud with a large Indian force under Crazy Horse. The country between Crook and the Yellowstone swarmed with hostiles, and he had no way of letting

Terry and Gibbon know the Indian strength. Confident they had adequate forces to overwhelm any Indians they might encounter, Terry and Gibbon proceeded with the campaign as scheduled in spite of Crook's unaccountable absence. Neither general thought the number of hostile warriors exceeded fifteen hundred; working estimates of Indian strength actually figured at around one thousand.

A council of war was held aboard the *Far West,* a supply steamer brought to the military rendezvous from Fort Abraham Lincoln. Reporting on a reconnaisance up the Rosebud, Major Marcus A. Reno of the Seventh Cavalry announced that Arikara trackers had struck a fresh Indian trail that seemed to lead toward the Little Big Horn. Gibbon, Terry, and Custer mapped out an enveloping maneuver to counter possible Indian attempts to disperse and scatter in the inaccessible Big Horn range.

Terry gave Custer written orders directing the Seventh to follow up the Rosebud until the Indian trail was struck, then to follow it across country to the Little Big Horn. Gibbon's troops, mostly infantry, would simultaneously march upstream from the mouth of the Little Big Horn. With Custer's regiment driving downstream, the hostiles would be caught and crushed between the two forces. The date set for the combined attack was Monday, June 26.

Knowing Custer was still smarting from his set-to with Grant and anxious to allow him ample leeway in dealing with the hostiles, Terry carefully worded his orders to give Custer more or less a free hand in their execution. However, the Seventh Cavalry was expected to co-operate to the fullest extent with Gibbon's column.

On the afternoon of June 22, Custer started off up the Rosebud at the head of his regiment.

"Don't forget, General, to wait for us," Gibbon called.

"Don't worry, General, I *shall* wait!" Custer shouted back, standing in his stirrups and waving his hat in a jaunty farewell.

As white men figure dates it was June 24, the eve of battle, the night before the great fight which Long Hair Custer wanted. Standing alone on the jutting ridge which, by tomorrow, would be stained with white men's blood, Sitting Bull

Sitting Bull performing the *hanblake oloan*, the Sioux prayer for advance knowledge.

raised his hands in supplication to Wakan Tanka, "The Great
Holy Spirit," who always guided the Indian, had brought the
Sioux chief a vision of victory over white soldiers during the
intertribal sun dance on the Rosebud ten days earlier. "Many
soldiers falling into camp," the vision had promised. Although
the Sioux had beaten Crook, Sitting Bull sensed an even
greater victory might soon be forthcoming. Now he prayed
and wailed aloud: "Wakan Tanka, hear me and pity me! I
offer you this pipe in the name of my people. Save them. We
want to live! Guard them against all misfortune and danger,
I beg you. Take pity on us!" Soon Sitting Bull left the lonely
ridge to return to camp. Behind him he had stuck slender
wands in the ground to which tiny buckskin bags of tobacco
and willow bark were tied. Next day Custer's horse soldiers
would knock them over and trample them in the dusty grass.
But tonight—although he did not yet realize Custer was
marching against him—Sitting Bull knew his offerings to
Wakan Tanka would not be in vain.

On the morning of June 25, dry summer heat hung like a
dusty shroud over Fort Abraham Lincoln. From a streaked
window in the commandant's house on Officers' Row, Elizabeth Custer looked out across the barren parade ground and
tried to visualize the triumphant return of her husband. He
would come through the main guard gate to the north, just
as he had ridden out that day over six weeks ago. When he
returned this time, of course, he would be victorious, riding
on Vic or Dandy, his favorite horses, at the head of the old
Seventh, with the regimental band blaring out the familiar
jubilant strains of "The Girl I Left Behind Me" or the
regiment's own "Garryowen." The band had remained here
at the fort, their gray mounts taken over by E Company's

43

fresh recruits. But they did not play often these days. It was just as well, Elizabeth thought. She was not sure how much of their raucous blaring she could take—at least until "Autie," as she called the General, was safely back.

Elizabeth Custer's nightmare of an Indian warrior brandishing her husband's scalp.

"It's do or die this time, Libby," Autie had told her that last day, when the regiment rode out across the dry Dakota prairie and he had stayed behind with her a final moment before dashing away to join his command.

Looking out at the shabby weathered buildings of the fort, Elizabeth's vision blurred with sudden tears. When she wiped

44

them away, the drab parade ground was empty after all. Then in her mind's eye loomed again the frightful dream figure of the old nightmare. An involuntary gasp of horror crossed her lips as she saw once more the terrible naked red warrior, brandishing aloft the long yellow hair that was, she knew, her husband's scalp.

Before he left, Autie had patiently tried to quiet her fears, even going so far as to have Lieutenant Varnum whack off his shoulder-length curls and run horse clippers over his hair to make his scalp less worth the taking. For a while the gory picture was out of her thoughts—until this very day. Though strangely agitated by the shock of the all too real dream, which she was later to consider a premonition of the General's death, Elizabeth Custer could not have guessed that before the day was done Sioux and Cheyennes would be chanting kill-songs in which she would be named as Long Hair's widow.

Midmorning

Summer had come late to Montana. Late melting snow in the mountains caused the Little Big Horn to run bank full—wider and deeper than it normally did at this time of year. Where the Indians camped it was some forty yards in width and deep enough to swim a horse. Here and there were pebbly natural fords where the water ran swift and shallow. Although the ground was bone-dry a few yards away from the river, the steep clay banks oozed soft with unseasonal moisture.

Along the western bank of the Little Big Horn, fifteen miles or so from its mouth, the undulating prairie sloped up several feet to a level grassy bench, which provided an ideal camp site. Beyond it to the west the land rose gradually to an upland plateau nearly two hundred feet above the river. Here thousands of Indian ponies grazed, tended by a few half-naked Indian boys. Off to the south sloughs in the flat bottomlands showed where the river had formerly followed a different course. In the far distance in the southwest rose the hazy bulk of the Big Horn Mountains, while nearby, up the river, chalk buttes and bluffs looked ash-gray above the dense growth of green cottonwoods.

The camp extended nearly four miles, north to south. Hundreds of tanned buffalo-hide tepees were pitched in seven great camp circles, each well over half a mile in diameter. On the outskirts of the tepee circles were temporary brush shelters and shades of evergreen boughs brought down from the mountains. Open stretches of prairie were dotted with fresh-killed antelope hides, pegged out to dry in the sun. Here and there hobbled horses were grazing, while slinking dogs lurked around every camp. Nothing was haphazard about the arrangement of the village. Each tribe camped according to the order in which it traveled—a pattern never broken as long as the tribes were together. Ancient custom governed the placement of each camp circle, the allotted place for each band within the circle, the location of every lodge within the band. In this great metropolis of the Plains, every Indian had a definite address known to everybody else in the camp.

Located farthest north were the Cheyennes, three hundred lodges of them, nearly eighteen hundred people. Their place of leadership in the line of march west from Dakota Territory had been a courtesy extended by Sitting Bull, who had welcomed wholeheartedly these hard-fighting allies of the Sioux. Camped with them were several families of Gros Ventres and five stray Arapaho warriors, members of related tribes who spoke a kindred dialect.

Away from the river, just southwest of the Cheyennes, was the camp circle of the Ogalala Sioux, a branch of the Teton-Dakota or Sioux Nation that often lived and fought closer to the alien Cheyennes than to its own cousin tribes.

On the river was a small irregular camp of Brûlé or Burnt Thigh Sioux.

Below the Cheyennes and Brûlés were the Sansarc Sioux, another of the seven Teton tribes. With them were about one hundred and thirty Two Kettle Sioux, also Teton.

47

Across a small stream to the south were the powerful Minneconjou Sioux.

Near them, but away from the river, was the Blackfeet Sioux camp circle, which included smaller bands of Assiniboins and Yanktonnai, Yankton, and Santee Sioux.

Back on the river, at the extreme south end of the village, was the largest camp circle of all—that of three thousand Hunkpapa Sioux. Their place in the line of march was traditional, that of rear guard, and so they were the last to make camp.

The Little Big Horn was a valley of giants that day. Many great leaders were here to govern the largest Indian encampment ever seen on the North American continent—upwards of twelve thousand people, of whom at least a third were fighting men.

Two of the Cheyennes' "old-man chiefs" were present, Dirty Moccasins and Old Bear. The tribe's other two old-man chiefs, Dull Knife and Little Wolf, were not here at midmorning, although Little Wolf showed up later in the day. Leading war chiefs were Crazy Head and Lame White Man, Old Man Coyote and Last Bull.

Big Road and He-Dog led the Ogalalas. Their head chief was Red Cloud, who had remained peacefully at his Nebraska agency, although he was represented here by his young warrior son, Jack. Leading spirit of the tribe, followed by many warriors throughout the village, was an Ogalala fighting man not yet made a chief. His name was Crazy Horse.

The head chief of the Brûlés, Spotted Tail, had also remained in Nebraska. Among minor leaders present was his future slayer, Crow Dog.

Spotted Eagle and Fast Bear led the Sansarcs, while Runs-the-Enemy headed the small band of Two Kettles.

48

Lame Deer was head chief of the powerful Minneconjous, whose fighting chiefs included Hump, Fast Bull, and High Backbone.

Inkpaduta, perpetrator of the Spirit Lake massacre of Minnesota whites in 1857, led the Santees. Scabby Head was chief of the Blackfeet Sioux.

War chiefs of the Hunkpapas were Gall, Crow King, and Black Moon. Their head chief was probably the greatest Indian leader of all time—Sitting Bull.

A visionary and a healer, Sitting Bull was no ordinary medicine man. But it was not only his mystical power that brought red men to the Little Big Horn from every quarter. Nor was it his courage alone—although he was a brave fighting chief whose daring and vigor in battle were known to every Indian in the Northwest. Above all others—even the reckless Crazy Horse—Sitting Bull stood as a clear, unspoiled symbol of the old free way of life that the Indian held sacred and that was passing so fast into oblivion. The example he set gave him dominion over the entire encampment.

The tribes had no nefarious purpose in gathering on the Little Big Horn. They were not rebelling against any authority they recognized at the time, but simply exercising their age-old custom of following the buffalo herds northwest in the animals' annual migration. Scarcity of game, brought on by the white man's ruthless waste and destruction of the herds, had brought various tribes and bands into closer contact than usual.

Pte, the buffalo, gave the Plains Indian all he needed to exist: fresh meat for immediate cooking, fat and dried flesh for making pemmican, robes for beds and winter apparel, tanned hides for leggings and women's garments and tepees.

Tough old bull hides could be used for making light bull-boats to cross rivers, or cut into circular shields that would ward off sharp lances and arrows. Sled runners could be made from rib bones in winter, fleshing tools could be fashioned from cannon bones, axes could be made from shoulder blades.

Women scraping hides in the village.

Boiled hoofs produced a fine glue for feathering arrows. Bones furnished needles, sinew provided thread, horns made ladles and spoons. Even the tail was useful as a switch for brushing away flies. No part of a buffalo carcass went unused. Although *pte* was not technically a deity, he alone—of all animals regarded by the Indian as brother creatures—was honored by the Sioux title of respect: "Uncle." Little wonder the tribes followed the buffalo West; their very lives depended on the herds.

50

Generosity was a cardinal virtue among the Sioux, ranking higher than courage. Hospitality on the part of an Indian could not be denied to another red man. The starving bands from the prairies to the east were welcomed on the Little Big Horn with open arms. And so the tribes gathered to form the powerful hoop—the mythical circle of the universe that bound the Sioux Nation and their allies together.

Religion played no little part in bringing the tribes and bands close to one another. Early summer was the time of the annual sun dance, when the Sioux and Cheyennes gathered normally to do penance to Wakan Tanka—the Great Mystery. Only ten days had passed since the year's observance of the ceremony on the Rosebud, at which Sitting Bull fulfilled a vow and gave one hundred pieces of flesh (skin) from his arms to Wakan Tanka. It was shortly after this painful sacrifice, during the actual ritual of daylong staring at the sun, that the chief had seen a vision of white soldiers and enemy Indians falling head-down into the Sioux camp like so many grasshoppers. And it was then that Sitting Bull had heard a voice from above, crying, "I give you these because they have no ears!"

Sitting Bull mulled over his vision. Eight days ago, on the Rosebud, Sioux warriors under Crazy Horse had badly beaten the troops of the Gray Fox (General Crook) and had driven them back to the south with heavy losses. Many Indians thought the Rosebud victory was a fulfillment of the vision. But Sitting Bull knew better. He had seen the earless soldiers and enemy Indians falling into the Sioux camp. The Gray Fox had not come within twenty miles of the encampment. Although he had as yet no warning of Long Hair's approach, Sitting Bull was confidently certain the Sioux would soon win another great victory—perhaps here on the Little Big Horn. The death of such an important woman as the aged wife of Four Horns at dawn that morning made the chief wonder if the victory might not occur that very day.

The Cheyennes were also forewarned that an attack might come. A tribal prophet named Box Elder (also called Dog-on-the-Ridge) sent a mounted crier around the camp to announce that everyone should keep horses tied up near his lodge. "In my dream I saw soldiers coming," Box Elder said. But few Cheyennes took him seriously. Several howled like wolves in ridicule—meaning that their prophet was crazy and no better than wolf bait.

A crier in the Sansarc camp kept warning his tribe that enemies were approaching. Yesterday, June 24, about noon, he had gone around the camp circle, shouting, "Soldiers are coming! They'll be here tomorrow!" But no one got much excited. The Gray Fox and his soldiers were still running away, according to scouts' reports, and no one suspected other soldiers were near.

Throughout the village many people did not even hear the scattered warnings. Most of them were sleeping late after the all-night scalp dance celebrating their victory over the Gray Fox a week ago.

The sun was already high and heat shimmered across the valley as a small scouting party rode into the Hunkpapa camp circle at the south end of the village. They had been out for several days, watching the continued retreat of the Gray Fox and his troops to the south, and so approached the camp from the up-river end. Because of throbbing victory drums in the village, buffalo were scarce in the vicinity. The scouts had been seeking game while they kept an eye on the Gray Fox, but, other than a small band of pronghorn up the valley, they had sighted nothing. Their leader, Eagle Elk, guessed the buffalo herds had been frightened away by soldiers somewhere in the country, but now he was anxious to report to the chiefs and let other scouts take over the futile search for game.

A "wolf," or outriding scout, who often wore a wolf hide over his head to mislead his enemies as he watched them.

Eagle Elk was an Ogalala and, at twenty-five, a veteran warrior and skillful hunter. His prowess as a scout had earned him the reputation of a top specialist. But even he had little inkling that morning that a column of soldiers was approaching the Little Big Horn from the east.

As Eagle Elk and his brother-friend and fellow scout, High Horse, were crossing the Hunkpapa camp circle, people were just beginning to stir around. Judging from prone bodies visible under the walls of the lodges which were raised for freer ventilation, many were still asleep. But one old woman was up and about, cooking meat in an iron kettle. Eagle Elk recognized her as a friend of his grandmother; the two old ladies visited back and forth, and liked to help each other. When Eagle Elk rode near she said something to him, something the sudden swelling of the wind kept him from hearing. He motioned High Horse to slow down and when they stopped the old woman spoke again.

"Attackers are coming!" she said.

"Where are they coming, Grandmother?" Eagle Elk asked.

"Grandson, I said attackers are coming!" And she went on stirring her kettle.

"Does she know anything?" High Horse asked.

"I know this old woman," Eagle Elk said. "There's something to what she says, I'm sure of it. I'm going on home to get ready."

High Horse was a Minneconjou. By different routes, the brother-friends headed toward their respective camps.

Though not among the revelers, Sitting Bull had been awake most of the night. He had spent many hours on the lonely ridge overlooking the village, praying and meditating. Upon his return to camp, his uncle Four Horns had asked that he attend his dying aunt. Through the late hours she sank fast and by daybreak she was dead.

Now, with the morning half gone, the chief sat talking with friends in the council tepee. Even in everyday clothes Sitting Bull was an imposing figure. He wore a fringed smoke-tanned buckskin shirt, decorated with green porcupine quill-work and tassels of human hair. His leggings and moccasins were also smoke-tanned, matching the dark color of his shirt. His long breechclout was deep red. He wore a single eagle feather upright at the back of his head, although on more formal occasions he often donned a trail war bonnet made up of nearly a hundred honor feathers, each representing a brave deed. With a knife at his belt, he was otherwise armed only with a buffalo tail—for flies were bad on the Little Big Horn that summer. Like most of the Sioux and Cheyennes, Sitting Bull parted his hair in the center and wrapped his long heavy braids in otter skin. As was customary among the men as they rested in camp, he had his broad face painted red for good luck. But most of all, his firm heavy jaw and piercing gaze lent strength to his features. Not even the little twist at the left corner of his thin-lipped mouth could take away from his look of controlled power.

He listened quietly to the small talk of his companions, while gnawing at his thoughts was a growing conviction that something momentous—something terrible, perhaps—was about to take place.

As the morning wore on the village gradually came awake and stirred into its usual activity. Carrying hoes made of buffalo bone, many women moved out to the surrounding hills to dig for wild turnips. Others remained in camp, fleshing new antelope skins or catching up with their quillwork and beading. Some of the young men went fishing. It was a lazy day, and the pace was leisurely. Few people expected to encounter enemies, in spite of the warnings.

One Bull, Sitting Bull's twenty-three-year-old nephew and bodyguard, had arisen early to take the family horses to water at the nearby river. The stock had been picketed close to the chief's lodge all through the night, so One Bull and another bodyguard named Gray Eagle turned the herd loose on the grassy benches west of camp. As soon as the ponies settled down and began to feed, the two young warriors returned to the village. Sitting Bull then had only twenty

One Bull bringing the family stock to the river for watering.

head of horses, including buffalo runners, pacers, war horses, pack horses, brood mares, and colts, but all were choice animals. As a chief, Sitting Bull was often called upon to display his generosity, which kept him from getting rich like other men. One Minneconjou named Wounded Hand, for example, had accumulated over a hundred horses—one reason, perhaps, why Wounded Hand was not a chief.

One Bull's brother, White Bull, a Minneconjou, had left his wife's tepee in the Sansarc camp circle before sunup to take his horses out to drink and to graze. At twenty-seven, White Bull was a seasoned warrior—among the bravest of his tribe. In fact, few Indian fighting men ever equaled his record of over ninety battle honors. As a matter of precaution, he always carried his seventeen-shot Winchester rifle and two full cartridge belts. After seeing that his stock had drunk their fill, he drove them out north of the camp to graze, then went back to his tepee for breakfast, returning to his herd by midmorning. As the sun climbed higher in the sky, White Bull settled down to watch his grazing animals.

Iron Hail (Dewey Beard), aged seventeen, was also a Minneconjou. That morning he slept late like most of the other young people. By the time he awakened the sun was hot and his mother and aunt had gone out to dig turnips. Two uncles were also gone. A lone stray buffalo had been seen way off to the west and they had gone after it. His grandmother and another uncle were still in the lodge. A younger brother was herding the family horses on Muskrat Creek below the Santee camp. While Iron Hail ate breakfast, his uncle stirred around anxiously.

"When you finish eating," the uncle finally said ominously, "go help your brother watch the horses. Something might happen today. I feel it in the air."

Iron Hail obeyed, making a beeline for Muskrat Creek.

Although too young to be full-fledged warriors, Elk Head and his brother Two Runs had a special reason for family pride. Their father, whose name was also Elk Head, was custodian of the sacred Buffalo Calf Pipe of the Sioux Nation. For countless generations, the trusteeship of the pipe had

57

been handed down from father to son, always within the same blood line in the Sansarc tribe. The pipe was the most sacred object to all Sioux. This morning, as usual, it was wrapped in its special bundle of purifying sagebrush and hung from a special tripod in a medicine lodge which only the elder Elk Head might enter. His two sons mounted constant guard outside, however, within easy earshot of their father should danger approach.

The history of the pipe was ancient, dating far beyond the earliest winter count which went back less than a century and a half. Long winters ago, during a time of great hunger, two Sansarc hunters once went out in search of game. Buffalo and elk and deer were scarce. Even pronghorn were not to be found. After days of fruitless hunting, the young men were nearly ready to give up and return emptyhanded to their camp. Great was their surprise when they suddenly encountered a beautiful Indian maiden, garbed in flowing white buckskin and carrying a sage bundle. When one of the young hunters had carnal desire for the maiden and approached her, a cloud enveloped them both. As it lifted, the other hunter saw the sacred maiden again, and at her feet his companion who had had impure thoughts was a bare skeleton, his flesh eaten from his bones by bloated snakes.

"Behold!" cried the maiden to the good man who remained. "I am coming to your people, and will bring them something of great importance. Tell them to prepare for my coming."

The good hunter obeyed and the sacred maiden soon visited the Sansarc village. To Standing Hollow Horn, who was then chief of the tribe, she gave solemn instruction. From the sage bundle she took a pipe.

"With this sacred pipe," she said, "you will walk the

Earth, which is your Mother as the Great Mystery is your Father. The bowl of this pipe is red stone; it is the Earth. Every step you take upon Her should be as a prayer. The stem of the pipe is wood, and represents all that grows upon the Earth. These twelve feathers that hang from the stem are from the Spotted Eagle, and represent all the winged things of the air. All things of the universe are joined to you who smoke this pipe. All send their voices to the Great Mystery, for when you pray with this pipe you pray *for* and *with* everything!"

Presenting the pipe to Standing Hollow Horn, she said: "Behold this pipe! Always remember that it is sacred, and treat it as such, for it will take you to the end of time. I am leaving you now, but I shall always watch over your people. At the end I shall return to you again."

So saying, the mysterious sacred maiden walked away, the people looking after her in amazement. Then before their eyes a strange thing happened: the maiden suddenly sat down on the ground, and when she rose she had become a white buffalo which trotted away over the hill.

Elk Head and Two Runs knew the story well. Though not permitted to listen directly to religious talks that their father had with various holy men in the tribe, they had managed on several occasions to overhear him telling of the Buffalo Calf Pipe. And while they were not thinking of it particularly this morning, they remembered well the time two years ago when the pipe had been brought out for ceremonial smoking with a white soldier-chief.

The Sansarcs had been camped near the Black Hills that summer of 1874 when the soldiers came. None of the Sioux could understand then what the soldiers wanted in their country. But it did not seem the soldiers were interested in building towns or staying very long, so the Sioux made them welcome. Spotted Eagle and Fast Bear, chiefs of the Sansarcs, persuaded old Elk Head to arrange for them to smoke the Buffalo Calf Pipe with the long-haired leader of the soldiers, a ceremony which would serve the whites as assurance the Sioux wanted continued peace. It was a fine ritual. In smoking together, both parties pledged themselves to everlasting friendship and peace. The old days of war were gone forever, the long-haired soldier-chief promised, and no soldiers would ever attack Indians again. The Sioux took him at his word. But it was not long after that when the soldiers poked around in the ground and found much yellow metal considered sacred by white men. Thousands of whites poured into the Black Hills. The Sioux were shunted aside, even routed out of their old hunting grounds, so the whites could dig in the ground for the yellow metal. This time, the Sansarcs no longer bothered to assure the whites of their friendship, for they knew the white men did not mean what they said. Never again did the Sansarc chiefs invite a white man to smoke with them, but they always remembered that the *only* white man who ever did was the soldier-chief they called Long Hair.

Slight and sickly, Black Elk was dead for sleep when his father woke him at daybreak to help take the family horses to water and grass. The lad needed more rest than the exciting night-long kill-talks and victory dances in the Ogalala camp made possible. Knuckling sleep from his eyes, Black Elk obeyed his father's orders and uncoiled a long rawhide rope to tie on one of the ponies.

"If we tie one with the long rope, you can catch him easily, then round up the others," his father explained. "If anything happens today, bring back all the horses as fast as you can. Keep your eyes on the camp all the time."

With several other boys watching their horses nearby, Black Elk settled down for the day. By midmorning, however, he began to tire of sitting around with nothing to do, and thought of taking a swim. His cousin offered to stay with the horses until he got back.

Somehow, Black Elk did not feel just right as he and the other boys greased themselves with bear fat before plunging into the water. He felt a little sick, but more than that he felt strange. He thought of yesterday afternoon, when an old Ogalala medicine man named Hairy Chin had come to the riverbank and called him and five other boys into shore from this same swimming hole. The six boys were promptly enlisted in a curing ceremony. Though Black Elk, as a medicine man himself, was later to perform many acts of healing, this was his first participation in such a ritual.

The patient was a warrior named Rattling Hawk, who had been shot through the hip in the Rosebud fight with the Gray Fox eight days ago. People thought Rattling Hawk could never recover. If he did, he would certainly never walk again. Then Hairy Chin was called in. Because he had gotten his power to heal from a dream of a bear, Hairy Chin needed someone to take the part of bears in the curing ceremony. Black Elk and his companions were handy and willing.

Black Elk was painted yellow all over his body, and his hair was tied up to look like a bear's ears. The other boys were painted red and wore real bear's ears on their heads. Hairy Chin went all out and wore a complete bear's skin with the head intact. While Hairy Chin walked around on all fours and sang a sacred song, two girls entered the sick-lodge and gave Rattling Hawk a cup of water and some sort of herbs, which he chewed up and swallowed. Then the girls handed him a red stick. He stood up at once, leaning on the stick. The boys then began to jump around him, making growling sounds and pretending to be bears. Then, suddenly, feathers of different colors began to spill out of the boys' mouths. Rattling Hawk stirred a little bit and took a step. He hardly seemed like a sick man any more. He still was not well enough to fight, but it looked as if he would be able to walk again and he was past any danger of dying.

For Black Elk it had been a profound experience—one that he mulled over through the long morning. Somehow it seemed that because of the strange curing ceremony, something significant was about to happen.

Young Jack Red Cloud, aged eighteen, hardly dared show himself around the Ogalala camp circle during the Rosebud fight kill-talks. By now everyone knew that the son of the great Ogalala chief had not conducted himself as a warrior should in the battle with the soldiers of the Gray Fox. Now he sat in his lodge, sulking, and trying to put the onus of cowardice from his thoughts. But the persistent picture of that day on the Rosebud kept coming back. He had made at least three serious mistakes. First, of course, he had been foolish to wear his father's long trail bonnet. Any enemy might know by looking at him that he was hardly old enough to have won two or three honor feathers—let alone the hundred in the conspicuous headdress. His foolishness in wearing the war bonnet and carrying his father's Winchester with the name "Red Cloud" engraved on it (a weapon given the old chief by the white man's Government) made him fair game for the Crow and Shoshoni scouts who served the Gray Fox.

The first thing a warrior must do if his horse is killed, as any fighting man knows, is to remove the bridle calmly and coolly before running for safety. Red Cloud's failure to do so showed the enemy Indians how untried he was in battle. Running away on foot with the bonnet streaming out behind him made him a prime target.

The crowning disgrace, of course, was the refusal of the Crows to kill him after they had grabbed away his war bonnet and rifle as trophies. Instead of shooting him or riding him down with their ponies, they had simply struck him with their quirts—then rode away laughing, while he begged them to come back and finish him off.

Shamed and brooding, young Red Cloud very nearly joined four or five lodges of the Ogalalas' Bad Face band that were starting back toward Red Cloud Agency at midmorning. He might have to content himself with becoming an agency chief like his father, instead of a fighting leader like Crazy Horse or He-Dog. But something held him. Vowing never again to wear a war bonnet, Jack Red Cloud silently hoped for another battle—and a chance, perhaps, to redeem his honor.

Five uneasy strangers squatted around the breakfast fire of their host in the Cheyenne camp at the downstream end of the village. They were Arapahoes who had slipped away from their agency at Fort Robinson, Nebraska, to raid their enemies, the Wind River Shoshonis. Instead of finding Shoshonis, they had run headlong into a Sioux war party which had disarmed them and brought them in as prisoners to the Little Big Horn camp. Believing the stray warriors had acted as scouts for the Gray Fox, the Sioux wanted to kill them at once. But two Cheyennes, Black Wolf and Last Bull, happened by and took their part, advising the Sioux not to act too hastily. The Sioux chiefs decided to wait and ordered the captives put under tight guard for the night.

Next morning—June 24—the Arapahoes were taken to the lodge of Two Moon, a minor Cheyenne chief of the Fox warrior society, one of whose two wives was an Arapaho woman. Many Sioux followed, aiming cocked guns and drawn bows at the prisoners and insisting they must be killed. Women who had lost sons and husbands and brothers in the Rosebud fight asked for the death of the five Arapahoes. While the Sioux chiefs mulled it over, Two Moon spoke to the prisoners through his wife—since few outsiders spoke or understood Arapaho. After a while, Two Moon turned to the group.

"These Arapahoes are all right," he assured the Sioux chiefs. "They are our cousins and allies, and have come here to help us fight the soldiers if we are again attacked. Do not harm them, but give them back their property."

The Sioux were still undecided. The prisoners seemed doomed. One by one, the Arapahoes began to talk for themselves as Two Moon's wife interpreted for them. Yellow Eagle, Waterman, Yellow Fly, and Left Hand each spoke at length, telling of their friendship for the Sioux. Sage (Well-knowing One) talked last. Tense moments passed as he sparred for time. Then he remembered something the others had neglected to mention.

"On Powder River, before the Sioux took us prisoner, we

64

killed a white man—a rancher, I think," Sage told them. "That Sioux war party must have passed by the burned-out cabin before they caught up with us."

While the Sioux chiefs pondered Sage's statement, the leader of the war party recalled the fire-gutted ranch.

"No one scouting for the Gray Fox would kill a white man," the leader decided.

It was enough. With the flick of a buffalo-tail switch, the matter was dismissed. The prisoners were released and their weapons and ponies given back to them. Two Moon took them into his own lodge where, as his wife's relatives, they would be welcome. A minor tragedy had been averted.

Two Moon had done all he could to make the Arapahoes feel at home, Sage later remembered. The Cheyenne subchief took them all around the camp to meet various leaders. They even went with him last night to take part in a great victory dance at the Sansarc camp. But while the Rosebud fight kill-talks were going on, some of the Sioux treated them like interlopers and threatened to kill them.

Now, this morning, Two Moon's five guests squatted around the steaming breakfast kettle. While their genial host was occupied in cutting up willow-bark tobacco and mending feathers for a Cheyenne scalp dance planned for tonight, the Arapahoes cast wary glances toward the Sioux camps and hoped their captors would not cause them further trouble.

Not far from Two Moon's lodge was the tribal medicine tepee which contained the sacred Buffalo Head of the Northern Cheyennes—corresponding to the Buffalo Calf Pipe of the Sioux as a revered object. Like all the camps, the lodges were pitched in a great circle open to the east. The medicine tepee was along the western edge of the wide space within the circle, directly across from this gap. Guarding the sacred lodge was Roan Bear, a Fox warrior.

Cheyenne fighting men on the Little Big Horn were divided into three warrior societies: Elk warriors, Crazy Head warriors, and Fox warriors. At this time, the Fox warriors were on duty as camp policemen. It was up to them to enforce tribal laws—of which the Cheyennes had many—and to watch for the approach of enemies. The Sioux had a similar system.

While serving as guard for the medicine lodge, Roan Bear was permitted to talk to other warriors. Visiting him at midmorning were Bobtail Horse, an Elk warrior, and an Ogalala Sioux named White Cow Bull. The Ogalalas, as well as other tribes, had been invited to attend the Cheyenne scalp dance that night. White Cow Bull had ridden over to spend the day visiting friends in the Cheyenne camp.

Other visitors included a small contingent of Southern Cheyennes. Their chief was Lame White Man, aged thirty-eight, who had lived with the northern branch of the tribe so long he was no longer considered a southerner. Visiting him were eight Southern Cheyenne warriors and their families, led by thirty-one-year-old Brave Bear. They stayed in one big lodge next to Lame White Man's.

With the Rosebud fight fresh in their minds, Brave Bear talked to Lame White Man this morning of the dread winter eight years ago on the Washita River far to the south. At that time soldiers had come to destroy Black Kettle's band of Southern Cheyennes. There had been no warning of the surprise dawn attack. A hail of bullets had greeted Black Kettle's futile attempt to parley with the soldiers. A few warriors got away, finally; but Black Kettle lay dead, and the women and children of the tribe were led away into captivity at far-off Camp Supply on the North Fork of the Canadian River.

During the long winter trek officers commanding the victorious troops forced the younger prettier Cheyenne women, married and single, to come each night to their tents. Among the most attractive of all, Monahseetah (Meotzi) was picked to bed down with the soldier-chief, regardless of the fact that she was in deep mourning for her dead father, Chief Black Kettle. Strict Cheyenne morals counted for little with this soldier-chief, Brave Bear decided, for after they reached Camp Supply his white wife joined him and Monahseetah was discarded. Violated as she had been, no Cheyenne man now would take her as his wife.

"She was a proud woman," Brave Bear told Lame White Man. "For long months she kept silent as the child of the soldier-chief grew within her womb. At last, when the Cheyennes were all together again and the soldier-chief was talking peace with us, Monahseetah told him she was happy to bear his child. After that, he shunned her as though she had the white man's dreaded spotted sickness (smallpox).

"It was then that we chiefs met with this soldier-chief and smoked the pipe with him, for by now we were all ready for peace. The soldier-chief solemnly promised he would never attack us or fight us again. Someone explained to him that our smoking with him made the peace promise binding on us as well. The pipe was in my charge that day. It was my honor to light it first and smoke it last. Looking about me, I saw from their faces that the hearts of the Southern Cheyenne leaders were warm with hope. For a moment I, too, felt warm toward the soldier-chief and all white men. Then my mind darkened with thoughts of Monahseetah's disgrace. I took the dead ashes from the pipe and spilled them on the boots of the soldier-chief, placing upon him the endless curse of the Everywhere Spirit."

Brave Bear broke off suddenly as a gangling boy of seven with light streaks showing in his lank hair crept through the oval flap of the big tepee and stood blinking in the morning sun. A moment later a young woman whose face was still fair to look upon followed. At the woman's silent touch, the boy turned away to accompany her toward the river, where they went each day to gather kindling for the breakfast cook-fire. Lame White Man waited until they were out of earshot before he spoke.

"The boy with Monahseetah now—the lad called Yellow Bird—he is the son of the soldier-chief who killed Black Kettle?"

Brave Bear signed yes. "He goes with her everywhere, not caring to be around full-blooded children. Yet only his hair shows pale streaks, the light color such as white men often have. Otherwise, he could well be one of us."

Lame White Man signed agreement. For a while he remained quiet, for he wondered how his own wife might react if he told he was thinking of taking a second wife—and that he was considering Monahseetah, whose name was darkened by a cloud of white conquest eight years ago. At last he asked a question of Brave Bear. "Yellow Bird was fathered by the white soldier-chief?"

"It is so," Brave Bear answered. "The soldier-chief who had yellow locks hanging to his shoulders, the one we all called Long Hair."

Midday

THE SUN WAS straight overhead when Long Hair and the scouts came down from the Crow's Nest. The horse soldiers had already finished weapons' inspection. For the second time that day a bugle blared, sounding officers' call. Since trumpet calls had not been allowed the last two days, it was now plain to everyone that Long Hair no longer expected to take the Sioux by surprise.

The officers gathered around Custer, whose words could not be heard by the scouts. But they knew the entire command was getting final marching orders for the day. Presently, the officers separated to form their companies along the Lodgepole Trail.

As troopers jangled into a column of twos for the march, Long Hair's manner betrayed no lack of confidence. His earlier mood of introspection and doubt seemed to have vanished. With the return of his customary verve, he was once again the dashing *beau sabreur* of American arms. He had even discarded the shirt of blue-gray flannel in favor of his old campaign jacket of fringed buckskin with brass buttons. Under the turned-down collar he sported the bright blood-red cravat reserved for parades and other formal functions. Sleek and shiny from an orderly's quick rubdown, Vic danced under the saddle like a two-year-old colt.

At his side, quiet and observant, was the middle-aged newspaperman, Mark Kellogg—better known to the Indians as

Man-Who-Makes-the-Paper-Talk. The correspondent from Bismarck had ridden all the way out from Fort Abraham Lincoln on a little short-legged gray mule that brought many a smile to Arikara lips. The animal was so small that Kellogg's feet touched the ground, but for a mule he was fast and surefooted, and he had no trouble keeping up with the big chargers of the troopers.

Kellogg traveled light. He had no weapons and his only gear was an old black leather satchel slung over his shoulder. One or two Arikaras had gotten close enough a time or two to see that he carried tobacco and pipes and light clothing in the bag. Far more impressive was a supply of blank paper and pencils used by the correspondent to make picture writing. From Kellogg's scribbling, other white men were able to read words and whole messages that were sometimes sent back by runner to Dakota Territory. The Arikaras were still talking about the dispatch Kellogg sent back yesterday. They could not have read the words, but Girard had told them the contents. It had stated:

"We leave the Rosebud tomorrow and by the time this reaches you we will have met and fought the red devils, with what results remains to be seen. I go with Custer and will be at the death."

The Arikaras felt it was a strange way to talk of an impending victory—even in word pictures. It added to their growing uneasiness about the coming encounter with the Sioux. The scouts suddenly became attentive as Long Hair rode toward them.

"You there," Custer called, "the tall Crow with stripes on his face."

White-Man-Runs-Him kicked his pony's ribs until the

animal edged forward, Mitch Bouyer coming up behind him.

"You know the country," Long Hair went on. "Go ahead and look for me and see where I can make a success."

White-Man-Runs-Him looked questioningly at Bouyer until Custer's words were explained to him in Crow. Then he smiled faintly. Earlier, Long Hair had rebuked him sharply, belittling him in the eyes of the other scouts. Now, here was Custer asking him to show him the way.

"All right," White-Man-Runs-Him agreed. "Tell Son-of-the-Morning-Star I'll show him the way to go over into the valley."

The tall Crow looked neither right nor left, but led out the column, kneeing his pony into a lope up the slope of the divide. The troopers, with Custer and Kellogg in advance, followed at a sharp trot. Within minutes they reached the summit of the divide. The valley of the Little Big Horn lay before them.

A mile or so past the summit, Custer reined to a halt, signaling the adjutant to draw up alongside for further instructions. Lieutenant William W. Cooke, Adjutant of the Seventh Cavalry, came trotting up, patting trail dust from his luxuriant and normally dark Dundreary whiskers.

The next few minutes were busy ones for Cooke as Custer sent word to his battalion commanders to divide the regiment as previously arranged. Presently, Captain Frederick W. Benteen led his battalion of three troops (or companies) off to the left of the column. Heading southwest, they were soon lost to view in rough badlands. No Indian scouts rode with Benteen, but it was generally understood that his battalion was to head off any attempt by the Sioux to escape up the Little Big Horn valley.

71

The rest of the regiment was further divided. Major Marcus A. Reno and his battalion of three troops were ordered across the head of a small stream known to the Crows as Upper Ash Creek (Reno Creek). Captain Thomas

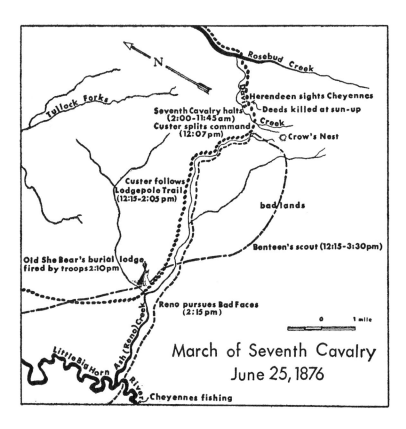

March of Seventh Cavalry
June 25, 1876

M. McDougall and his single troop held back to act as escort for the pack train, by which extra ammunition and supplies were transported. The other five troops remained on the right bank under Custer's personal command.

As white men tell time, it was seven minutes past noon when Custer's and Reno's battalions moved out, following parallel courses and staying within hailing distance across Upper Ash Creek. White-Man-Runs-Him and the other Crows were now far out ahead, riding along the right bank. He and his tribesmen were drawing closer with each hoofbeat to their home camp in the Big Horns off to the west. They knew this valley as well as their native mountains, for the Little Big Horn basin was Crow hunting ground—when the Sioux and Cheyennes were not around. They intimately knew every hill and bluff, every lone cottonwood and willow, every twist and turn of the little winding stream they now followed.

Nearly half a day had passed since Scout Herendeen had spotted the lone warrior on the ridge and had seen the jumble of pony tracks in the ravine by the regiment's back trail. At a half-mile's distance, Herendeen could not have guessed that the Indian he saw was *not* a member of a Sioux war party, but a Cheyenne outrider, Big Crow, scouting the trail for Little Wolf's band of seven lodges.

Little Wolf was an "old-man chief" of the Northern Cheyennes and the most respected leader of his tribe. But his personal following was then small. Seven lodges represented fewer than forty people, only fifteen of which were men of fighting age. For many days, the little band had been constantly on the move, hurrying to join their tribesmen on the Little Big Horn. Late yesterday afternoon, Little Wolf's scouts had stumbled onto the soldiers camped on the Upper Rosebud. With the utmost caution, he had kept his people hidden back in the hills while the horse soldiers had pushed on through the night. In the small hours of the morning the band had

gingerly followed, managing to avoid discovery by the soldiers
only through the most artful cunning.

An Indian outrider giving the alarm.

Although fifty-five, Little Wolf was a fighting leader of unlimited courage. His prowess as a strategist was unexcelled
in a tribe of great fighters. But he was too prudent a tactician
to venture into conflict with the soldiers he followed, who
clearly outnumbered his little band more than fourteen to one.
He was further bound by his duty as a chief to safeguard the
women and children above all else. Some of his warriors—
young bucks such as Black Horse and Medicine Bull, Big
Crow and Two Birds, and his son, Young Little Wolf—chafed
at the restraint. They repeatedly urged attacking the regimental pack train which brought up the rear of the column,
but Little Wolf was firm and held them back each time.

Unwittingly, Little Wolf's strategy paid off for the hostiles in more ways than one. The pony tracks found by Herendeen were those of Little Wolf's people hiding in the ravine, not a Sioux war party encircling the column as Herendeen guessed. And it was Custer's fear that the hostiles were beginning to flank him in an escape attempt that caused him to change his tactics and push on for a premature daylight attack on the Little Big Horn camp.

Keeping well out of sight, yet watching the soldiers' every move as they marched down Upper Ash Creek, Little Wolf's Cheyennes cautiously dogged the heels of the column.

The lone Sioux in the burial lodge had come close to dying as he had lived—on the field of battle. Old She-Bear was a Sansarc, a brother of Chief Circling Bear. As a warrior under the aegis of Crazy Horse, fighting genius of the Ogalalas, he had played a prominent part in the triumph over Crook on the Rosebud, and had suffered a critical wound—a soldier's bullet through both hips. Circling Bear's cohorts had brought him here to the band's temporary camp on Ash Creek, where he had lingered on for several days. Then, while the life slowly ebbed from him and most of the band moved on to the Little Big Horn four miles downstream, only his wife and a few kinsmen stayed on to the end.

Later on in the day Old Eagle and Two Bears had gone out to kill a badger. They brought back the carcass and slit open the belly, after an age-old Sioux custom. Removing the entrails, they allowed the blood to congeal. Then they propped up the wounded warrior so he could use the coagulated blood as a mirror. It was an ancient device for predicting the future. If a warrior saw a youthful image in the jelled blood, he would die young. If he saw the reflection of an aged person, he might count on living a long time. Old She-Bear stiffened perceptibly as he saw himself much as he was—a relatively young man. As he drew back in dismay, Two Bears stooped over him. He, too, saw his own youthful image reflected in badger blood.

Before many hours had passed, Old She-Bear breathed his last and in the early morning of the new day, Old Eagle and Two Bears painted the dead warrior's face red, and dressed him in his ceremonial buckskins. His widow cut off her heavy braids and gashed her legs with a sharp knife. Her keening could be heard for over a mile up and down the creek. Once her husband's body was ready and placed on a cottonwood-log scaffold six feet high, she pitched the lodge over him for the last time.

Using face paint, Old Eagle and Two Bears marked sacred symbols on the outside of the tepee. They would help to draw Wakan Tanka's attention to Old She-Bear's departing spirit and insure its arriving safely in the Last Hunting Ground. Normally, the process of decorating the lodge for burial would have taken several hours. But the variety of clay pigment in the area was limited, so they had to make out with few colors. The painting and ornamentation were completed soon after midday, just as Old She-Bear's widow and her aging aunt were striking the other lodges and loading their belongings on the pony drags for the move downstream to the Little Big Horn.

Kse e sewo istaniwe itatane—"Where the Young Girl Saved Her Brother's Life"—the Cheyennes already called the fight with the Gray Fox on the Rosebud. It had been Crazy Horse's victory and a triumph for the Sioux, but their Cheyenne allies were not without moments of glory. Such as the time, for example, when the horse of Comes-in-Sight was shot from under him, leaving the Cheyenne chief helpless in the path of the Gray Fox's charging Crow scouts. As the Crows whooped in triumph and came galloping to ride him down, the tall chief had stood facing them alone, defiantly chanting his death song. Then, suddenly, Comes-in-Sight's young sister, Buffalo Calf Road Woman, had dashed out on her fast little pinto. Before any Cheyenne fighting man could stop her, she was riding headlong between the opposing warriors. Bullets spat and arrows hissed all around, as she turned the little horse and swung low beside her brother to help him up behind her. The dumfounded Crows stopped dead in their tracks at such brash courage, while a wild cheer rose among the ranks of the Cheyennes as Buffalo Calf Road Woman carried Comes-in-Sight to safety. *Aiee,* it was a moment to remember long and well.

The details were fresh in the minds of Little Chief and White Shield as they sat fishing on the banks of the Little Big Horn not far from the mouth of Ash Creek. White Shield's little nephew had been sent to hunt for grasshoppers to be used for bait, and while the lad chased around through the tall grass up the bank, the two young warriors talked long of the courage of Buffalo Calf Road Woman. Not often did young bucks such as these have occasion to admire a woman for her bravery. But the sister of Comes-in-Sight had so encouraged her tribesmen that what had started as a Cheyenne rout ended as a Cheyenne victory. Instinctively, every Plains warrior lived and hoped for that supreme moment when courage and honor in battle stood above all else as a thing of unsurpassed beauty.

It was two hours past noon when White-Man-Runs-Him and his Crow companions loped to the top of the low ridge parallel to Ash Creek and looked down on the lone burial lodge. Though of an alien and enemy tribe, the tepee's purpose was plain to the scouts. Even some of the markings on the outside were similar to Crow symbols. Somewhat in awe, the scouts headed down the slope to the camp site vacated minutes earlier by Old She-Bear's family.

While the Crows were looking over the ground which showed circles of trampled grass where other lodges had been pitched, the Arikara scouts appeared at the top of the ridge. All the way downstream they had cautiously held back, letting the Crows lead the way and risk first contact with the Sioux. Now, seeing the camp site empty of enemies, they came whooping down the hill. Behind them Girard called out, "Long Hair says for you to run!" So they whipped their horses into a dead run and thundered toward the burial lodge.

"What does it look like we're doing?" Two Strikes shouted back between war cries.

Two Strikes reached the lone tepee first and struck it with his quirt. At his heels, Young Hawk rode up and also lashed at the cowskin cover. Then he dismounted at the tepee's north side, away from the door flap to the east, and stabbed at the tepee wall with his knife. Running the blade clear to the ground, he peered inside, then drew back hastily when he saw the painted corpse. Red Star rode up alongside and shouted, "He's coming! Long Hair's coming!"

Young Hawk leaped onto his pony and followed the other Arikaras into a dry coulee beyond the burial lodge, where they assembled to wait for Custer. Presently, the horse soldiers appeared on the ridge and started marching down the slope.

With Girard and Man-Who-Makes-the-Paper-Talk beside him, Long Hair rode at the head of the approaching column. The troops were shouted to a halt, but Custer and Girard rode on past the lone tepee to the coulee. Through Girard, Long Hair spoke to the Arikaras:

"Boys, I want you to take the horses from that Sioux camp up yonder. Make up your minds to go straight to their camp and capture as many horses as possible."

Stabbed turned to harangue the younger scouts. "Obey Long Hair's words and take many horses," he commanded solemnly.

"I know you're going to have a hard day of it," Long Hair went on. "You must keep your courage up, for you'll earn battle honors today."

Stabbed was rubbing some reddish clay in his fingers. Calling the young Arikaras around him, he had them lift their war shirts, one by one, while he spat on the clay and daubed sacred marks on each brawny chest.

"Father," Stabbed intoned, "I remember your promise to me this day; it is for my young men that I call upon you—"

His prayer was interrupted by the bugle, sounding the unfurling of the battle flag. Girard explained the trumpet call to the Arikaras and tense excitement swept through them as they made last-minute preparations for battle. The troopers had reassembled across the camp site. Reno's battalion, its formation intact, had crossed the stream, and soldiers throughout both commands were tightening saddle girths and discarding excess equipment.

Custer sat his horse quietly, watching Bloody Knife put on the black neckerchief with blue stars that he had given him. Once the dark cloth was in place, the Arikara scout tied the chin thong of his war bonnet under his jaw. Presently, Mitch Bouyer jogged over to speak with Custer.

"The Crows keep saying you'll find a good many more Sioux down there than you'll be able to handle," the half-breed warned. "The way they put it, there are more Sioux than all your soldiers put together have bullets."

Custer's eyes flashed. "You going soft on me, Bouyer?"

"Soft?"

"Yellow. Cowardly. Like an old woman. Call it anything you like."

The half-breed blinked and shook his head. "If we go in there, we'll never come out."

At his elbow, Bloody Knife made sign talk, saying, "His tongue is straight. What he says is true."

Long Hair cast a narrow glance at his old favorite. "You, too, Bloody Knife?"

In answer, Bloody Knife looked up at the sun, signed farewell, saying, "I shall not see you go down behind the Shining Mountains tonight."

Meanwhile, Girard had ridden over to the crest of a small knoll overlooking Ash Creek. Until now, the column had seen only scattered hostiles, mostly outriding scouts. But Girard suddenly spotted a band of some forty Sioux between the camp site and the creek, apparently in flight downstream toward the Little Big Horn. They were members of the Ogalala Bad Face band, who had started out that morning toward Red Cloud Agency, then had turned back sharply upon sight of the soldiers. Taking a second look, Girard noticed that although the Sioux kept moving, the warriors who brought up the rear did not seem to be afraid of the soldiers or much surprised at the sight of them. Girard turned in the saddle to call out to Custer, "Here are your Indians, running like devils!"

Long Hair snapped an order to the Arikaras, while his spurs jabbed Vic into motion, "After them, boys! Charge!"

But not an Arikara left the coulee. Girard came trotting over, but the scouts stayed motionless as though rooted to the ground. Custer looked around him in desperation. Mistaking the returning Bad Faces for the main group of hostiles, he believed they were slipping through his grasp. Time was running out, he thought; soon the Sioux would be scattered to the four winds, all chance of spectacular victory vanished into thin air. Calling Girard to his side, Custer had words of scorn for the timorous Arikaras:

"You're supposed to go right on to the Sioux village. I told you to charge and stop for nothing. You've disobeyed me. Move aside and let my soldiers pass you. If any of you is afraid to make a charge with them, I'll take his weapons away and make a woman out of him!"

Two Strikes shouted back an answer, "Tell Long Hair if he does the same to all his white soldiers, who aren't as brave as we are, it will take him a long time indeed."

Most of the Arikaras laughed nervously, refusing to quiet down until, scowling and silent, Bob-tailed Bull rode back and forth among them to restore order. But by that time Long Hair had turned away in disgust. Looking around, he saw Reno across the camp site. Beckoning to Cooke, Custer snapped sharp orders unheard by the scouts. After saluting, the adjutant cantered across to Reno and promptly relayed the orders:

"The General directs you to go after the hostiles, Major. Take your battalion and bring them to battle. Charge the

Indians wherever you find them. The General will support you with the whole outfit." Then he added, "He further directs you take the scouts with you."

As Reno led out his battalion at a sharp trot, Girard and Reynolds and Herendeen followed with most of the Arikara scouts. Two or three had fallen behind owing to poor mounts and were bringing up the rear with the pack train and Captain McDougall's troop. With Girard and the Arikaras were two mixed-blood Picunnies (Blackfeet), the Jackson brothers, and Isaiah Dorman, a Negro interpreter who had lived some years with the Sioux and knew their language.

Bouyer and the Crows, at Custer's suggestion, held back and did not join the Arikaras and Reno's battalion. Then Half Yellow Face saw a dust cloud rising and pointed it out.

"The Sioux are running away," he said.

Advised of this, Long Hair ordered Half Yellow Face and White Swan to go up on the next ridge for a look-see. The two Crows were confused by Custer's attempt at sign talk. Misunderstanding his orders, they turned sharply off to the left and rode after Reno's battalion. Bouyer shrugged, then led the four remaining Crows up the ridge.

Custer turned his full attention now to his own battalion of five troops. Following Reno's course, but taking a more leisurely pace, he moved out at the head of his immediate command. Soon Reno's battalion was so far ahead it was no longer in sight. As the tail end of Custer's command passed the lone tepee, a four-man detail swung out of the column long enough to set it afire. Glancing back over their shoulders as they trotted on, the troopers could see the blaze dancing in the still air a long time as Old She-Bear's burial lodge went up in flames.

Afternoon: Reno

RENO'S command crossed the Little Big Horn shortly after
2:30 P.M., as white men tell time. Custer was a full three-
quarters of a mile behind as Reno re-formed his battalion in
thick timber across from the mouth of Ash Creek. Stragglers
looking back caught a last glimpse of Custer as he came up
the stream at the head of his troops. With boyish exuberance
the General waved his hat in his old beloved gesture of confidence, and no one doubted he and his battalion would be
close behind Reno in the charge down the valley.

Out in front, where the timber gave way to open prairie,
Half Yellow Face tapped Charley Reynolds's arm and pointed.
The Ogalala Bad Faces were ahead and off to the left, but
no longer running. Another smaller band—Old She-Bear's
family—was moving slowly over to the right, skirting the
edge of timber that fringed the river all the way along. Reynolds called Girard over.

"Someone better tell Long Hair the Sioux are no longer
running," the scout suggested.

Girard found Reno, who sent an orderly back to Custer,
advising him of the change in the behavior of the hostiles.
Reno added in his message that the Sioux might be in greater
force than anticipated.

In a matter of five or ten minutes, Major Reno set up his
attack formation. The Indian scouts under Lieutenants Var-

num and Hare formed the left front. Two troops, A and M Companies, rode abreast in columns of fours, while the third troop, G Company, followed in reserve. Altogether, Reno had a battle strength of 112 officers and men, and 21 scouts. Riding some twenty yards in advance, Reno led his detachment out into the valley at a brisk trot.

Reno's battalion at the charge.

White Shield's young nephew, Dives Backward, caught grasshopper after grasshopper for his uncle and Little Chief to use as fish bait. He grabbed the insects off tall grass stems, then carried them, one by one, in cupped hands down the bank. Kept busy, he wondered why it was that the Sioux liked to catch fish well enough, but seldom ate them. In some ways, Dives Backward thought, the Sioux were much wilder people than his own tribe, the Northern Cheyenne.

Just after catching another grasshopper and starting down the bank with it, the lad heard hoofs rumble on the hard ground of the flat above. It sounded like thousands of horses thundering past. Running up the slope, Dives Backward got his first look at the enemy Arikaras, who had a distinct and unfamiliar look. One war-bonneted rider, probably Bloody Knife, caught the boy's eye. Sensing danger at once, he quickly forgot all about grasshoppers and fish, and clambered down the bank. "I saw someone wearing a war bonnet go by!" he shouted to his uncle. "They're looking for someone."

White Shield and Little Chief hurried up to higher ground to look. By that time the Arikaras had all ridden past, but soldiers dressed in Army blue were visible through the haze of dust.

"The camp!" cried Little Chief. "They're going to attack the camp!"

White Shield agreed, and the three ran back down to the Little Big Horn. By keeping in the defile of the river, they hoped to reach the Cheyenne camp circle nearly six miles downstream.

The Arikaras kept well to the left as Reno's battalion swept down the valley. The first tepees of the village were visible two miles down-river, while on high ground to the west the vast Sioux pony herds earmarked the rugged course the scouts would have to follow. As the soldiers drove head-on toward the village, the Arikaras were to swing westward to capture the horses of the hostiles. In a spurt of speed the battalion took the gallop, G Company moving up into line with the other troops. Reno kept his position to the front and center of the line.

As the valley floor leveled out, a stand of timber jutting west of the riverbank momentarily cut off Reno's view of the village. Clouds of thick dust added to the detachment's difficulty in making out its target.

Old Eagle later explained that he and Lone Dog and Two Bears had sent their women hurrying on ahead with Old She-Bear's widow and the loaded pony drags. Then the young warriors quickly tied sagebrush clumps to their ponies' tails and sashayed back and forth many times, raising dust in the path of the oncoming soldiers. Once, Two Bears rode wide, clashing headlong into the Arikara scouts. Old Eagle and Lone Dog scurried off to safety, but Two Bears never joined them. Like Old She-Bear, he had seen his face reflected young in badger blood.

Darting toward the milling pony herd, Bloody Knife rode far ahead of the other scouts. Swallowed up in a swirl of dust, he soon came galloping back to the others, herding three Sioux horses ahead of him.

"Someone take these horses," he shouted to Red Star and Boy Chief. "One of them is mine."

Then he turned his horse to dash back through the rising clouds of dust. This time, several of the other Arikaras and the two Crows followed him.

Among Sitting Bull's visitors in the council lodge after the midday meal was a prominent young Hunkpapa warrior named Rain-in-the-Face. Though not yet a chief, Rain-in-the-Face had a wide following as a fighting leader among the Hunkpapa and Blackfeet Sioux.

He had a further distinction. Some months previously, an Army veterinarian and a post sutler had gotten lost from their command. Lonesome Charley Reynolds had guided a young Army captain to Rain-in-the-Face's camp near Standing Rock

Agency, where the warrior was arrested by the captain for the murder of the missing whites. He was taken in chains to be confined in the guardhouse at Fort Abraham Lincoln. While troops held the Sioux prisoner, the captain slapped and kicked him into insensibility. One night, the young Hunkpapa broke out with several other prisoners and joined the hostiles. Rain-in-the-Face took a solemn vow, swearing eternal vengeance against the captain, remembering everything about his appearance, even learning that he was Tom Custer, the brother of Long Hair. In all the great camp on the Little Big Horn, no one, not even Sitting Bull, had a deeper hatred for the white man than Rain-in-the-Face.

Also in the council lodge that afternoon were Crow King, Black Moon, chief of the Fox warriors doing camp police duty that day, and a Blackfoot Sioux chief named Kill Eagle. Conspicuously absent was Gall, a Hunkpapa fighting chief better known throughout the tribe for his jealousy of Sitting Bull than for his courage. Also away from his usual place in the circle was old Four Horns, alone with his grief since early morning.

The business at hand centered about Sitting Bull's wily efforts to persuade Kill Eagle and his band to stay on with the hostiles. Although the Blackfeet Sioux chief had repeatedly stated his intention of returning to Standing Rock Agency, the bitter comments of Rain-in-the-Face about the white man's road had a telling effect. Numerous presents of ponies and fine buffalo robes had been received gracefully enough by Kill Eagle's people, but it was the evidence of the white man's brutality and injustice that held him and his twenty lodges on the Little Big Horn. For Sitting Bull, of course, it was another routine diplomatic coup. Under the

87

pall of intense heat that hung over the camp, the crafty head chief of the Hunkpapas flicked at flies with his buffalo-tail switch as Kill Eagle decided at last to remain.

At that moment Fat Bear burst into the council lodge. Four Horns's grandson had stumbled into camp after a full fifteen-mile run across country. Brown Back, returned at last, brought word of the killing of Deeds by white soldiers! For long hot hours the wiry lad had dog-trotted over hills and across ravines to spread the alarm back in camp. Once he had lain hidden for better than the time it took to run six miles when a column of soldiers rode past. The sun was high and hot before he felt safe to move on. By then the soldiers were between him and the camp. More precious time was lost when he was forced to make a wide circle to avoid them.

Black Moon sprang to his feet and hurried out to marshal the camp police upon whom the initial defense of the entire village might well depend. Sitting Bull followed, limping from a twelve-year-old wound—a soldier's bullet in his left hip.

One Bull was at the river, tending the family horses after the midday watering, when he heard shooting at the Hunk-papa camp. Since camp police did not permit offhand firing, he recognized the shots as a warning of approaching danger. In the near distance he saw dust rising, heard the pounding of iron-shod hoofs. Quickly catching his best pony, One Bull turned the other stock loose. Well trained, the horses headed back toward camp as soon as their hobbles were removed. One Bull raced for the tepee he shared with his uncle.

The camp was in an uproar. Everything was confusion and noise. While warriors dashed away to catch their ponies, older men shouted advice at the tops of their lungs. In head-

88

long flight, women and children were rushing away on foot or on horseback toward the north end of the village. All too often, stumbling children and scurrying dogs got in the way of the warriors and their plunging mounts. The women had no time to strike their lodges. Grabbing up babies and clutching young children to their sides, they hurried off to safety. Belongings had to be left behind. Old people hobbled away, leaning on sticks, moving as fast as creaking joints permitted. Here and there, a lost child stood crying, knuckling tears from its eyes. As yet, the chiefs had had little time to organize a defense. In spite of the various warnings, no one really expected an attack today.

One Bull reached the family lodge just ahead of his uncle. The young warrior grabbed up his old muzzle-loader and checked it over quickly. It really was not much of a weapon for close-in fighting. Just then, Sitting Bull entered the tepee and abruptly took the old rifle away from his nephew. Handing One Bull a stone-headed war club, he took his own rawhide shield from its buckskin case and hung it over the warrior's shoulder. The shield was not only for protection; this particular one was a badge of the chief's own authority.

"You will take my place and go out and meet the soldiers," Sitting Bull ordered. "Parley with them, if you can. If they are willing, tell them I'll talk peace with them."

Firing sounded in the near distance as the soldiers kept coming. Bullets whined overhead. As a stray shell splintered one of the tepee poles above, One Bull glanced up doubtfully.

"What if the white soldiers refuse to talk peace, Uncle?"

"Then go right in. Don't be afraid. Go ahead."

Sitting Bull buckled on his cartridge belt as they hurried from the lodge. Another bodyguard named Iron Elk had caught the chief's war horse, a black stallion with a blaze face and white stockings. Armed with a .45 revolver and a '73 Winchester carbine, Sitting Bull leaped on the bare back of the stallion. Loping to his aged mother's lodge, he helped the old woman on her horse and saw her safely on her way.

Sitting Bull's war shield.

In front of a nearby lodge, old Four Horns forgot his sorrow long enough to grab up a bow and arrows, and climb on a bony roan horse nearly as ancient as himself.

"Hoka Hey!" the old chief shouted out the Sioux call to battle. When the camp was threatened no leader, however old, could shirk his duty.

By this time, a number of young warriors had gathered around One Bull. Raising his uncle's shield high, he led them out to meet the soldiers.

Peace talk was far from the minds of the soldiers as they galloped down the valley in battle line with pistols cocked and carbines at the ready. The three troops managed to stay well abreast during the charge, but the Arikaras were far to the front and left, attempting to cut off the hostile pony herds.

A vast number of horses was being driven back toward camp by the youths who watched the herds. Even a few women, who had been out digging wild turnips, joined in the drive, waving shawls and sticks and hurling earth clods to keep the horses moving close enough to the village to be caught by the warriors.

Soldiers in the line opened fire, utterly disregarding the slight young warrior with war club and chief's shield who came riding out with his hand raised in the peace sign. Quickly aware that peace, or even talk of it, was out of the question, One Bull led his warriors out in a counter charge. To his right, Chief Black Moon rode up with a large body of camp police, bent on saving a large part of the pony herd now threatened by the Arikaras.

Several scouts under Bob-tailed Bull and Bloody Knife had succeeded in cutting out a big bunch of horses and were turning them back up the valley. Seeing Young Hawk ride up, Bloody Knife shouted to him:

"What Long Hair wanted is being done! We are taking the enemy's horses!"

Camp by camp, the alarm spread through the village. "Chargers are coming! Chargers are coming!" went the warning. The Hunkpapa crier was hoarse from shouting at the top of his lungs.

The cry was picked up at the Ogalala camp circle. From camp to camp, the people could hear the cry going all the way north to the Cheyennes. Everybody ran to catch horses. The first thought was to get away.

"Chargers are coming! They are charging!" echoed the cry again and again.

Bullets rattled like hailstones through the tepee poles in the Hunkpapa camp. The cowhide lodge covers were peppered with bullet holes.

"Brave up!" shouted Sitting Bull, trying to be everywhere at once to see to the camp's defense. "We have everything to fight for. If we're defeated, we'll have nothing to live for. It'll be a hard time, but fight like brave men! Brave up!"

The camp defenders stood their ground. A warrior named White Beard forgot the age-old taboo against talking to his mother-in-law when he saw her running for safety with a child dragging after her. He gave her his horse, helping the little fellow up behind her.

Iron Hawk, a young Hunkpapa, hurried out to the family horses grazing apart from the main herd close to camp. He succeeded in roping one before the bunch stampeded toward the Minneconjou camp. Jumping on the horse he had caught, he and his older brother finally managed to round up the spooked horses. Children came up from the river wringing wet from swimming. An old man hobbled by on a stick and shouted to Iron Hawk:

"Take courage, boy! Would you see these little children taken from me like so many dogs? Brave up!"

Iron Hawk hurried to the family lodge and dressed for war as fast as he could. He had to hold the pony's rope all the time he was getting ready, and the little horse kept jerking and trying to get away. Between the horse and bullets rattling all around, Iron Hawk was so shaky it took him a while to braid an eagle feather into his hair. After that he painted his face red, grabbed up his bow and arrows, hurried out, and climbed on his horse again—ready for battle at last. A big party of warriors rode up.

"It's a good day to die!" they yelled.

Iron Hawk was ready for death, too, if it came.

It was blazing hot. Black Elk's cousin had just brought the horses to water when the alarm went up. Black Elk and his brother hurried out of the swimming hole, not taking time to dry themselves with bunch grass or leaves as they usually did. They felt lucky to have their horses handy at a time like this. Black Elk's brother leaped on his favorite mount, a fine sorrel, and loped off toward the Hunkpapa camp. After he had left, their father rushed up.

"Your brother has gone to fight without his gun. Catch him and give it to him. Then hurry right back to me."

He had two six-shooters. One was Black Elk's own, a gift from an aunt. Taking the two handguns, Black Elk singled out a fast buckskin horse, mounted, and galloped after his brother.

After Black Elk delivered the revolver, he rode on a way with his brother. They could see a big dust cloud coming, and out of the dust were riding blue-clad troopers on their big chargers. They came shooting at everything before them, but they kept aiming high. Some of the younger soldiers were so excited they were shooting straight up into the air. Black Elk refused to leave when his brother told him to go back. They made a dash for a clump of timber and brush where some other warriors were gathering. The soldiers were shooting at these warriors, but aiming high so that leaves fell on them from trees where the bullets struck. Behind them in the Hunkpapa camp, a new cry went up:

"Take courage! Don't be women! The helpless are out of breath!"

It was the voice of Gall, fighting chief of the Hunkpapas. Around him the warriors began to rally. The soldiers were close now, but coming on more slowly as the Sioux resistance built up.

In the Ogalala camp a fighting leader flinched at the sounds of alarm. Unlike his usual self, Crazy Horse was jumpy at reports of attacking soldiers. Only a week had passed since he had led his warriors to victory on the Rosebud. Yet somewhere in the dark of his mind lurked an old silent fear, a harkening back to his early boyhood when Worm, his father, had tested his courage by forcing him to cut open a snapping turtle and eat its beating heart raw. Few of his tribesmen knew of his vulnerability, few guessed the calf of his left leg bore the scar of an old wound from a fight with the Skidi Pawnee long ago. People throughout the tribes thought him bulletproof and impervious to enemy arrows, but Crazy Horse knew better. The hours of combat ahead called for cautious preparation if he was to survive and come through another battle unscathed.

With deliberate care the Ogalala opened a soft buckskin bag, taking from it the fooling gopher dust with which he must sprinkle himself and his war pony. Then he got out the rawhide parfleche in which he kept a small kit of earth pigments. Selecting yellow ocher, he daubed spittle-wetted fingers into the powdery pigment, then dotted his lean, stripped body with protective hail spots. Gradually he regained his normal composure. Stepping from his lodge, he moved lithely across the open camp circle, calling his warriors around him.

"My friends," he shouted, handsome with his light complexion and small aquiline nose, "remain cool and fight until your last arrow and shell are released. Keep in mind that our women and children will be in great danger if the soldiers reach our village. As soon as you are mounted, follow me toward the river. *Hiyupo!* Come on!"

Suddenly the Sioux onslaught began. The Arikaras forgot all about taking enemy horses and fell back like leaves before a high wind. Reno halted his troops. As he did so, Black Moon's force turned from the rescued pony herd and charged his left flank. Two troopers failed to hold their skittish mounts as the howling horde bore down on the line. Frantic with excitement, the two cavalry horses bolted, carrying their riders straight into the Sioux charge. The warriors' line simply opened up to swallow the hapless soldiers in a gaping, dusty maw which closed in around them.

A few of the Arikaras tried to hold their ground. Bloody Knife and Young Hawk joined the soldiers at the left of the line. Bob-tailed Bull was cut off by a whirl of yelping warriors. He went down under a hail of bullets. The rest of the Arikaras seemed to have vanished into thin air.

With his left all but enveloped, Major Reno looked to the rear for Custer's promised support. The rest of the regiment was nowhere in sight. With every moment, the Sioux horde ahead of him increased. Here were already more warriors than Sitting Bull was supposed to have with him. No Indian fighter, Reno did what seemed to the Sioux a strange thing.

He ordered his troops to dismount, save for every fourth soldier who held the mounts of three other men. By fighting on foot, Reno sought to penetrate the stand of timber jutting out from the river. Even with a trimmed-down force, the dismounted skirmishers managed to advance for a quarter of an hour or so. But now the Sioux had not only turned Reno's left back on itself, they were threatening his rear and might try at any moment to stampede his led horses—which would be disastrous for his battalion.

Looking down the valley, Reno still could see no sign of Custer's five troops, the promised support behind his own initial attack. The entire valley seemed to be swarming with hostiles. Already most of the Arikaras had turned tail and were running for safety back the way they had come. Reno called Lieutenant Wallace of G Company to his side.

"Send one of the scouts to Custer," he ordered. "If we're going to get out of here ourselves, we'll need help—and fast."

Wallace cast about for someone to go. Mixed-blood Billy Jackson was firing offhand at a Sioux rider who kept riding close. The lieutenant tried hard to talk him into going, but Jackson waved his hand to the rear, Indian fashion, signing refusal.

"No man could get through alive," he countered.

With no way to reach Custer or send for help, Reno ordered the battalion to change front, putting the river at its rear, the south end of the village on its right. The troops pivoted on the double, falling back into the edge of the timber, while the Sioux closed in from all sides. With more warriors pouring up the valley by the minute, Reno's position had now become strictly defensive. Further attack on the village was simply out of the question. The battalion was already outnumbered more than ten to one.

White Bull, watching the family horses out north of camp, heard the criers yelling the alarm. He leaped on his fastest horse, a sleek bay, and chased his stock back to the village. Off to the south the Army blue of the soldiers and the glint of sunlight on their gun barrels were already visible through the dust. Confusion had now reached the Sansarc camp circle, with fleeing women and children running everywhere, young girls clutching blankets over their heads in bewildered fright, fat old women panting and sweating to get away. A few very old people were hobbling away on their sticks, hurrying off to the safety of the grassy benches to the west toward which all noncombatants now headed. It was everyone for himself White Bull saw to it that his wife got away safely, then raced upriver to join his uncle, Sitting Bull, in the defense of the village.

White Bull's father, Makes Room, Sitting Bull's brother-in-law, had his lodge pitched on the north side of the Hunk-papa camp circle. By the time White Bull rode up, the warriors had rallied under his brother, One Bull, and Gall. A brisk battle was in progress with the soldiers, and the Sioux seemed to be gaining a little ground. The soldiers had dismounted and were gradually falling back. Forming a line, the troopers set up a guidon. Then White Bull saw that part of the troops was falling back again while others stayed near the guidon.

"Whoever is brave, get that flag!" White Bull shouted.

No one seemed to hear him just then—at least no warrior volunteered to capture the guidon. Before White Bull, himself, could do anything about it the soldiers fell back again, taking the guidon with them.

Four miles north, in the Cheyenne camp circle, the people milled about uncertainly. The alarm had already gone up and a few families had started for the benches to the west. But most of the tribe stood around, uneasily watching the tower of dust rising beyond the Hunkpapa camp. As yet, there was no sign of the soldiers.

Sage, one of the five Arapahoes, had gone with Two Moon to help water his host's horses at the river. One by one, the sweltering animals were swabbed down with cool water. The men even splashed around in the river themselves before leading the horses back to camp. Two Moon and his guest both walked the short distance in order to leave the horses fresh. Then, suddenly, they saw the dust down at the Sioux camp. Presently, a Sioux horseman came riding through the Cheyenne camp at a gallop.

"Soldiers are coming!" he shouted. "Plenty white soldiers are coming!"

Two Moon ran toward his lodge, picking up the cry, *"Nutskavebo!* White soldiers are coming! Everybody run for your horses!"

While the warriors hurriedly prepared for battle, the women stirred into activity, beginning a mass exodus from the camp. A few managed to strike their lodges and load them on pony drags before starting west toward the benches. But most of the camp circle was left standing. In all the excitement, people kept running back to get things they had forgotten and left behind. A few of the oldsters stood dazed and motionless, as though rooted to the ground.

"*Hay-ay! Hay-ay!*" started the Cheyenne battle cry. Some of the warriors were ready and massed in a group to wait for their leaders.

The Sioux horseman came back again and rode around, shouting to the women, "Get out of the way! We're going to have a big fight!"

Some of the Cheyennes did not understand his words, but his meaning was plain enough. Everyone scrambled out of his path.

Two Moon called the young men around him. "Warriors, don't run away if the soldiers charge you," he told them. "Stand and fight them. Keep your eyes on me. I'll stand even if I am sure to be killed!"

It was a brave fighting talk. With Two Moon leading the way, the warriors dashed off in a body to the Hunkpapa camp. Fewer than a handful remained to guard the Cheyenne circle.

Reno's behavior was proving to be a puzzle for Sitting Bull. The Hunkpapa chief could not figure out why such a small band of soldiers had come to the very outskirts of the camp, then had dismounted and fallen back, when only by charging could they hope to fight their way through the village. Too shrewd a strategist to underestimate the whites, Sitting Bull sensed some sort of trap.

"Watch out for a trick!" he warned, riding back and forth among the Sioux warriors who now held the ground between the camp and the troops.

In spite of his uncle's warning, One Bull had his hands too full of fighting just then to think the white soldiers were carrying out any sort of subterfuge. When the enemy retreated, it was time to charge. One Bull and Black Moon combined their

99

forces and led a charge against the soldiers in the timber. Almost at One Bull's elbow, Good Bear Boy was shot from his horse. An instant later Black Moon fell. The chief of the camp police was dead, but Good Bear Boy was only wounded. One Bull commanded Looking Elk to rescue him, but Looking Elk either did not hear or did not care—he paid no heed. Good Bear Boy was trying to crawl back to the Sioux lines. With bullets hissing all around him, One Bull halted and jumped off his horse long enough to pick up Good Bear Boy and get him on the excited animal. Then One Bull leaped on the horse's back behind the wounded man. Together, they rode back to safety.

Shot through both thighs, Good Bear Boy was bleeding heavily. One Bull and his mount were quickly covered with the wounded man's blood. Thinking he had reached a safe place, One Bull got down again, swinging the horse broadside to the line of fire. Suddenly the horse screamed. A bullet had struck one hind leg. They were still out in the open, so One Bull led the horse on toward the Sioux lines until he could turn Good Bear Boy over to friends who would take care of him. Then One Bull hurried back into the fight.

In spite of a steadily mounting assault against his position, Reno had lost only one man aside from the Arikara scouts, most of whom were dead or missing. Sergeant Heyn of G Company had been shot through the chest during the change of front. Now the major saw he was about to lose another man—through desertion. A trooper was defying orders to hold fast and was making a run for it through the timber.

"Stop that man!" shouted Reno. "No man leaves this line, dead or alive, until I give the order!"

White Swan, one of the two Crows with Reno, may have misunderstood. Or perhaps Bloody Knife, next to Reno, misinterpreted the major's words as an order for the Crow to overtake and kill the deserter, and passed it along as such in sign talk. At any rate, White Swan got up quickly and took after the trooper. Snaking his way through timber and brush, it did not take the scout long to run down the fugitive. The trooper's death cry as White Swan's knife plunged into him was lost in the din of battle. In a little while, the Crow quietly resumed his place in the line. Reno had his hands too full to notice what had happened.

Reno's position in the timber was fast becoming untenable. Several of his led horses had been hit by flying bullets, and overwhelming numbers of hostiles now surrounded the timber. A few, in fact, were already beginning to infiltrate his thinly held line. There was still no sign of support. Although he was not close enough to report the fact to Reno, Lieutenant De-Rudio of A Company now saw mounted troops moving along the bluffs across the Little Big Horn. Even at that distance he could recognize Custer's buckskin clothing and Adjutant Cooke's immense whiskers. Lieutenant Varnum also caught a glimpse of the gray-horse troop marching along the bluffs, but *away* from Reno's position. It was not until later that Varnum remembered the gray-horse troop had been assigned to Custer's battalion. All this, of course, was unknown to Reno. His ammunition was getting low, his reserves already dipped into, and no way of getting through to the pack train to replenish. Unless he got out of the timber fast, it added up to disaster. He gave the order to stand to horse. In the noise and confusion, many failed to hear him.

In the center of the timber was a small clearing of ten acres or so, formerly used as a camping place by a Sioux medicine man. Here, Reno re-formed his command. With Bloody Knife at his side, the major shouted out the order, "Mount!"

At that moment, a large number of hostiles broke through the timber, firing point-blank on the troops in the clearing. In the melee, Reno lost his hat. With frenzied haste, he tied a white neckerchief around his head to keep the hair out of his eyes.

The Arikara with the war bonnet had attracted the attention of the Cheyennes since they had joined in the assault. Breaking into the clearing with the Sioux, Turkey Legs and Crooked Nose kept angling for a sure shot at this enemy "chief." At last Crooked Nose drew a careful bead and fired.

Trooper Lorenz of M Company was first hit. Hollering, "Oh, my God, I have got it!" he toppled from his mount. Caught in the same volley was Bloody Knife, less than ten feet to Reno's right and slightly to his front. The Arikara was struck square between the eyes, his brains and blood spattering in Reno's face, bits of feathers dancing crazily for a moment in the smoke-fogged air.

Completely disconcerted, the major ordered the troops to dismount, then immediately countermanded with an order to remount. Giving no further orders, he whirled his horse and broke through the timber into open plain, the confused troopers close on his heels. There was no chance to re-form the battalion. In a straggling column they stampeded up the valley at a dead run, Reno well to the front, his eyes frantically set on the upstream ford where he and his command had crossed hardly more than an hour earlier.

102

Hard pressed in the timber, six Indian scouts had their hands too full to be aware of Reno's withdrawal. Young Hawk and Goose crawled through thick brush, trying to join Forked Horn and the two Crows, Half Yellow Face and White Swan (Strikes Enemy). Already the hostiles had spotted them and were peppering them with bullets. Giving up their attempt to reach the others, Young Hawk and Goose made a run for their horses, tied to trees in the grove. Just after they mounted, a groan of shocked pain passed Goose's lips. Young Hawk reined up sharply.

"Cousin, I am wounded," said Goose.

His right arm was badly shot up. Young Hawk hurried to his side, taking his cartridge belt and buckling it around his own waist.

"You'd better get down," he told Goose.

Before the wounded man could dismount, his horse was shot down. Young Hawk propped Goose against a tree, handing him the reins of his own pony. Seething with hot anger, Young Hawk stripped off his blue Army coat and prepared to fight for his own and his kinsman's life.

Off through the trees the two Arikaras saw a duel in progress. White Swan rode out to face the enemy and a tall Cheyenne (named Whirlwind) came charging from the hostile ranks. Running their horses at each other full tilt, the antagonists fired almost simultaneously. Both men toppled from their mounts. The Cheyenne lay dead, but the Arikaras could see their Crow friend trying to crawl back to safety. White Swan had a bullet through his leg and one hand had been nearly shot away. Half Yellow Face dashed out to help his tribesman. A minute later he came creeping through the brush to find Young Hawk.

"My friend is being killed," he said. "He is just at the edge of the timber."

Young Hawk followed him back, the two men crawling through dense undergrowth until they reached White Swan, who lay on his back. Taking him by the arms, Young Hawk and Half Yellow Face dragged the wounded Crow back to where Goose was sitting with his back against the tree. White Swan smiled above his pain.

"I am not afraid," he said. "I am glad to be wounded."

Young Hawk felt a quick surge of emotion. He did not want to see his wounded comrades mutilated by the hostiles, and decided to get himself killed. He put his arms around the neck of his horse, saying, "I love you," to the animal. Then he crawled out to the edge of the timber and stood facing scores of hostile warriors who knelt ready to shoot. Young Hawk fired first, receiving a volley of bullets in return. He was not hit. Seeking a new position, he moved forward to a pile of dead brush. Behind it he found Forked Horn lying face down to avoid being shot. Forked Horn scolded him severely for drawing the fire of the hostiles.

"That is no way to act. This is not the way to fight at all, to show yourself as a target."

After this scolding Young Hawk lay quiet a long time. Out in the open the Sioux were trying to fire the grass to smoke the scouts from their cover, but the grass was too green to burn. Presently, a Sioux on a gray horse came charging in close. Young Hawk fired at him, but missed. Then he jumped to his feet and fired again, killing him. Gradually the hostile counterattack mounted, sweeping past them on all sides.

104

By blood First Lieutenant Donald McIntosh, commander of G Company, was as Indian as any of the hostiles he faced. A Mohawk, he was a member of the Iroquois Six Nations, a onetime resident of Canada. For many years he had followed the white man's road. It came to him here on the firing line plainer than ever, as people of his own race came charging, that there was no turning back to Indian ways—now or ever. Too long ago he had cast his lot with the whites, and now he was stuck with them.

Looking over at Lonesome Charley Reynolds and Fred Girard, he wondered a little at his choice. Reynolds was trying to get his canteen open for a pull of whisky, and both men were more interested in that than in fighting Indians. It made McIntosh a little bit more proud of his blood. He came close to wishing the Army had left these poor hostile devils alone. After all, they had come here first—long before the whites. Maybe they had a right to the wild land, living simply as they thought God intended.

Suddenly, he heard a commotion behind him. With alarm he realized the Sioux were moving in through the timber all around him. Something had gone wrong. Seemingly without warning, most of the battalion had withdrawn from its position. Charley Reynolds yelled something unintelligible and ran for his horse. Reno's retreat had come off with such alacrity that McIntosh and most of G Company had no idea the rest of the command was quitting the timber. The order to mount had not even been heard by all the troops and seventeen men were left behind.

As senior officer of the isolated detachment, McIntosh in his slow-poking way debated what to do. Charley Reynolds was in no mood to wait for him and made a quick dash to overtake Reno. His horse had barely left the timber when a bullet toppled the scout from his saddle. His rifle flew out of his hands. One foot caught in a stirrup and he was dragged over a hundred yards by his frenzied mount.

Rallying his men and keeping them well together behind him, McIntosh led out at last. At the edge of the timber a bowstring twanged at close range. The lieutenant's horse crumpled under him, an arrow through its skull. McIntosh darted back into the timber.

"Take my horse, Lieutenant," Trooper McCormick of G Company offered. "We're all dead men anyway, way it looks. I might as well be killed afoot as on horseback."

By this time Reno and the battalion were far ahead, already lost in a blur of dust. The hostiles were rapidly closing in behind them. But McIntosh decided to try to break through. Once more he led out. This time a large party of warriors cut him off and forced him over toward the river. There on the banks of the Little Big Horn, McIntosh was pulled from his saddle and killed. Most of G Company died with him. A few troopers broke through to Reno, and a mere handful made it back to find cover in the timber.

Hundreds of warriors swarmed around the fleeing battalion like angry gnats. The hostiles needed little urging to take full advantage of the soldiers' panic. Left behind at first, Lieutenant Varnum raced forward, trying to slow the rout, knowing that to run away in a fight with Indians was to invite disaster.

"For God's sake, men, don't run!"

But the troopers were taking their cue from Reno, far ahead, and the headlong retreat continued without letup. All along the way troopers and horses were down. But no one dared stop to rescue a wounded comrade or pick up a trooper whose horse had been shot from under him. It was every man for himself all the way.

By sheer weight of numbers, the hostiles turned the ragged column toward the river. With the ford hopelessly out of reach upstream, Reno had no choice but to cross the river and make for the bluffs on the opposite side. There, at least, he might make a stand, put up some sort of defensive fight. There, by some remote chance, Custer might come to his rescue.

Reno and the forward troopers looked in vain for a shallow place to cross. A sharp cut-bank edged the river; it was a sheer six-foot drop to the water. The foremost horses refused to jump until the increasing pressure from behind forced them over the crumbling brink. Into water four feet deep plunged Reno and his troops in a splashing welter of men and horses. From both banks of the river, from all sides, the hostiles poured in a deadly fusillade of bullets.

It was as easy as running buffalo. The warriors were all over the panic-stricken soldiers, chopping down with war clubs or gun butts, sometimes striking out with lances or bows or old-fashioned coupsticks. Many were the honors won during the rout of Reno's battalion. And many were the soldiers killed—often with one sharp blow. Eagle-bone whistles shrilled the victory.

A great cry suddenly went up among the warriors: "Crazy Horse is coming! Crazy Horse is coming!"

And the way opened for a flood of fresh fighters—Ogalalas, Brûlés, and Cheyennes—under the great fighting leader, Crazy Horse. Mounted on a buckskin-and-white pinto, the famous Ogalala was stripped down to a breechclout, bare as usual of war adornment save for the skin of a red-backed hawk tied in his hair. His body was dotted with pale hailstone marks, his face streaked with blue lightning. Seeing him, the warriors massed for a new charge. He was the Invulnerable. As everyone knew, no enemy bullets could touch him, so powerful was his medicine. He rode close to the fleeing soldiers, inviting their fire, shouting encouragement to his followers all the time.

"Friends, save your ammunition! Make the *wasicun* (whites) shoot fast so their guns will stick! Then you can knock them over with clubs! *Hoka hey!*"

For a while the warriors held their fire. But this was a phase of the fighting that required no leadership. No one needed to give orders. No fighting leader needed to challenge a reluctant enemy. Now, every warrior knew what to do without being told. Every fighting man did as he thought best. It was the age-old way in which Plains Indians made war.

A large number of Sioux had already crossed the river downstream and now came riding up the opposite bank, shooting back at the soldiers all the way. A few had even plunged into the river and were swimming their horses toward where the soldiers were crossing.

One Sioux rider dashed in bravely to grab at the reins of an officer's mount. The officer (probably Captain French, commander of M Company) fired his pistol at point-blank range, and the warrior went down.

The Indians had other casualties as well. Dog-with-Horns was killed in the running fight. Chased-by-Owls was mortally wounded. But the soldiers were too preoccupied with getting across the river to the bluffs to fire accurately.

Stripped, his face carefully painted, mounted on his fastest war pony, a fine roan with a crooked white patch over its left eye, Eagle Elk rode into the fray. The Ogalala warrior carried a Winchester repeater that was almost new. Striking out right and left, he knocked soldier after soldier from their saddles. It was as easy as killing buffalo cows. He saw one Sioux wielding a heavy saber, captured from one of the Gray Fox's troopers during the Rosebud fight. It was probably the only saber on the Little Big Horn that day, since none of Custer's Seventh carried sabers in this campaign.

Sometimes a soldier and an Indian would wrestle each other, each trying to dismount the other, like the old Sioux game of "throwing-them-off-their-horses." With much practice, the warriors had every advantage. Even in the water they kept it up. Occasionally the fighting Indian and soldier would go under water, then bubble to the surface, finally go under again.

Eagle Elk killed two or three soldiers who were trying to get across the river. His was one of the better guns, and he used it with telling effect. He stayed out of the water, however, for he was looking for his Minneconjou brother-friend, High Horse. Glancing around, he saw an Arikara scout trying to get through to the river. (This may have been Stabbed, who had already been wounded in the timber.) A Sioux jumped from his horse onto this Arikara. He had a long knife ready, and when he stood again, it was covered with blood all the way up the blade. Eagle Elk then saw the Sioux was High Horse. He was breathing hard and talking crazily.

"I cut off his neck," he kept saying. "I cut off the neck of that Arikara cur!"

Suddenly a large party of Cheyennes galloped up, chasing a big cavalry horse straight toward High Horse. The Minneconjou reached out and caught the bridle and leaped into the saddle.

Downstream, near the timber, Indians were setting the brush afire to drive out the soldiers hiding there. Racing back that way, Eagle Elk and High Horse saw some Sioux boys shooting arrows at a soldier who dodged around in the burning brush. He seemed to have lost his gun, and was trying to keep from being caught in the flames.

Now that the Sioux were firing the brush, Red Bear and Little Brave, two of the Arikaras, knew they would have to leave the timber.

"Let me fire one more shot at the camp," said Little Brave, over Red Bear's insistence that they get started.

Red Bear held the other's horse, though, as Little Brave went on foot to fire his one shot. But it seemed now as though the village were almost empty, that most of the Sioux were between the timber and the place where Reno was trying to get the battalion across. At last Little Brave got off his shot and came running. Mounting, the two Arikaras dashed out together. They ran headlong into heavy fire from some Indians on foot. Doubling back fast, they narrowly avoided running into an ambush. They darted back toward the river. There they saw about ten troopers in full rout, riding at a dead run toward Reno. Red Bear saw the soldiers head straight for a deep cut, a washout of some kind, and plummet headlong into it.

"Whoa, whoa!" the troopers shouted, trying to control their mounts. Red Bear guessed it would have taken top riding to avoid being thrown as the horses fell into the cut. Not waiting to see what happened to the soldiers, Red Bear yanked his own horse around to keep from falling in, and kept going.

Suddenly Red Bear's horse stumbled and went down, throwing the Arikara, who picked himself up and chased after the animal, but could not catch him again. Then a piece of deadwood caught in the cheek strap of the bridle, and Red Bear was able to get him this time. Red Bear's left hand had been hurt in the fall. With the carbine in his right, it was hard to control the horse now.

Hearing a war cry behind him, Red Bear whipped around to see a lone Sioux warrior with a face painted half yellow, half red, bearing down on him. Swinging up his carbine, the Arikara fired from the hip. The warrior's pony reared up, throwing the Sioux to the ground. Red Bear did not wait to see if he had killed the Sioux. He started out again to catch up with Reno. By this time, Little Brave was nowhere in sight.

With loose reins flying, a riderless horse raced snorting past Red Bear. The Arikara recognized it at once as the horse of his chief, Bob-tailed Bull. He saw the front of the saddle was all bloody. The animal was terrified at the shrill scream of the eagle-bone whistles, used in battle by the Sioux.

Seeing confusion and fighting ahead, Red Bear turned down the riverbank and swam his horse to the other side. Five or six troopers had crossed the river ahead of him and now were riding through the brush to his left. Up ahead he saw Reno, his head tied up with a white kerchief, his beard frothy white with foam, his eyes wild and rolling. The soldiers with the major aimed their guns at Red Bear, taking him for a hostile. He kept riding in toward Reno and tapped his chest.

"Scout! Scout!" he shouted in English.

Then Reno kept yelling words. It took Red Bear a while to understand them.

"The Sioux? The Sioux? Where are they?" Reno kept asking. And in answer, Red Bear merely pointed down the ridge. There were, after all, plenty of Sioux in that general direction.

An officer with three stripes (a sergeant) came up to Red Bear and gave him a handful of cartridges for his gun. He had an armload of cartridge boxes on his arm and, as he was passing out bullets, a whole box spilled out on the ground. Red Bear picked up most of them. He kept loading them in the carbine and pulling the trigger, firing up at the ridge where he guessed some of the hostiles were. The officer kept calling him "John," and for a while he fired every time the soldier called this name.

Glancing down at the river, Red Bear saw a lieutenant (Benjamin Hodgson, Reno's adjutant) hit as his mount leaped down the far bank. The bullet pierced his thigh and went through the horse, killing it instantly. As his mount sank under him in the water, the lieutenant struggled to keep afloat, grabbed at the stirrup strap of a passing trooper, and let himself be dragged across the river to the near shore. The trooper tried to help him out of the water but failed. Unable even to crawl out, the lieutenant drew his pistol and faced the hostiles—fighting bravely until a shower of bullets cut him down.

On the riverbank opposite, One Bull killed two soldiers with his war club. Jumping his horse into the water, the young Hunkpapa struck another trooper, knocking him from his saddle with a single blow. Climbing out again, One Bull loped back to the field of battle, hoping to earn more honors. Only three troopers, probably horse holders, were left and they were running fast toward the river. In the heat of victory One Bull let out a war cry and started after them, when he heard the voice of his uncle, Sitting Bull.

"Let them escape!" shouted the chief of the Hunkpapas. "Let them live to tell the truth about this fight!"

One Bull obediently turned back. Then his uncle noticed the blood all over his nephew, the blood of Good Bear Boy.

"Nephew, you are wounded. Go back to camp and have your wounds treated."

One Bull only laughed, saying he was not wounded. Sitting Bull was relieved to know his nephew was still in one piece. But now the Hunkpapa chief had seen the full array of Reno's forces, dead and running away, and guessed from the small size of the battalion that Reno's action had not been the main attack, but a mere diversion. At this very moment, perhaps, other soldiers might be menacing the village.

"Go back and help defend the women and children," Sitting Bull told his nephew.

Most of the village was deserted. The women and children and old people had gathered along the benches west of the village, where they could look down across the valley and watch the battle. One Bull did as he was told and joined the people there.

Meanwhile, as his warriors began stripping the bodies of thirty-two soldiers and Arikara scouts, Sitting Bull looked after his own casualties. So far, they had been remarkably light, although the death of any fighting man was an occasion for deep sorrow. Seven Sioux and one Cheyenne had been killed outright, two other Sioux mortally wounded. As opposed to these losses, Reno had lost nearly half his command in dead, wounded, and missing—counting several men still cut off in the timber. Sitting Bull was willing to let it go at that. After all, this fight had not been of his choosing. The whites had come shooting. They had fired the first shot. And now they had taken the drubbing they deserved for their foolish aggression. The issue already seemed settled. Now, perhaps, the soldiers would stop coming to fight the Indians, and would let them live in their old way, free and undisturbed. The chief of the Hunkpapas hoped it could be so as he started back toward the deserted village.

Many of the warriors also seemed willing to let the soldiers go now that they had been beaten. Only a few bothered to cross the river and harass Reno's men as they climbed the bluffs and dug in for a defensive fight. A handful of other warriors, who happened to have good firearms, sniped away at the bluffs long-range. But the rush, which the disorganized remnants of Reno's command clearly expected, never got under way. While the soldiers dug trenches on the crest of the bluffs and waited for the worst, the warriors continued to loot and strip the bodies of their enemies and recount their deeds of honor.

Black Elk was riding all over, trying to see everything and share in the excitement and elation of the older warriors. He was so small and slight that he was often shunted out of the way before he could see very much. Dead or alive, white men were still a curiosity to the boy. He was much impressed by the paleness of their naked bodies, but even stranger was the hairiness of the white men. Their faces and chests and arms—sometimes even their backs—were covered with hair. As he sat his pony, looking wide-eyed all around him, a Sioux warrior rode up.

"Boy, get off and scalp that soldier."

A soldier lay on the ground, kicking and squirming, wounded but not yet dying. Black Elk obeyed, getting down from his pony and drawing his knife. The blade was not very sharp, and the soldier had short hair. He ground his teeth as Black Elk began to take his scalp. At last, the Ogalala youth drew his pistol and shot the soldier in the forehead. After that, the scalping operation seemed easier. Wanting to show the scalp to his mother, Black Elk jumped on his pony and rode toward the benches west of camp, where the women and children and old people waited. On the way he passed through the Ogalala camp circle. Rattling Hawk, the warrior wounded at the Rosebud, was sitting up in his tepee, a gun across his lap. He seemed to regret the fact that he was unable to get out and fight. He was singing this song as Black Elk rode by:

"Brothers, what are you doing that I can't do?"

Reaching the benches, Black Elk heard all the women singing and making the high tremolo sound to cheer on their warriors. His mother made a loud high tremolo just for her son, when she saw Black Elk's first scalp.

At the edge of the timber a black man lay dying. His breast was bloody and a gaping wound showed through his shirt. He was Isaiah Dorman, civilian interpreter for the Seventh Cavalry, the Negro who had once lived with the Sioux and knew their tongue. Now, as he sprawled out on the ground, an old Hunkpapa woman pointed an ancient muzzle-loader at his head, ready to fire at any instant. She was one of a handful of women who had stayed in the Hunkpapa circle, the first to come out after the fighting let up.

"Don't shoot me, Auntie!" he begged. "I'll be dead soon enough, anyway."

"You're a sneaking cur!" the old woman screamed at him. "Why did you bring the soldiers here?"

"I only wanted to see this Western country once more before I died," the Negro explained.

Just then Shoots-Walking, Two Bulls, and several other warriors rode up, intending to strip the Negro's body.

"Don't count coup on me, my friends," Dorman begged. "You've already killed me. I was shot early in the fighting."

At that moment Sitting Bull arrived. He recognized the Negro as "the black white man"—known to the Sioux as *On A ẓinpi* or Teat.

"Don't kill that man!" the Hunkpapa chief said sharply. "He is Teat. He used to be a friend of our people."

With that the warriors rode away. Dorman then asked for water. Sitting Bull got him some water in his own drinking cup of polished buffalo horn. After he had drunk from it, the old Negro died.

Leaving Dorman's body there in the brush, Sitting Bull rode on north through the deserted village. He passed the abandoned camps, one by one, where skulking dogs prowled, looking for meat. A few tepees in the Hunkpapa camp were damaged by soldiers' bullets and burned, but otherwise the village was intact. Thus assured, Sitting Bull turned the black stallion sharply to the west and headed for the benches. As a chief it was also his duty to look after the women and children, and to see that they made an orderly return to their lodges. In a little while the camp police would be calling everyone to go back to his own tepee—now that the fighting seemed to be over.

116

Afternoon: Custer

SHORTLY AFTER the last of Reno's battalion disappeared from view in the thick timber on the Little Big Horn's far shore, Long Hair Custer dismounted and knelt a minute or so in prayer. Mitch Bouyer and the four Crow scouts were respectfully solemn as they grouped around him. The troops moved up noisily behind. Then, seeing the General, they quieted down, and there was no sound except the squeak of saddle leather and the tinkle of bit-irons. Finally, Custer stood up and, turning, shook hands with each of the Crows.

"My scout," he said to Goes Ahead, "if we win this battle, you will be one of the noted men of the Crow Nation. If I die today, you'll get this land back from the Sioux and stay on it, happy and contented. If you should die, you'll be buried on your own land."

He spoke similarly to each of the Crows, then addressed them as a group, Bouyer translating rapidly.

"I am a great chief," Custer said matter-of-factly, "but I do not know whether I'll get through this summer alive or dead. I do not know whether I'll pass through this battle or not. But if I live, I'll recommend you boys, and you'll be leaders of the Crows—all of you. My other scouts are worthless. The Arikaras are like women. But you Crows have helped me find the enemy. I'll tell you one thing: There will be nothing more good for the Sioux. If they massacre me, they will suffer. If they do not kill me, they will suffer, for they have disobeyed the orders of the Grandfather in Washington. Now, let's take a look-see from that near ridge, and find out how the camp shapes up from there."

Mounting again, Custer let the scouts lead out to the top of the ridge. From there they could see that the village was farther away than any of them had thought. They signaled Long Hair they were moving on ahead. Custer followed, leading his command along the ridge.

By that time they all saw that Reno's attack on the south end of the village was well under way. The firing of the soldiers' guns was so continuous that it sounded like a taut blanket being torn.

The scouts rode on, beginning now to see glimpses of the distant lodges through breaks in the timber across the river. They could make out the great camp circles spread out down the valley. It was now plain they had been right all along in warning Custer. Presently, he would see for himself how many hostiles were arrayed against him.

Spurred by the din of the battle across the river, Custer speeded up the column, leading it out at a gallop along the ridge. It was all the small ponies of the Crows could do to keep ahead of the soldiers. The scouts had to quirt the little animals constantly to keep them at a dead run. Then they came to a break in the ridge, where the column halted. While the Crows rested their mounts, Custer and his brother Tom rode on past and drew up on a nearby knoll. From this point, Reno's command was out of sight beyond the timber, although firing could still be heard up the valley. Looking across the other way, several hundred tepees were in plain sight, but most of the village lay hidden behind the dense cottonwood growth along the river. Custer studied the camp a while with field glasses. The village seemed nearly deserted. A few old people hobbled about on sticks, dogs slunk here and there—the usual lazy activity of a hot summer afternoon.

"We've got them!" Custer exclaimed. "We've caught them napping!"

Slapping his thigh, he turned in the saddle, took off his hat, and waved it at the troops waiting at the base of the hill.

"Custer's luck, boys!" he shouted. "We've got them. We'll finish them off, then go home to our station. Come on!"

A hoarse cheer went up among the troopers. It had been a long hard day and they were all anxious to get the job over and done. By the watches some of them carried it was just three o'clock.

Riding from the Reno battlefield toward the benches where the women and children stood huddled, One Bull was among the first to see Custer's column on the bluffs across the river. His first inclination was to gather warriors together wherever he could find them and lead them through the village to meet this newest threat. Then he remembered his uncle's orders. Halfway through the camp, he swung west across the flats to the benches. Here Sitting Bull already waited on the big black stallion, the women bunched close around him. One Bull pointed excitedly toward the bluffs.

"Come, Uncle," he urged, "we must fight these new soldiers."

But the chief raised his hand in a gesture of caution. "No, I want you to stay here and help me protect these women. This is the second party of soldiers to march against us today. More may come. It may be some sort of trap for us, so be wary, Nephew." He pointed up the valley to the flat where Reno had been overwhelmed. "There are plenty of warriors yonder to take care of these soldiers on the bluffs."

One Bull saw it was so. Other Indian leaders had sighted Custer's column. Masses of warriors were breaking off from looting Reno's dead and rushing downstream to face the fresh danger. The soldiers' strategy was suddenly plain. Having divided into comparatively small forces, the soldiers had obviously planned to strike simultaneously at both ends of the great encampment. Though their timing was somewhat off, the situation as One Bull saw it was still precarious. This new band of soldiers stood poised at the head of Medicine Tail Coulee, which gave on a shallow ford directly across from the north end of the village. By moving fast down the coulee and across the ford, the soldiers could drive like a hunting arrow into the heart of the camp—with time to spare before the warriors could reach the endangered area.

On the near side of Medicine Tail Coulee, the Crow scouts found a hilltop from which the whole valley was visible. From its head the coulee sloped down almost a mile to the ford across the Little Big Horn. Halting the command at the base of the hill, Custer galloped up to the crest with Trumpeter John Martin at his side. From here the General got his first look at the entire sprawl of the hostile village. With the scouts and trumpeter he went back down the hill and led the column on to the head of the coulee, riding grim-mouthed and silent. From where they left Reno's trail, the command had trotted or galloped a full three miles. With drawn carbines and cocked pistols, the troopers waited for the long charge down Medicine Tail Coulee. Custer turned to his trumpeter.

"Orderly, I want you to take a message to Captain Benteen. Ride as fast as you can and tell him to hurry. Tell him it's a big village and I want him to be quick, and to bring the ammunition packs with him."

"Yes, sir." As he turned to go the adjutant, who had been listening, rode forward.

"Wait, I'll give you a message." He wrote a hurried scrawl in a little notebook, tore out the page, and handed it to the trumpeter. "Now ride as fast as you can to Captain Benteen," he said. "Take the same trail we came down. If you have enough time, and there is no danger, come back. Otherwise stay with Benteen."

Trumpeter Martin was the last white man to see Custer and his command alive. As he rode away at a gallop, the Crow scouts flushed out five Sioux horsemen hidden near the head of the coulee. Lookouts posted along the bluffs, these hostiles banded together to see what the soldiers would do. Once discovered, they whooped and fired their rifles and waved buffalo robes to frighten the cavalry horses. Then they whirled into the coulee and scurried off down toward the river. Custer shouted the column into rapid pursuit, the gray-horse troop, E Company, leading.

Off to one side Mitch Bouyer was talking to Curley, youngest of the Crows.

"Curley, you're young yet," he said. "You don't know much about fighting. I advise you to leave us. These five Sioux are just a decoy. But Son-of-the-Morning-Star will stop at nothing. He'll take us right into that village, where the Sioux have thousands more warriors than we do. We have no chance at all."

He handed Curley a pair of field glasses. "Ride back over

the bluffs a ways, then head east for one of the high points yonder. Watch a while, and if it looks like the Sioux are besting us, go to No-Hip-Bone (General Terry) and tell him we are all killed. Now go!"

The young Crow quickly shook Bouyer's hand, then swung his bald-faced bay pony around and headed back upstream. The others raced down the coulee to catch up with Custer. It was hard going down to the ford. Piles of shale made the footing slippery for the small horses of the Crows. With the battalion moving at a fast trot, the scouts were hard put to get ahead of the troopers and come up with Custer. Then they rode up beside him and moved on with him a way, until he called out to them above the clatter of the troops descending the coulee behind him. "You are not to fight in this battle. Go back and save your lives."

They seemed not to understand, even after hearing his words. Mitch Bouyer left Custer's side and rode over to them.

"You scouts need go no farther," he explained. "You have guided Son-of-the-Morning-Star here, and your work is finished. So you'd better go back to the pack train and let the soldiers do the fighting."

To White-Man-Runs-Him and Hairy Moccasin and Goes Ahead, Mitch Bouyer was as much a member of the Crow tribe as they were.

"Then you must come away with us," Hairy Moccasin urged. "Your Crow woman, Magpie Outside, is waiting for you back in our home camp in the Big Horns. And she will—"

He broke off short. From the timber across the river a Sioux voice called, *"Wica-nonpa!"*

Bouyer turned to listen.

"The Sioux call someone?" Goes Ahead wondered.

122

Bouyer signed yes, and tapped his own chest.

"*Wica-nonpa!* Two Bodies!" the voice called again. "Go back or you die!"

"The Sioux have not forgotten me," the half-breed explained to the scouts. "They tell me to go back—but I cannot."

Without added leavetaking, Mitch Bouyer swung his horse around and galloped off down the coulee with Custer.

The Cheyenne camp was all but deserted. A bare handful of oldsters, too feeble to get away under their own power, was left behind in the shadows of the silent lodges. A few mangy dogs, sensing danger, cowered at their feet. In one tepee lay the warrior White Elk, who had accidentally shot himself through the left thigh in the Rosebud fight. Only four other fighting men who were able-bodied remained out of nearly seven hundred. The others had raced off to join the Sioux in defending the Hunkpapa camp.

Bobtail Horse, an Elk warrior, was also an "elk dreamer," and, like most members of his warrior society, had had a vision of an elk some years earlier, and from this now derived long life and power as a fighting man. As any Cheyenne knew —and any Sioux, for that matter—an elk's tooth was indeed holy medicine, for it endured after all else crumbled to dust. All afternoon Bobtail Horse had been drilling a hole through an elk tooth, preparatory to tying it onto a hair ornament to wear as a battle charm. When the alarm had gone up at the far end of the village, he had held back—not through any reluctance to fight, but simply because the charm was not yet ready. He would have been foolhardy indeed to charge into battle without it.

At last he drilled through the tooth, using a scrap of white man's steel to enlarge the hole. Threading it on a rawhide thong, he attached it to a small hoop decorated with porcupine quillwork. He then fixed the hoop to his scalp braid, close to the head. Ready for war, he grabbed up a handful of bullets and his old muzzle-loader and left the lodge. Striding toward his hobbled pony, he fiddled with a twenty-foot rope of rawhide, fashioning a crude bridle to slip over the horse's head. Suddenly he stopped short. Looking above the tepee tops to the tumbled ridges across the river, Bobtail Horse could see most of Medicine Tail Coulee. Down it rode dusty blue soldiers at a dead run.

"Nutskavebo!" he shouted. "White soldiers are coming!"

The words seemed a hollow echo of Two Moon's earlier warning; few heard them. From his guard post in front of the medicine lodge, Roan Bear came running, at his heels White Cow Bull, the Ogalala, who had stood by him through the long day. Both had been regretting the circumstances which had kept Roan Bear at his post when so much excitement was going on at the far end of the village. Yet this saved the day for them. With the soldiers obviously bent on attacking the all but defenseless Cheyenne camp, Roan Bear was justified in leaving his post in an effort to keep the troops away from the sacred Buffalo Head in the medicine lodge.

"They're coming this way!" Bobtail Horse warned. "Across the ford!"

While Roan Bear and White Cow Bull caught their hobbled ponies, a fourth warrior darted out of one of the lodges where he had been carefully painting his face for battle. Jumping on his own mount, he quickly joined Bobtail Horse. He was Calf,

124

a Crazy Dog warrior, one of a soldier band looked down upon by the Elks and Foxes as uncouth fighters who lacked responbility. Crazy Dog or no, Bobtail Horse was glad to have him on hand.

Just then, Mad Wolf, an older man, rode up on a bony spavined nag. Though poor, he was known throughout the tribe for his wisdom. But he was no fighting man. Long years away from the warpath had made him old and soft.

"My sons," he called out, as they moved at a steady jog trot to meet the soldiers at the ford, "my sons, do not charge the soldiers now. They are too many. Wait until our brothers come back to help."

As he rode along with the warriors, he kept up an incessant whining about the uneven odds of any clash they might have with the soldiers. At last Bobtail Horse turned on him. "Only Earth and the Heavens last long, Uncle. If we four can stop the soldiers from taking our camp, our lives will matter little."

Mad Wolf was rebuffed and humbled. With bowed head, he wheeled his old horse back toward camp.

The four warriors rode on. White Shield, hurrying back from his fishing upstream, joined them with a whooping challenge to the soldiers who were now almost at the ford. Taking cover behind a low ridge near the river, the four with guns opened fire on the troops. White Shield, carrying only a bow and full quiver, saw a vantage point a few yards downstream and rode off to the left. The others alternately loaded and fired, all of them whooping incessantly to make it sound as if a thousand warriors were hidden behind the ridge. Armed only with antique weapons and fighting courage, these five men faced two hundred and fifteen.

Even after Custer ordered them to go, the three Crow scouts were undecided what to do. Climbing the bluff flanked by Medicine Tail Coulee, they dismounted and fired at the five Sioux warriors racing ahead of the soldiers. With troopers clattering almost at their heels, the Sioux plunged into the ford and splashed across the river at a dead run. The soldiers reined up at the water's edge, giving the Sioux time to join the embattled Cheyennes on the far shore. Meanwhile, the Crows had fired several volleys in the general direction of the camp, their target well past carbine range. With their repeating Spencers, they were barely able to spat up dust along the low ridge behind which the ten hostiles were now concealed.

Three Cheyennes and one Sioux held off Custer's column at the ford.

Goes Ahead looked down and saw the soldiers halted in a straggling column all the way back up the coulee, although there seemed little to stop them either side of the river. He wondered why Custer hesitated. The battalion could easily ride over the ten hostiles defending the camp. Of course, the ford was not much as fords went. The near bank was gravelly and gradual enough, but the opposite side of the crossing was a good two feet above water level—and miry and precipitous as well. Perhaps Custer feared that his big cavalry horses with their iron shoes might slip on rocks in the ford and go down before they reached that steep bank yonder. Then he realized that Custer was uncertain as to how many hostiles lay hidden behind the ridge, and while it seemed unlikely a mere handful would have the audacity to oppose him, ambushes were routine hazards in fighting the Sioux. And so Custer waited before finally giving the order to charge.

At last he turned to shout an order, and the command was echoed by his officers back up the coulee. Custer led out. Even in shallow water his horse Vic had a mincing, prancing gait that had the other mounts trotting to keep up. Mitch Bouyer rode on one side of Custer, an orderly carrying the General's battle flag on the other. For a moment there was a lull in the firing from the hostiles behind the ridge. As the foremost ranks of troopers took to the water, the Crows heard a frenzied yelping upstream. Looking up sharply, Goes Ahead saw hundreds of mounted hostiles coming on fast, streaking through the cottonwoods that fringed the river. Having whipped Reno, the warriors were taking a short cut to the ford, racing to meet the new danger.

"They're coming fast!" cried White-Man-Runs-Him.

Hairy Moccasin leaped on his pony and started back upriver. The ten hostiles on the other side again opened fire, shooting with pin-point accuracy now that the soldiers began to ride into closer range. A trooper on a gray horse toppled from his saddle, his blood making a dark stain on the swirling water.

Custer and Bouyer were firing as they advanced, the General using his favorite weapon, a Remington Sporting rifle with octagonal barrel. Two English self-cocking Bulldog pistols were ready in unsnapped holsters at his belt. The troopers coming up behind were already building up a heavy wall of gunfire; the air was thick with white gunsmoke as shot after shot rang out.

Just then, at midstream, the unbelievable happened.

Custer—the great invincible soldier-chief, golden-haired hero of the effete East, self-styled swashbuckler of the Plains, Son-of-the-Morning-Star to the Crows, Long Hair to other tribes—fell, a hostile bullet through his left breast. No Indian, Crow, Sioux, or Cheyenne, could say whether he died at once or later, after his men carried him up the ridge from the river. The wound, in any case, was mortal.

As the troopers splashed to a halt around their fallen commander, Mitch Bouyer quickly jumped off his horse into knee-deep water to keep Custer from going under. A moment later, the orderly with the flag crumpled from his saddle. A trooper grabbed at the flag and kept it from falling.

The three Crow scouts on the bluff did not wait to see more. With Son-of-the-Morning-Star down, the fight was already over. Jumping on their ponies, White-Man-Runs-Him and Goes Ahead joined Hairy Moccasin, now well out in front, in a pell-mell dash for safety back the way they had come.

Though a mature man and a full warrior, White Cow Bull had never before seen or encountered white soldiers. As he fired from behind the low ridge near the ford, he had very little idea what to expect from these strange bearded troopers in blue, so caked with dust they seemed nearly as pale as the gray horses they rode. He did not know how much longer he and the others could hang on here between the attackers and the camp. But a voice kept shouting, "Fight on!" and he stayed put, firing and loading as fast as he could.

Now he saw one of the soldiers drop into the water. Then as another white man on a sorrel horse, out in front of all the grays, fell in midstream, the oncoming soldiers did a strange thing—they stopped in the middle of a charge. White Cow Bull could not see all that happened then, for he was kept busy dodging bullets as the soldiers fired volley after volley into the ridge. But it seemed as though some of the soldiers dismounted there in the river and were dragging something from the water, while others, still mounted, kept shooting. With gunsmoke hanging thick in the still air, with no letup in the firing, they fell back to the far bank where the entire troop dismounted. The troops backed up into Medicine Tail Coulee also dismounted.

By this time the first of the Sioux and Cheyennes from upstream were riding up to help out the ten warriors behind the ridge. As more and more of them reached the ford a great cry went up.

"*Hoka hey!* They are going!"

It was true. White Cow Bull saw the soldiers falling back as though seized with sudden panic. The number of warriors was increasing every minute, and they were massing for a countercharge across the ford. But it was something else that seemed completely to demoralize the soldiers just then—something that occurred within their own ranks.

From his lookout on a ridge a mile and a half east of the Little Big Horn, young Curley watched the soldiers fall from their saddles into the river. Even with the field glasses, he could not tell who they were or much about them. Then he saw the troopers fall back from the ford and dismount. In no time at all, the will to attack seemed gone from Custer's men.

As the steadily increasing horde of hostiles swarmed across the river to surround the dismounted soldiers, the troopers frantically climbed out of Medicine Tail Coulee and ran on foot toward higher ground back from the bank. Leading their mounts and firing at the Indians all the way, the soldiers reached a little knoll where they tried to make a stand. With troopers dropping all along the route, it was plain the fight could end in only one way.

Convinced that Mitch Bouyer's words were soon to come true—that Custer's men would all be killed—Curley left the ridge and rode north to look for No-Hip-Bone, the other soldier-chief.

Soon after the soldiers dismounted and fell back to higher ground, the tiny holding force behind the ridge was joined by other Sioux and Cheyennes. Among the new arrivals were the son of Chief Ice, one of the Cheyenne fighting leaders, and Yellow Nose, a Ute. Captured as a four-year-old boy by a Cheyenne war party some eighteen years earlier, he was now as much Cheyenne as any of his captors. Today Yellow Nose seemed bent on taking chances, no doubt in an effort to redeem himself for having lost Spotted Wolf's borrowed shield on the way from the Rosebud to the Little Big Horn two days ago.

"Come on!" shouted Bobtail Horse, running to his pony. "They're running! Hurry!"

He led the way across the ford, the camp defenders now foremost in the Indian countercharge. White Cow Bull dashed forward with the others. Riding beside him, the son of Chief Ice sang out, "Only Heaven and Earth are eternal! I am not!"

As the warriors charged the knoll, the troopers opened such a heavy fire that the Indians had to fall back. Only Yellow Nose charged up close to the soldiers. Then he, too, raced back to safety. The son of Chief Ice was not so lucky. White Cow Bull saw his horse running away riderless and covered with blood. The Cheyennes massed for another charge. As Chief Comes-in-Sight and a warrior named Contrary Belly rushed in close, fear-crazed troop horses plunged and bolted and reared, causing their handlers so much trouble that the soldiers held their fire a moment or so. Just then, Yellow Nose, charging in again, snatched a company guidon from its place in the soldiers' line. As he carried it away, he counted coup on a nearby trooper—striking him with the captured guidon, thereby proving his courage by riding close enough to his enemy to hit him without necessarily killing him. A great cry of approval and encouragement went up among the Indians. At this, some of the frenzied mounts of the gray-horse troop broke away from their handlers and stampeded.

"The soldiers are running!" a Cheyenne yelled.

But it was not yet so. Though hard pressed from all sides, the troopers were standing their ground.

In getting out of Medicine Tail Coulee, Custer's command split into two battalions. Last to go down the coulee, I and L Companies—both mounted on bay horses—were now farthest back from the river in a solid formation of a column of fours. They scrambled up a ravine toward the main hogback ridge, a continuation to the north of the bluffs and hills that edged the river. As senior captain of the detachment, Captain Myles Keogh was in command.

Under attack since the fallback at the ford, the other battalion—consisting of F Company mounted on bays, C Company on sorrels, E Company on grays—moved dismounted and in echelon formation north along the hogback's western slope: F as the spearhead of the advance, C as the right or contact wing with the other battalion, E as the left, holding the position nearest the river. Captain George Yates of F Company commanded the maneuver.

The two battalions made a co-ordinated attempt to reach a high knob on the north end of the hogback ridge (present location of monument), where they could take up the strongest available defensive position and make a stand until help came. As more and more hostiles surged around them, they found themselves fighting hard for every inch of ground they covered.

By this time the principal Indian fighting leaders were coming up, bringing their contingents of warriors into the fray. Crow King led a big party of Hunkpapas and Blackfeet Sioux up Medicine Tail Coulee to envelop the smaller battalion from the east. Gall and a huge horde of Hunkpapas, Minneconjous, and Sansarcs also used the coulee as an avenue of attack, keeping a relentless pressure on the soldiers from the rear. Comes-in-Sight and Brave Wolf led a main Cheyenne attack along the left flank.

Once on the field of battle, warriors began to fight independently of their bands and leaders, moving freely as they pleased. Seeing the enemy, the leaders charged, knowing their followers would try to emulate them. There was no time or need for plotting strategy, no giant trap to be sprung, no formulation of battle plans. Whether chief or warrior, all any Indian could do to win war honors and tribal acclaim was to rush into the fight, strike the enemy, capture the enemy's horse or weapon, or rescue a friend in danger.

Here, today, were chances aplenty to perform deeds of the highest valor. For the Sioux and Cheyennes, the battle had all the excitement of a buffalo hunt, with opportunities for every fighting man to cover himself with glory.

By this hour the greatest glory hunter on the field slumped, dying or already dead, his body carried forward in the tortuous advance by subordinates who dared not leave him to an ignominious fate. Propped in his saddle or slung across it, Long Hair Custer was taken along up the ridge by C Company, his brother's troop. No man lived to say if he ever issued another order after the hostile slug slammed into his chest at the ford.

After the Reno fight, many of the Indian ponies were jaded and a change of mounts was needed with more hard riding and fighting ahead. Among the warriors who stopped at the camp to get fresh horses was Pine, a Cheyenne. His aging father was the only person at the family lodge in the Cheyenne camp circle. Pine had already killed a trooper and had captured a carbine and cartridges. The old man was proud of his younger son.

"You've been brave," he said. "I think you've done plenty for one day. Now you should take a rest."

"I must go and fight the other soldiers now," Pine insisted. "With this captured gun, I can fight all the better."

"But your horse is played out," the old man argued.

"Then I will take yours—the one hobbled back of the lodge."

"Your elder brother is already up on that ridge fighting the soldiers. There are plenty of warriors around to beat them now. It's not necessary for a man to send both his sons into battle. And you do not have your eagle-bone whistle or your shield, my son."

"Get the horse," Pine ordered his father. Then he darted into the lodge in search of his shield and whistle. Outside, the old man brought up the horse and waited.

"Now I'm ready." Pine looped the carrying strap of the shield over one shoulder and leaped on the horse.

"Stay back as far as you can," cautioned his father. "Shoot from a distance. There's no need to get in too close. Your brother can ride in ahead of you."

But Pine was already on his way. He passed two or three other warriors who were hanging back in the camp.

"Come on!" Pine shouted.

"We're not going," one of them said.

Pine rode over to them. He showed them the carbine and the shiny cartridges. "One can take many things from the white soldiers after we kill them. They carry much with them. You'd better come along and see what you can get."

At last they gave in. Pine led the way to the ford, crowded now with a great throng of warriors going across to fight the soldiers. Once across, every Indian went his own way, picking his own route to bring him close to the troops.

As they began to close in around the soldiers, the warriors

134

dismounted. While riding, they used only a rawhide lariat, wrapped around the pony's jaw or looped over the head to form a simple bridle. The loose end of the lariat was coiled and tucked in the warrior's belt, so that if he fell from his pony, the coil would jerk loose and unwind. Now, as they got down, the warriors automatically yanked the coils from their belts and let them drop. With a long rope trailing, no horse would be hard to catch.

Just north of Medicine Tail Coulee the forces of Crow King closed in on L Company. In the van of warriors rode Rain-in-the-Face, charging into the fray on a buckskin horse. Shooting from the saddle, a trooper opened fire. The buckskin dropped, a bullet through its skull.

A vast flood of warriors came down the valley to join in the counterattack on the soldiers on the ridge. With four or five arrows clenched in his teeth, Iron Hawk lashed his pony into a dead run with the flat of his bow. Another Hunkpapa, Little Bear, rode abreast of him on a big pinto horse.

"Take courage, boy!" Little Bear shouted. "The Earth is all that lasts!"

Iron Hawk stayed close to Little Bear for a while. Presently a Cheyenne wearing a spotted war bonnet, a spotted robe of young mountain lion skins, and a spotted belt joined them. Then someone shouted:

"He's charging! He's charging!"

The Cheyenne had broken away and was racing up the hillside alone, straight toward the line of soldiers along the ridge. The Sioux followed part way, then reined up sharply in the face of heavy fire. But the lone Cheyenne kept going. The soldiers were on foot, holding their horses and firing steadily, as the Cheyenne charged almost close enough to touch them. He rode several circles as the soldiers' bullets spat up dust all around him. Finally he galloped back to where the Sioux waited in speechless admiration.

"Ah! Ah!" the Cheyenne said.

Then he unfastened his belt and shook a number of spent bullets out of his robe. He had not been scratched. Iron Hawk and Little Bear decided at once that he was *wakan* (holy) and immune to soldiers' bullets.

Suddenly a cry went up among the Indians, "They're going!"

Up on the ridge gray cavalry horses were stampeding. Little Bear's horse reared. Bringing him under control, Little Bear raced up the slope toward the soldiers. A few yards short of them, his horse was shot from under him and he went down in a swirl of dust. A bullet through his leg, Little Bear started hobbling back down the hill with soldiers shooting at him all the way. His brother-friend, Elk Nation, breaking away as was his duty, rode up the slope to take Little Bear up behind him and bring him back to safety. For even though he knew he might be killed, Elk Nation was obligated to attempt a rescue of his brother-friend.

Now a strange thing happened. A whole group of soldiers started running on foot down the hill toward the Indians. It was obvious they were so terrified that they did not know what they were doing. They fired guns into the air and made meaningless motions with their arms. At first, the Indians around Iron Hawk fell back, so weird was the performance of the soldiers. Then someone yelled:

"Hoka hey!"

It was a signal to charge and the warriors rushed in. In no

time at all the soldiers were all down. Most of them put up no fight at all but let themselves be killed without a struggle.

A soldier on horseback came riding aimlessly down the slope. Iron Hawk set an arrow to his bow and let fly. The arrow penetrated the soldier's chest, part of the shaft protruding on each side. The soldier screamed, grabbing the cantle of his saddle. Head down, he rode on until Iron Hawk came alongside and knocked him from his horse with the heavy bow. The warrior dismounted and, standing over the prostrate trooper, beat him to death with his bow. Even after the soldier was dead, Iron Hawk continued to hit him, shouting, *"Hownh!"* with each blow, for now his blood was hot with the lust for battle.

Nearby, Brings Plenty had unhorsed another trooper and was killing him with a war club. Almost the entire gray-horse troop was now wiped out. A few Indian women, mostly Cheyennes, had already ventured back to camp and were in the river bottom trying to catch the big gray cavalry horses as they stampeded down the hillside.

Hemmed in on three sides, with E Company chewed to pieces, Custer's command was forced along the ridge. What had begun as an orderly advance under fire was rapidly disintegrating into a complete rout. L Company was enveloped by hundreds of massed warriors, most of them Sioux. Caught in a slight hollow on the eastern slope of the hogback, halfway between L and the rest of the command, I Company's turn came next. Three-fifths of the command was now cut off and threatened with piecemeal destruction.

So far, the leading troops, F and C, had suffered the least casualties and maintained almost intact formations. Approaching the knob at the north end of the hogback, the two companies had almost reached it when a full thousand Ogalalas and Brûlés under Crazy Horse charged up out of a deep ravine that encircled the end of the ridge. Minutes earlier, Crazy Horse had crossed the Little Big Horn farther downstream to head off any attempt of Custer's men to escape to the north or make a successful defense on the knob.

Another powerful force of Indians—Cheyennes under Two Moon—circling the end of the ridge by way of the ravine, swarmed up over the crest of the ridge to strike the soldiers from their exposed flank on the uphill side. The envelopment of Custer's command was now complete. Having brought the soldiers to a standstill, the Indians held back from further massed mounted charges which might well prove costly to themselves and settled down to long-range sniping at the contained foe. Getting off their ponies, many warriors carefully worked their way on foot up the gullies and ravines, taking full advantage of every twig of available cover. By simple attrition, they began to thin out the ranks of the soldiers.

Only a daring few among the Indians continued to fight on horseback. Soldier Wolf, a Cheyenne, stayed mounted through most of the fight. Among his own tribesmen his daring was unsurpassed. Fighting the troopers nearest the crest of the ridge, Soldier Wolf rode straight at a soldier who aimed his carbine at the Cheyenne and would have shot him dead had the weapon not failed to discharge. Seeing the trooper was having mechanical difficulty with the carbine, Soldier Wolf simply rode him down. Wheeling his horse, the warrior charged the same soldier again. By this time the man had regained his feet and was trying desperately to fire his gun.

The trigger merely snapped, a faint click in all the uproar. Now Soldier Wolf leveled his own gun at the soldier and fired, killing at last an enemy he had first given ample opportunity to kill him.

Courageous as he was, Soldier Wolf's performance was not mere derring-do. As every Indian who knew him was aware, he never went into battle without his special protective charm —one well known to the entire Cheyenne tribe. On Soldier Wolf's left breast today was tied the tiny figure of a man, a four-inch-high cutout of deerskin with bits of buffalo wool for hair. So great was the power of this war medicine, that its wearer could never be touched by an enemy bullet unless the charm itself was hit. As the Cheyennes all knew, in battle the little rawhide man *became* the real Soldier Wolf.

Always in the thick of the fighting, Sitting Bull's elder nephew White Bull was all over the field, jerking soldiers from their horses, counting one coup after another. As part of Gall's following, he had stopped only once to unsaddle his horse and strip off his leggings so as to fight better. With Has-Horn, Iron Lightning, Shoots-Bear-as-He-Runs, and two Cheyennes, he rode up Medicine Tail Coulee. They all joined a horde of warriors in the pursuit and encirclement of L Company which was bringing up the rear of the fleeing battalions.

The Indians kept up a constant fire. Two soldiers fell from their horses. The other troopers opened such an intense fire from their saddles that the Indians were forced back. While the soldiers halted and dismounted to fight on foot, White Bull rode around to the south, then east of the surrounded troop. As the Indians momentarily held back, a few soldiers tried to break through to reach I Company, similarly cut off, but farther up the ridge. Spotting the running troopers, White Bull charged across their line of flight, the soldiers firing at him all the while. No bullet found its mark and White Bull circled back to his friends.

"I won't turn back this time!" he shouted to his comrades.

He charged at a dead run between the scattered troopers, many warriors following. This broke the spirit of the L Company survivors. They no longer tried to keep formation but ran to join I Company. Indian marksmen dropped them right and left along the way.

One mounted trooper was badly hit. As he swayed in the saddle, White Bull dashed forward to strike him with his quirt, thus counting a first coup. Jumping from his horse, he grabbed the soldier's cartridge belt and pistol. A Sansarc named Did-Not-Go-Home struck the dying soldier for a second coup. White Bull leaped on his horse and galloped on. The whole ridge had become a dusty sea of struggling men and horses. The warriors rode around the little knots of surrounded soldiers like water swirling around rocks.

Few troopers, however, were actually killed by mounted Indians. The largest number of casualties, by far, were those inflicted on the soldiers by Indian marksmen hidden in every little gulch and ravine and behind every patch of brush around the ridge. Many whites were shot in the back or side. While their hands were full defending themselves against mounted charges, the soldiers often exposed themselves to long-range gunfire from a totally unexpected quarter.

The Indians were not without a minor share of mishaps. One Sioux stumbled away from the ridge toward a nearby gulch. His lower jaw had been completely shot away. Another wounded Indian, an Ogalala named Long Elk, was riding around with bright blood gushing from his mouth. He seemed to know he was soon going to die, but he was too weak to keep on fighting.

Dives Backward, with some other Cheyenne boys, stayed close to a Sioux wearing a war bonnet who kept firing at the soldiers from a sagebrush clump near the north end of the ridge. The Sioux would look up a moment, then fire, then duck down behind the brush. Apparently he did not move fast enough. Once, when he had his head up, a soldier's bullet caught him square between the eyes. His legs and arms jerked spasmodically a while before he died. Dives Backward quickly crawled back down to a little ravine, then jumped to his feet, and ran to safety.

In the heat of the battle Left Hand, one of the Arapahoes, mistook a wounded Sioux for a Crow or Arikara scout serving the soldiers. Riding him down, the Arapaho thrust his lance through the Sioux's chest, killing him instantly. Several of the slain warrior's comrades saw what had happened, came running up to try to take Left Hand's horse away from him. They were ready to kill him for killing their friend. Left Hand rode away fast to another part of the field. As he rode up the ridge, a soldier lying on the ground handed his gun to the Arapaho. Left Hand did not kill him, leaving that to some Sioux following after him. Then Left Hand went back and got the cartridge belt off the dead trooper.

At the peak of the fighting the warriors noticed a pretty Ogalala girl named Walking Blanket Woman riding among them in full war dress such as a man would wear. Her brother had been killed in the Rosebud fight and now she carried his war staff and fought as hard as any male warrior. Riding into battle, she sang:

> *"Brothers, now your friend has come! Brave up!*
> *Brave up! Would you see me taken captive?"*

While it was rare for a girl to fight, Walking Blanket Woman was out to avenge her brother's death, since there was no longer a man of fighting age in her family. Catching sight of her, Rain-in-the-Face shouted to all the warriors within earshot:

"Behold, a brave young woman rides with us! Let no warrior hide behind her!"

A bugle blared on the ridge. The surrounded troopers of I Company, with a few survivors from L, were about to attempt a break-through to reach the rest of the command. Soldiers who still had horses quickly mounted. Among the Indians it was also a signal for action.

White Bull now found himself next to Crazy Horse, widely known among the tribes as the bravest of all Sioux. With sheer bravado, White Bull dared Crazy Horse to lead a charge. When the Ogalala refused, White Bull led the charge. His horse having played out, one trooper was left behind after the other soldiers broke through. White Bull promptly picked him as a target. Crazy Horse followed close behind White Bull. Seeing the Indians coming up behind him, the trooper twisted in his saddle to fire his carbine at them. But White Bull was too fast for him, grabbing his blue coat and jerking him from his horse. The soldier fell screaming to the ground. Crazy Horse counted a second coup. White Bull had already outdone the famous Ogalala fighting leader.

A few soldiers still fought on foot in this sector, having

been unable to join in the break-through with those who still had horses. One soldier with a carbine kept turning from side to side, threatening any Indians who advanced toward him. While other warriors kept their distance, White Bull dashed straight in at this soldier. When the soldier fired at him, he simply dodged aside, the bullet narrowly missing him. The next moment White Bull rode him down with his pony. A second coup on the fallen trooper was counted by a Minneconjou named Bear Lice.

Now most of the soldiers were in a struggling mass on the north and west slopes of the hogback ridge. Aside from these, only a scattered trooper here and there was alive.

One soldier, bleeding heavily from a lance wound in his left thigh, kept fighting on alone, a pistol in one hand, a carbine in the other. No Indian could come close to him. Coming up behind him unseen, White Bull rode him down. Following on White Bull's heels, Brave Crow struck the man for a second coup.

Halfway down the slope of the hogback toward the river, about forty soldiers of C Company mounted their sorrel horses and broke out of encirclement. Charging west, they came galloping toward the deep gulch held by most of the Cheyennes and many Ogalalas and Brûlés. The Indians fell back, drawing them on. When the troopers reached a low ridge just vacated by the Indians, they halted and dismounted. Down in the gulch, Lame White Man, the Southern Cheyenne chief who had to fight because he had no sons, rallied the warriors.

"Come on!" he shouted. "Now we can kill them all!"

143

Working their way carefully up the low ridge, the Indians closed in for an attack. Suddenly the soldiers went crazy. Instead of firing at the attacking Indians, they began shooting at one another and at themselves. Before any warrior could charge them, all but four were dead.

These four remounted and tried to escape back the way they had come. Three of them were easily overtaken and killed by the pursuing warriors. The fourth broke away and galloped up the river. A handful of Indians kept after him, although his sorrel horse was fast and long-winded and kept well out ahead. At last only three warriors were left in pursuit. Two were Cheyennes—Old Bear and Kills-at-Night. The other was a Sioux. They raced on, trying hard to bring their quarry to bay. But the soldier kept lashing his horse, making him go faster.

The Sioux fired several times at the white man, but missed him. Old Bear also fired, thinking he had hit his fleeing target. But the soldier was well out ahead.

Suddenly the soldier drew his revolver. Instead of turning to shoot at his pursuers, he jerked his gun arm up to his head, pulled the trigger, and fell dead from his horse. According to available records this may have been Lieutenant Harrington of C Company, whose body was never identified.

By this time many of the Indians were arming themselves with captured guns, much prized as the spoils of battle. However, bows and arrows continued to be in greater favor for this sort of fighting. To fire a gun, an Indian had to jump up and expose himself as he fired. Arrows, on the other hand, could be shot in a long high arc to fall on the soldiers and their horses. With arrows sticking in their backs and rumps, the cavalry horses bolted and plunged every which way, knocking soldiers aside and contributing greatly to their demoralization. Added to this was the fact that the Indians largely stayed concealed, while the soldiers were exposed on the open hillside.

Low on the western slope of the ridge a handful of soldiers fighting on foot held out in a shallow ravine. Past them swept a turmoil of mounted Indians and stampeding cavalry horses. Though the afternoon sun was bright, the valley seemed dark as evening from dust and gunsmoke. These soldiers presented a solid phalanx against frontal attack, and Indian sharp-shooters could not see them well enough to pick them off.

Eagle Elk and his brother-friend High Horse rode up on the ravine without warning. It was not the best place to choose for a fight, but neither warrior was inclined to turn back. Eagle Elk lashed out with his quirt at High Horse's pony and shouted:

"It's a good day to die! Brave up, brother! *Hoka hey!*"

And the two brother-friends charged straight in. Riding with his knees, Eagle Elk clubbed his rifle and struck at the soldiers with his gun butt. High Horse was slashing right and left with his long knife.

With aimed carbines, two soldiers rushed out at them. Then, when the warriors were almost on top of them, they fired straight up in the air and went down under the Indian ponies' flying hoofs.

Just then three mounted soldiers rode in on the warriors' flank. As his pony reared and wheeled, Eagle Elk struck out at one of the troopers with his gun butt, knocking him from his saddle. The trooper's gun flew out of his hands. High Horse leaped onto another soldier with his knife ready. A shot was fired at point-blank range. The third soldier had fired, but had already gone down in the dust. High Horse and his antagonist were struggling on the ground, rolling around in the dust. Eagle Elk jumped down from his horse and tried to hold him quiet, but the animal reared and jerked on the reins, pulling his owner back. By the time Eagle Elk got back to High Horse, his brother-friend's knife was across the soldier's throat and blood was pumping from the soldier's jugular vein.

Eagle Elk pulled High Horse away, but he had suddenly gone limp. Blood came out of wounds in his back and chest. He was dead. Eagle Elk's pony jerked away at the smell of death.

Eagle Elk carried High Horse's lifeless body on his back and took it to a hill apart from the field of battle. There Eagle Elk wept freely in his sorrow. Then a fierce anger swept over him. He only wanted to kill many soldiers, then die.

"My brother," he cried, "look back as you go. I am following. Look back and wait for me, for I'll be coming soon."

Running back into the fight, Eagle Elk saw four cavalry horses, tied together in fours by their reins, running in a tight circle and rearing and yanking at one another. After getting one loose, Eagle Elk mounted and dashed into the dust cloud that told him where the fighting was thickest. He looked now for soldiers to kill, wanting them to kill him. Cavalry horses were breaking away from their holders, and other warriors were chasing after them. But Eagle Elk wanted no horses now. He only wanted killing. Time after time he rode into a shrinking knot of soldiers, flailing out with his gun butt until none were left standing. He had little idea how many he may have killed—but even that mattered but little, as long as he was killing.

Meanwhile, the troopers up the hill were letting their horses go. Quite a number of mounts had already been shot by the soldiers themselves as well as by the Indians, and their carcasses were used as crude barricades behind which the troopers lay prone and partly shielded. But now the horses that were turned loose ran in all directions—bays, sorrels, grays—and many Indians stopped fighting long enough to chase and catch them. The cavalry horses were big and strong, capable of hauling travois with far heavier loads than the scrubby little cayuses could drag.

Just east of the surrounded soldiers White Bull left the side of Crazy Horse to make a lone charge through the troopers. With no cover anywhere at hand, he bent low over his pony's neck, passing to within three or four yards of the firing soldiers. Though bullets whistled all around him, he came through unscathed. After that charge, he grabbed at the reins of a fine big sorrel cavalry charger. But under heavy fire, his own horse was suddenly hit, shot through the head and chest. White Bull was now afoot. Dauntless as ever, he ran toward the soldiers to engage them in hand-to-hand combat.

One soldier, attempting a bluff, aimed his gun at White Bull as if to fire. But as the young warrior dashed toward him, he hurled the weapon at him without firing. At close quarters, the two men grappled in a fierce, well-matched struggle. The soldier almost got White Bull's gun away from him. Using his quirt, the warrior lashed out at the white man's face, forcing him to let go. When the soldier made another grab for the gun, White Bull again lashed him back. With his fists, the soldier pounded away at White Bull's head and shoulders, then suddenly grabbed at the warrior's long hair and jerked his face close in an attempt to bite off his nose. White Bull

147

yelled for help. Crow Boy and Bear Lice came running, but their frantic pummeling fell largely on White Bull, rather than on the enemy. Finally, the warrior yanked free of the soldier's grasp and struck him down with his rifle butt. As the spoils of war, he took the soldier's carbine and cartridge belt. A Hunkpapa named Hawk-Stays-Up counted second coup on the soldier.

Feather Earring, a Minneconjou, lay concealed behind a clump of sagebrush pumping bullets into the dwindling circle of soldiers up the hill. From time to time he moved about, changing his hiding place so the soldiers would not detect it by the gunsmoke from his rifle. His brother, Dog-with-Horns, had already been killed by the white men, and Feather Earring was fighting mad. Firing from long range, he could not be sure how many he had killed. As the resistance of the soldiers began to wane, he moved up closer to their barricade of dead horses, shooting almost constantly.

Only once did he turn back. Five gray cavalry horses with empty saddles came running toward him. He spent a few minutes herding them on down the hill and across the river. Then, on the other side, he noticed they were badly shot up and trembling from their wounds. Chances were, they would soon die. So he let them go and turned his attention back to the soldiers on the hill.

On his way back up the slope, he came upon two bodies. One was a dead Sioux. The other was a soldier, but Feather Earring could see no wounds on him. It looked as though he were still breathing. Feather Earring called to a young Sioux with a bow and arrow, and showed him the dead Indian.

"Your grandfather has been killed by that soldier lying over

148

there. I don't think he's dead. As I don't want to waste a bullet on him, you'd better shoot him with an arrow."

The warrior obligingly shot an arrow into the soldier, who had been playing dead all the time and now jumped to his feet with a scream of pain. He ran a few steps before a second arrow killed him.

With captured weapons and ammunition, as well as his own, White Bull was helping to make it hot for the soldiers. Aiming for the heart with every shot, he was in on the final phase of the battle, having hidden in a ravine down the slope toward the river. Without warning, some soldiers seemed ready to give up their hillside defense. A squad of ten troopers jumped to their feet and came charging straight at White Bull's position. Only White Bull and a Cheyenne stayed in the ravine to face them. Of two soldiers in the lead, White Bull shot one who was already wounded and bleeding at the mouth. The Cheyenne took care of the other. Rushing forward, White Bull counted first coup on one, but was beaten to the other by the Cheyenne. Each warrior got a second coup on the other's kill.

The eight other soldiers kept coming on, firing until they forced the two Indians out of the ravine. Grabbing up one of the dead soldiers' guns, White Bull scrambled up the wall of the ravine. On the hillside above, he stumbled and fell. His leg was numb, and his ankle was swelling painfully. He found there was no wound, his ankle was only bruised. He realized he had been hit by a spent bullet. But he was unable to walk. Crawling into a shallow draw, he lay waiting until the end of the battle.

The last survivors of C and F Companies made their stand in a dwindling knot on the hillside. Under a hail of arrows and bullets, their strength was fast decreasing. They fell one by one, their bodies slumping across those of dead comrades. With little shelter from enemy fire, many of them sold their lives dearly, fighting on bravely to the end.

Shrilling the challenge with eagle-borne whistles and war cries, a large party of warriors charged these soldiers. A Cheyenne named Bearded Man led them, getting almost within the soldiers' lines before they cut him down.

Two soldiers of F Company were shot dead near the top of the ridge by Sage and Left Hand, Arapahoes fighting under the Cheyenne subchief, Two Moon. No soldier was now left standing. Desultory fire from the dead-horse barricade had fallen off to a few scattered shots. With Indians shooting on all sides it was hard to tell how many soldiers were still able to fire a gun.

Hundreds of older men and young boys on horseback watched the end of the fight from surrounding hills, keeping far enough away to be safely out of gun range of any soldiers who remained alive. Behind them, many women were coming up to look on, sensing the battle was almost over and feeling, no doubt, a little of the importance of the day's happenings. A swell of excitement surged through the onlookers when on the north slope of the battle ridge a tall soldier jumped to his feet and ran across a little gulch toward the high knob to the north. Perhaps he thought some of his comrades might be alive there, still holding out, or that the gulch beyond the knob might provide him with an avenue of escape. He stopped short when he saw hundreds of warriors still in the gulch. Standing there on the hillside, he put his revolver to his head and pulled the trigger. A moment later, a Cheyenne boy named Big Beaver raced his pony up the hill from the gulch, jumped down to grab the soldier's pistol and cartridge belt, then leaped back on his pony and galloped off in triumph to a nearby hill.

Across the crest of the ridge a Sioux had crept up close to the barricade of dead horses and was grappling with one of the surviving soldiers. The Indian was clearly getting the best of the white man and had a knife poised above his chest, ready to stab. Knowing he was doomed, the soldier cried for mercy.

"John! Oh, John!" he sobbed, as the Sioux stabbed him.

The name was commonly used by frontier whites to address any male Indian, but from that time on it became the warrior's proper name. He considered he had fairly earned it on a field of battle.

Way down the hill near the river a soldier with stripes on his sleeves—Sergeant Butler of L Company, most of which had been wiped out earlier—struggled to his feet in spite of serious wounds. Standing out on a little knoll, he began shooting at Indians all around him. He seemed determined to go down fighting. A number of warriors dashed to the attack, eager to accommodate him, for such a brave antagonist might well bring on a fine display of courage among them. For a long time he stood there, holding the Indians at bay singlehanded. Then, when it looked as though they might have to let him go, he was dropped by a long-range bullet. No other white man showed such fierce fighting courage that day. Truly, of all the soldiers, he with the stripes on his sleeves was the bravest.

The warriors were crazy with excitement. One Indian lay dead on his face.

"Scalp that Arikara!" went the cry. Everyone took the dead man for an enemy Indian scout. A Sioux jumped off his pony and quickly scalped him. Then he turned him over and saw he had made a terrible mistake. The dead Indian was Chief Lame White Man, the Southern Cheyenne. Nearly forty, he was old for a fighting man, but had been forced to fight because he had no sons of fighting age. The Sioux, saddened by this unforgivable error, stole off, saying no more about the matter. A short time later, a Cheyenne named Wooden Leg found the body and soon many Cheyennes knew Lame White Man had been killed and scalped by their Sioux allies. They were doubly grieved because now Monahseetah and Long Hair's son, Yellow Bird, were again unwanted in the lodge of any man.

A similar predicament arose when Little Crow, brother of Chief Hump of the Minneconjous, took the scalp of Bearded Man, also mistaken for an Arikara scout. Swallowing his pride, and with much ceremony, Little Crow later presented the scalp to the dead warrior's mother and father.

Elsewhere on the field, the brother of Chase-in-the-Morning, an Ogalala, was found horribly wounded. Black White Man, the warrior in question, had been shot down through the shoulder, the bullet lodging in his left hip. His curious wound was due to the fact that he had been hanging from the neck of his pony when hit. There seemed little anyone could do for him, so terrible was the wound and so intense the pain. The warrior's father was so angry about it that he and some other Sioux butchered a dead soldier as they would an animal. But although the meat looked edible, no one was seen to eat of it.

Black Elk was among hundreds of boys who rode down from the hills to shoot arrows into the soldiers. By this time only a handful of whites was still alive and kicking, and all

152

the soldiers were down. Black Elk shot an arrow into the forehead of one soldier. After he stopped quivering, the boy rode on. Another soldier was stuck full of arrows but was still squirming a little. Black Elk got down and began to remove his blue coat. Then an older man came up and pushed the boy away, taking the coat for himself. But Black Elk saw something bright and shiny fastened to the soldier's belt and got it. It was gold and round and very pretty. Since it had a long chain on it, Black Elk hung it around his neck as a charm. At first it made a strange ticking sound, but finally it stopped. It was a long time before the young Ogalala learned how to wind it up and make it tick again.

Another boy, younger than Black Elk, asked him to scalp a soldier for him. After taking the scalp and handing it to the little boy, Black Elk watched him scamper off to show it to his mother. By this time a great mass of women had swarmed up "Battle Ridge" to look at the dead soldiers and see whether any of their own men were among the Indian casualties. As they came on, they were singing victory songs and sounding the tremolo.

The stench of blood was strong in the still air. While warriors stripped the uniforms from the dead soldiers, several mounted Indians with lances rode around jabbing their spear points into the left thighs of the naked bodies. In this fashion the fallen enemies were officially counted dead. Here and there along the ridge, warriors were administering the final *coup de grâce* by firing the soldiers' own pistols at their heads at point-blank range.

Two fat old women were laughing as they stripped a wounded soldier. Once he was naked, they started to cut off his genitals with their knives. Suddenly, inexplicably, he was on his feet. Convulsively, he lunged at his tormentors. A third woman heard her companions shouting for help and ran up to shove her own knife into the soldier, killing him at last. Warriors all around laughed loud and long to see the soldier playing dead, then trying to fight the two fat women.

Among the bravest of the soldiers was a big man with a stubby black beard and long mustaches which curled up at the ends. Several Cheyennes, including Turkey Legs, had ridden him down toward the end of the fight. He had acted much as the leader of the soldiers might have been expected to act, although the white metal bars he wore had little meaning to the Indians—they assumed the captain's insignia was some sort of personal medicine. His body lay among those part-way down the slope, near the barricade of dead horses.

Amazingly he seemed to come to life right before their eyes. He propped himself up on one elbow and looked around him as though he had just arrived from another world. Looking about with a wild expression on his face, almost like that of a madman, he gripped a pistol in his right hand.

A courageous Sioux warrior ran forward, grabbed the revolver out of the white man's grasp, then turned it on him and shot him through the head. The Cheyennes mustered up enough courage after that to strike and stab him until they were all sure he was dead. He was the last man of Custer's command to be killed on the ridge. This brave man may well have been Captain Myles Keogh, gallant Irish soldier of fortune, former papal guardsman and Civil War hero.

Not far from this spot lay the body of a soldier whose sweeping side whiskers at once caught the attention of the sparse-bearded Indians. So luxurious was the growth of beard covering all of the dead man's face save only his chin, that

Wooden Leg who was leading his horse among the dead stopped and "scalped" the dead soldier's *cheek*.

"I have a new kind of scalp," he announced proudly to his companion. He tied the strange scalp to an arrow shaft and carried it about as he wandered on among the bodies. Lieutenant Cooke, Custer's adjutant, had had such a beard.

A cry went up all around as a horseman rode through the crowd still watching from the hills. It was Sitting Bull on his great black stallion, his face grave, his manner not at all that of a victorious conqueror, but rather that of a father concerned about the well-being of his children.

"Are they dead—all?" he asked.

And from those near him came the answer: "Yes."

"All right, let's go back to our camp. Take nothing belonging to the soldiers. Leave everything here. *Hiyupo!* Come on!"

As Sitting Bull started back toward camp, many Indians— Hunkpapas, Blackfeet, Yanktonnais—followed. Dead horses and troopers of Reno's command left near the south end of camp were beginning to bloat and smell in the heat of the afternoon. Women belonging to bands from that end of the village were already rigging up temporary shelters on the grassy benches west of the bottoms. So there was much work to be done getting things straightened around. Furthermore, the wounded had to be taken care of and the dead laid to rest.

In spite of Sitting Bull's warning, hundreds of Indians stayed on Battle Ridge, looting the bodies of the soldiers, stripping off the uniforms, taking the weapons and ammunition. A few responsible fighting men remembered the remnants of Reno's command surrounded on the bluff upriver and rode off in that direction to renew the siege.

All this time the Indians had no idea who commanded the

soldiers they had been fighting. Even by name, Long Hair Custer was known only to a scattered handful. Aside from a few leaders, most of the warriors thought it was the troops of the Gray Fox come to fight them again. Inconsistent with this idea was the fact that these soldiers had Arikara Indians fighting with them, indicating they might have come from Dakota Territory where the Arikaras lived in earth-mound villages along the Missouri River. Crook's forces, on the other hand, had come north from the direction of Wyoming; he had had both Shoshonis and Crows as his allies. And so now the people wondered. . . .

In thick timber on the banks of the Little Big Horn near the Brûlé camp, Woman-Who-Walks-with-the-Stars wandered, looking for stray cavalry horses. Since the now dead soldiers on the ridge had turned their mounts loose, many of the thirsty chargers had been rambling through the brush, trying to get to water. As the wife of Crow Dog, ranking Brûlé chief in the village, Woman-Who-Walks-with-the-Stars well knew the value the big sturdy horses would assume now that the fighting was over. During the kill-talks and honor giveaways which were sure to follow such a great victory, nothing would add more to her husband's prestige than gifts of fine horses to chiefs of other tribes.

Suddenly a flash of dusty blue caught the woman's eye. There in a thicket close to the water crawled a man—a uniformed white soldier. Badly wounded, he was struggling through the undergrowth to get to the river's edge. As he inched along over the ground, the woman saw he was carrying a carbine. For some reason he was trying to get back across the river, though he seemed at times too weak to crawl any farther. Every so often he was forced to stop creeping and lay panting a while until he could build up strength again. At last he was near enough to the water to push his carbine over the bank. While he lay prostrate, weary from this last exertion, Woman-Who-Walks-with-the-Stars picked up a

Crow Dog's wife killing the last of Custer's command.

heavy branch of deadwood. For a moment she watched the soldier curiously. White men always seemed strange with their hairy faces and bodies and their pink skin. She found herself wondering what their women were like, for she had only seen pioneer women at a great distance, when they were cloaked in mother hubbards and sunbonnets hid their faces. Perhaps some white woman loved this very soldier. A strange tenderness swept over Crow Dog's wife.

The soldier stirred a little. Dragging himself along again, he slipped over the bank's edge and plunged into hip-deep water. Watching him, the softness left the eyes of Woman-Who-Walks-with-the-Stars. After all, the soldiers had come attacking. Women, even children, would not have been spared by them, for had not entire Cheyenne families been wiped out by the soldiers in the south? It was always the whites who were the aggressors, seeking to destroy *Pte,* the sacred buffalo uncle of the Sioux, crowding the Indians out of the land Wakan Tanka had given them. Taking a tighter grip on the driftwood club, Woman-Who-Walks-with-the-Stars moved swiftly to the river's edge, where the soldier now saw her for the first time. Stark terror widened his eyes. A hoarse scream started in his throat. But his cry was lost under the loud crash of driftwood about his head and shoulders. In a little while he sank beneath the surface as the woman kept striking at the roiled water where his head had been.

It was slightly past midafternoon. Less than a half-hour had passed since Custer's fall at the ford. During that brief interim, the two hundred fifteen members of his command had been wiped out to a man.

Sundown

Now that the fight on the ridge was over, wounded warriors began making their weary way back toward camp, leaving the field to curious youngsters or women bent on venting their sorrow for slain warriors on the bodies of dead soldiers. Ever since his injury by a spent bullet, White Bull had waited patiently in his small shallow hollow for the battle to end and help to come. At last Has-Horns spotted him and rode over to help him up on his own horse, then led him across the river to the new makeshift camp of the Hunkpapas on the flats west of the bottoms.

Here Makes Room soon saw to it that White Bull lay down in the shade of a tent fly, and sent word for Sitting Bull to come quickly. When his uncle showed up, White Bull played down the "wound." It really was nothing at all, he explained over and over again. But when Sitting Bull bade him stand on the injured leg with his full weight he could not. In no time, the chief of the Hunkpapas had applied powdered sage and other curatives to the injured ankle and had it wrapped in the shed wool of a buffalo bull.

"You should be more careful, Nephew," warned Sitting Bull. "Sometime you might take one chance too many."

White Bull smiled proudly above the obvious pain of his swelling ankle and called for his horse. After he ate a bite, he insisted he would ride over to take another look at Battle Ridge where so many whites had been slain.

Sitting Bull moved on to look after other Indian casualties. Of these there were surprisingly few: nine Sioux and twelve Cheyennes reported killed on the ridge, with another two or three dying of wounds. While the day's fighting was not over, thirty-two warriors had been killed altogether, counting those slain in the bottoms. Joining the families of the Indian dead in their grief, Sitting Bull said solemnly, "My heart is sad for our fallen warriors—and those white soldiers who fell before us. This night we shall mourn alike for our own dead and those brave white men lying up there yonder."

For all his sorrow the chief of the Hunkpapas knew his fighting men had scored a great victory. To the chief of the white soldiers—whoever he might be—such losses must be staggering. Thirty-odd troopers lay dead in the bottoms. Using cut willow sticks to tally the enemy dead, subchiefs appointed to the task had counted one hundred ninety-seven soldiers' bodies on the ridge alone. Others were known to be scattered through the brush along the river. The Indians had delivered a devastating defeat to the armed forces of the Grandfather in far-off Washington. Such an overwhelming triumph brought jubilant smiles to the faces of all save those in actual mourning. Yet Sitting Bull's countenance remained grave.

"They compelled us to fight them," was all he had to say about the victory over the soldiers—even though it meant fulfillment of his vision.

A vague shadow already clouded his sense of well-being about the success of his warriors. Somehow, he could not help thinking, more soldiers must eventually come. A day of reckoning, a day of reprisal, lay ahead. The people here on the Little Big Horn would do well, he thought, to steel themselves against that time.

It was close to four o'clock when Forked Horn, Young Hawk, Goose, Half Yellow Face, and White Swan prepared to leave the timber where they had been cut off after Reno's retreat to the bluff across the river. Another Arikara, Red Foolish Bear, joined them.

"My grandson," Forked Horn said to Young Hawk, "you have shown yourself to be the bravest of us all. The flag on that bluff over there is where the white soldiers are holding out. We must try to reach them. It is up to you to lead us there."

Remembering Long Hair's instructions to them to avoid being mistaken by the soldiers for Sioux, Young Hawk cut a willow stick and tied his white handkerchief to it. He led the way across the river to the bluff. They made slow progress. Goose was mounted on the horse of Red Foolish Bear, who went on foot. They had put White Swan on another horse, and Half Yellow Face brought up the rear. The hostiles seemed to have left only a few marksmen around "Reno Hill," where Reno's depleted command were digging entrenchments against an expected renewed assault in force. As the scouts climbed the bluff, the soldiers fired over their heads at the distant hostiles. A few yards from the top, Young Hawk's horse was shot down. Scrambling to his feet and still carrying the white flag, the Arikara ran on to safety. Seeing Peaked Face (Lieutenant Varnum), Young Hawk solemnly shook his hand. The chief of scouts told him in signs that Bob-tailed Bull and Bloody Knife were dead.

Meanwhile, Half Yellow Face, making his way uphill, waved in the vanguard of Captain Benteen's battalion. Though their fruitless reconnaissance had failed to flush up a single hostile, Benteen's three troops were bone-weary from hours of wandering in rough badlands. Still, to the beaten remnants of Reno's battalion, they were a welcome sight and their arrival was cheered from the bluff. Not all of Reno's men had gained the summit, and more came straggling up the steep embankment as Benteen's command rode up. Half Yellow Face stared enviously at one G Company survivor who, though wounded, came striding up the bank proudly swinging a fresh Sioux scalp. This white man had had better luck getting a battle trophy than any of the Indian scouts.

Looking off downhill toward the mouth of Ash Creek, Half Yellow Face saw three or four Arikara scouts chasing a little band of captured Sioux ponies upstream. They yelled, *"Ota* Sioux! *Ota* Sioux!" *Ota* was the Sioux word for "plenty" or "many." To the Crow it seemed funny to hear these Arikaras using the enemy's language. By this time most of the Arikaras who survived were already on their way back to their earth lodges on the Missouri. Not many of them were brave enough to stay and fight for the soldiers.

As leader of the six Crows who had accompanied the Seventh Cavalry, Half Yellow Face prided himself on his choice of men. It had taken time and care, he reflected, but he had picked the best of the Crow "wolves" for this duty. He wondered what was happening to the four who had ridden off with Two Bodies and Son-of-the-Morning-Star.

All this time the hostiles kept the soldiers pinned to the bluff with long-range fire. It was plain they had left only a small holding force here, while the big masses of warriors had galloped off down-river—perhaps to fight Son-of-the-Morning-Star. Strangely enough, no firing came from the east. The way seemed open to ride off in that direction, if the soldiers wanted to get away.

But the soldiers apparently were determined to stay here on the bluff a while. They were digging at the hard, sun-baked soil with knives and tin spoons and mess kits. All the horses had been led to the center of the oval-shaped entrenchments and tied together in groups of four.

Meanwhile, sharp bickering had broken out among some of the officers as to whether or not they should follow Custer's trail down-river and try to find him. The whereabouts and fate of Custer and his command were still unknown to the rest of the regiment.

Major Reno refused to look for Custer. It had been up to the General to support his own initial charge, he argued. He and the remnants of his command seemed completely demoralized, Half Yellow Face thought. Once, during the most heated part of the argument, Reno whipped out his revolver to fire at half-hidden Indians a thousand yards away—nine hundred yards past effective pistol range. Varnum, too, was in bad shape. Almost in tears, he seized a trooper's carbine and blazed away at the distant hostiles. Coolest and calmest of the officers was Captain Benteen. It was soon apparent to Half Yellow Face that he rather than Reno was now in actual command. Reno's authority, in fact, was fast slipping.

A heavy volley of gunfire sounded off to the north where Custer had gone. The officers peered off in that direction, trying to see what was going on, but it was too far away and too much dust and gunsmoke lay between to see much of anything.

"Jesus Christ!" exploded Varnum. "What does that mean?"

"Custer!" said Captain Weir, commander of D Company in Benteen's battalion.

"We ought to go down there." Lieutenant Edgerly turned to face his superiors.

"If Reno won't take the command, are you willing to go with D Company alone?" asked Weir.

"I am," Edgerly answered.

Weir strode off to get permission from Reno. He and Reno spoke heatedly, then Weir rode north accompanied only by his orderly. Supposing permission had been granted for D Company to follow, Edgerly followed with the troop.

It was after five o'clock before Captain McDougall and the pack train reached Reno Hill. Reinforced by some 24,000 rounds of ammunition in the packs, Reno got up enough courage to follow D Company's advance, unauthorized though it was. But he had many wounded. They could not be left behind and six men were needed to carry one. So progress was painfully slow. Benteen actually led the advance with a trimmed-down battalion of three troops—H, K, and M Companies.

Not far from Reno Hill they were joined by the three Crow scouts who had been with Custer at Medicine Tail Coulee. Goes Ahead, White-Man-Runs-Him, and Hairy Moccasin had circled wide to avoid hostiles, had seen Weir and D Company only in the distance. Now they intended to cross over to the Rosebud and go back up to the Yellowstone, but Benteen ordered them to stay with the command.

Half Yellow Face seemed glad to see his tribesmen, and White Swan showed them his wounded hand. But no one would believe their story of Son-of-the-Morning-Star's fatal wounding at the ford, so they said little more about it—even to Half Yellow Face. None of the soldiers wanted to believe that Custer was dead.

Within an hour, the command reached Weir and D Company and took position on a high point along the crest of bluffs that edged the river, a point later known as Weir's Peak. Joined by D Company, Benteen's battalion was quickly engaged by hostile warriors returning in triumph from Battle Ridge. Benteen prepared to stand fast and fight as hundreds of eager warriors swarmed to the attack. Then frantic orders came from Reno to fall back. Slowly retracing its steps, the entire command retired under mounting pressure to Reno Hill.

During the withdrawal, Edgerly saw a D Company trooper lying wounded on the ground. Edgerly promised him he would form a line and return to rescue him presently. But once in line of skirmish, Edgerly was forbidden by Captain Weir to go back for the man. The trooper was left to his fate as the withdrawal continued.

Iron Hawk was one of many hundreds of Sioux and Cheyenne fighters who met the column and turned it back upriver. With his fellow warriors, he did his share of picking off soldiers and cutting off those left behind. At all costs, the Indians placed themselves between the camp and the attackers, but these soldiers from the hill were hardly more numerous than those just wiped out on Battle Ridge. Once again there was the thrill of the chase, the excitement of swift pursuit and flashing encounter with an enemy who was anything but indifferent.

The soldiers fell back slowly at first, fighting stubbornly

but steadily retreating. Although the retreat never developed into a complete rout, such as the day's two previous engagements had turned out to be, it was plain enough that the troops could go in only one direction—east. Strangely, they would not keep going eastward although the way lay clear and unobstructed as the war chiefs had commanded it should be. The soldiers had every chance to get away if they so desired. Instead, they stopped again on the hill where they had already dug trenches. This time the Indians closed in from all sides.

But it was not the way the Plains tribes liked to wage war. Fighting from trenches or other fixed positions had little part in their brand of battle. Dug in as they were, the troops could not be hurt much there.

Iron Hawk found cover down by the river. Soon he found that he had an excellent hunting blind as well, for soldiers were coming down to the riverbanks unarmed, equipped only with buckets. Indian boys came out of hiding in the brush and threw mud and stones in the faces of the soldiers, chasing them into the water, where Iron Hawk easily picked them off.

His swollen ankle dangling, White Bull rode around Battle Ridge looking for the saddle and leggings he had left there during the big fight. Finding them at last in a clump of brush, he called to his kinsman Bad Soup (or Bad Juice) to come help him saddle up. Once this was done, he and Bad Soup rode slowly over the field, telling each other the honors they had won.

A good many women and young boys were systematically looting the bodies of the soldiers from which warriors had already stripped the best clothing. White Bull managed to find two pairs of dusty blue breeches with yellow stripes down the legs. He saw no mutilation of the enemy corpses taking place, but here and there were scattered heads and arms and legs of the would-be conquerors. Such cutting up of a dead enemy was routine in Indian warfare—none could well come back from the Spirit Land to fight again if his body lacked a gun hand or trigger finger or eyes with which to see his foe.

The dead soldiers of Custer's command being stripped by the victorious Indians.

White Bull's biggest find was a buckskin jacket with long fringe on it. Searching the pockets, he discovered fresh-cut curls of long yellow hair. He showed it to Bad Soup, who quickly made a close examination of the dead white man who had worn the jacket. Bad Soup was quite wise about things pertaining to the whites, for he had spent much time around Fort Abraham Lincoln back in Dakota Territory.

White Bull also looked at the now naked body of the white man, trying to remember him during the fighting. One white man in buckskins, whose hair had been short, stood out in the still-fresh details of the battle. He had fired a pistol twice at

167

White Bull, missing him both times. Then White Bull had shot him dead. He could not be sure if this was the same man or not. He looked at the wounds on the pale body. One bullet had struck the man's left breast, inflicting what was almost certainly a fatal wound. Another bullet hole showed in the left temple. Dark with powder burns, it could have been inflicted by some warrior after the fight as he made sure all the soldiers were dead. The man's features were composed and calm, not contorted as the faces of so many other soldiers were. He had not been scalped; the hair on the crown of his head was too thin to count for much as a trophy.

For a while Bad Soup stood there looking down at the body. Finally he said, "That man there was Long Hair Custer. He thought he was the greatest man on earth, but he lies there now."

That was the first anybody knew that it was Custer himself they had been fighting. White Bull and Bad Soup moved on, telling other warriors that Long Hair had been chief of the soldiers they had wiped out on the ridge.

Accompanied by her aunt Mahwissa, the sister of the dead Black Kettle, Monahseetah wandered idly over the field. Tagging at their heels, the little light-haired Yellow Bird followed. Scattered over the ridge, the carcasses of some seventy cavalry horses and two Indian ponies lay bloating in the heat. Soon they would get fly-blown and the stench would be too great on Battle Ridge for the people to come near. Mahwissa was already complaining of the heavy odor which clung in the warm still air.

A few live horses still limped downhill toward the river, their wounds obvious even at a distance. The women needed

168

only a glance to assure them that the hopelessly injured animals were not worth bothering with.

Another horse stood head down, unable to move. Under the dust and blood, he appeared to be a claybank gelding—he was later identified as Comanche, Keogh's mount, supposedly the only living thing left on the field. His saddle had twisted under his belly and Monahseetah thought for a moment of taking the gold-edged blue saddle blanket. But it was mostly spoiled by bloodstains. Yellow Bird shouted at the horse and threw an earth clod his way, yet the animal would not move over.

Nearby, a circle of dead horses and a pile of naked white bodies showed where the white troops had made a valiant stand. A Sioux warrior was engaged in cutting off the first joint of a dead soldier's finger. The two women moved closer and suddenly there was an exclamation of grief that halted the warrior.

"Ohohyaa!"

The Sioux looked up sharply as he heard the name—"Ouchess." Once in a council meeting Black Kettle had called the great white conqueror by that name. It meant Creeping Panther and was a name long unspoken by the tribesmen.

Now standing above the body, Mahwissa had recognized in the dead soldier with the missing finger joint that same soldier-chief who had killed Black Kettle and wiped out the Southern Cheyenne camp on the Washita so many years ago. This had been the handsome dashing soldier who had once taken her niece and left her so that she could never have a Cheyenne husband. This was the father of little Yellow Bird.

Mahwissa motioned the Sioux away. "He is our kinsman,"

she told him in the sign language, and he moved off, grinning over what he considered a grisly joke. He knew that sometimes Indian women cut off the genitals of a fallen foe, believing that by so doing greater fertility would come to the tribe. He looked back over his shoulder, thinking he would catch the two women busy at such a task.

"Only one thing will we do," said Mahwissa, taking a bone sewing awl from her belt. Bending over Custer's body, she forced the sharp end of the awl into each ear of the corpse, jabbing deep.

"So that Long Hair, the Creeping Panther, will hear better in the Spirit Land," she said by way of explanation. "He must not have heard our chiefs when they warned him if he broke his peace promise with them the Everywhere Spirit would surely cause him to be killed."

Monahseetah gazed in silence at the naked pale-skinned body she had once loved. Now, here in the dust and blood and stench, she felt nothing but loathing for the soldier-chief who had come to kill her people and had himself been slain.

Of far more interest than Long Hair's remains to the people generally were several other bodies on the field. One was that of a soldier who also wore buckskin clothing, later thought to have been Captain Tom Custer. Once his head had been cut off and his clothing stripped from the body, bright red and blue picture writing was found all over his chest and arms. One such picture was of an eagle with outspread wings. Since the eagle was the supreme creature of the animal world and the most exalted symbol of the Plains tribes, many Indians believed this man had been the great chief of the soldiers. This was, of course, before it was learned that Long

Hair had been the soldier-chief. Later, someone stabbed the body of this man with a lance so that the entrails oozed out, an attempt no doubt to count a coup on the supposed dead leader of the soldiers.

Across the river, where Reno had advanced on the Hunkpapa camp, elders, women, and children alike were examining the body of their onetime Negro friend, Teat (Dorman, the interpreter). For years many of them had known him as a woodcutter for Major Galpin, the trader at Fort Yates, Dakota Territory. His Christian name, Isaiah, had sounded so much like *aẑinpi*, the Sioux word for teat or nipple, that Dorman became known among the tribes as Teat. Now, with the clothes stripped from him, the *wasicun sapa* or black white man was more fascinating than ever. Added interest was created by the fact that his legs from the knees down were peppered with tiny pistol balls. In bringing him down, his slayers had fired buckshot into his shins and ankles.

Reno's dead, having fallen closer to the village, were mutilated more than Custer's. Generally speaking, they had been regarded as a greater threat to the camp, and nearly all the bodies bristled with arrows, shot into them after death by small boys. Many were minus hands and feet and heads, with numerous stabs and slashes on limbs and bodies, done largely by enraged weeping women relatives of warriors who had been killed. Using hatchets and sheath knives, the women had completely dismembered several corpses.

Among the grim trophies was the head of an Arikara scout, cut off and carried to the new camp in the bottoms by two young Hunkpapa sisters who swung their grisly prize between them as they walked, each girl firmly gripping a bloody braid. The distinctive side part in the graying hair of the

Arikara's head caused considerable comment. Membership in a certain tribe was indicated by hair style among other features. While Crow men wore their hair cut short over the forehead, the rest standing in an erect ruff, the Arikaras merely combed their locks to one side or another. The Sioux and Cheyennes, on the other hand, usually parted their hair in the center, letting it hang in braids or loose hanks at the sides. The excited girls proudly showed the head to their mother who was half Arikara.

"*Aieee!*" the woman gasped in horror. "It is my brother Bloody Knife, who long ago became an Arikara. He and Chief Gall have feuded hard and long, and now Gall has killed him at last!"

But few people believed that Bloody Knife had been killed by Gall, since that Hunkpapa leader had not been among those Sioux warriors led by One Bull through the timber and into the clearing where the Arikara scout had been shot and the rout of Reno's men had begun. In any case, it was unlikely that any individual enemy could have been recognized in all the confusion and dust and gunsmoke, and it was not until after the fight that it was learned that the Indians who accompanied the soldiers were Arikaras.

Another head that attracted much attention was that of a trooper with many gold teeth in his mouth. The Indians could not understand how or why the man had covered his teeth with the shiny yellow metal and assumed it was part of the soldier's special and personal medicine.

Various military insignia, from a captain's bars to a corporal's stripes, were thought by most of the Indians to be personal battle charms rather than indications of rank. Many of the officers, including Custer, wore no insignia and had been dressed in buckskin clothing, which made the Indians think they were scouts rather than leaders.

No mutilation was performed on the last man killed on Battle Ridge, for when the corpse was stripped a tiny *Agnus Dei* was found hanging around the dead man's neck. This was at once believed to be some powerful charm which might bring harm to anyone who further disturbed its wearer, who was none other than Captain Myles Keogh.

During the fight, nine guidons and flags were captured, but the biggest medicine of them all was Custer's battle flag. Indians quickly sensed its special importance when they recalled that the soldiers had taken great pains never to let it touch the ground.

Rising Sun, a Cheyenne, was puzzled by a flat round metal object with glass on one side of it which he had taken from a dead trooper. The glass face had queer marks on it that seemed to move. Peering at it closely, he suddenly beckoned his comrade Red Fox.

"This thing is alive!" he said, certain that he had found some new sort of soldiers' medicine. He held it to his ear, listening to the tick-tick-tick sound it made. Then he handed it to Red Fox for him to hear. Other Indians came around and Rising Sun let them all listen, but at the same time he decided to keep it for his own battle charm. Presently, he listened to it again, but now it made no sound.

"This is not good medicine, after all," he said. "Now it is dead." He threw it from him, hurling it as far as he could.

Another soldiers' medicine object behaved better, although it made no tick-tick sound. It was larger than the thing found by Rising Sun and had a little fluttering arrow in it which always pointed north. By late afternoon there was beginning to be talk of other soldiers coming from the north up the valley so Little Shield, also a Cheyenne, decided the object might be useful. Later he gave it to High Walking.

Field glasses had an obvious use, but jointed muzzle-cleaning rods carried in the wooden stocks of captured carbines puzzled the Indians for some time. Several such weapons whose cartridges were caught in the breech were deliberately thrown away in the Little Big Horn as unusable, for the warriors had no way to extract the spent shells.

The leather parts of captured bridles were kept, but the steel bits were thrown away. The McClellan saddles were passed around among the older men. A new use was found for the soldiers' boots. Since Indians had low, flat arches they could not wear the white men's footgear. Cutting off the feet of the boots, they carefully saved the leather uppers for moccasin soles and pouches.

Another Cheyenne, Yellow Weasel, found a bugle. For a while he tried to get sound from it. He let other warriors try and they all puffed and blew with no success. When another captured bugle sounded from one of the Sioux camps, a Cheyenne said, "The one the Sioux have is good. Yellow Weasel might as well throw his away since it is no good."

But Yellow Weasel kept trying and finally succeeded in making loud squawking noises on his bugle.

Many soldiers had been carrying leather packages containing sheets of green paper with pictures on them. Some of them were kept by the finders, while some were given to children who enjoyed looking at the pictures. A seven-year-old Cheyenne boy named Spotted Hawk used one such sheet as a saddle blanket for a toy rawhide horse. But most of the bills were discarded as worthless bits of paper. Few Indians on the

Little Big Horn realized the green papers had any value. Even had they known, it could have meant but little to them that the Seventh Cavalry had received two full months' pay since leaving Fort Abraham Lincoln and so had carried some twenty-five thousand dollars into battle.

A far more significant discovery from the Indians' viewpoint was made by Wooden Leg, a Cheyenne, when he found a soldier's canteen half full of some liquid that definitely was not water. After sniffing the metal bottle, a more knowledgeable Sioux said, "Whisky."

Other such bottles were found scattered over the field and some Indians drank the contents. Many tried to drink but quickly spat out the fiery liquor. Bobtail Horse took a big swig from Wooden Leg's canteen, got violently sick, and vomited. The Indians suddenly had an explanation for the weird behavior of the soldiers—they had been made crazy with this drink. At last it was clear why the soldiers had attacked the great camp with an inadequate force, why they had hesitated at the ford and committed other tactical blunders, and why so many of them had fired in the air and waved their arms wildly and finally killed themselves rather than die fighting as brave men should. Several Indians wise to the ways of whites insisted that not enough whisky was gone from any of the bottles to make a white man crazy, but the idea persisted nevertheless. By early evening most of the people were convinced that the soldiers' downfall had been due to the white man's *mni wakan*—"holy water."

Sitting Bull was gravely concerned because his people had flagrantly disobeyed his orders not to mutilate or loot the dead soldiers. His immediate band had taken nothing, but others obviously had gone all-out in acquiring the spoils of battle. All through the village, Indians were saying to each other:

"I got a soldier gun."

"I got three horses."

"I got a saddle."

"I got tobacco."

"I got whisky."

No man could have controlled all the Indians on the Little Big Horn. Any conformity other than to age-old tradition was out of the question. Individuality, not regimentation, was the Indian way. Yet Sitting Bull gathered the leaders together at the new camp in the bottoms. Angrily, he spoke:

"Since you have taken the spoils, henceforth you will covet the things of the white man. You will be at his mercy and will starve at his hands. Someday his soldiers will crush you. Indians! There are no Indians left but me!"

Humbled and contrite, the leaders left the informal council, the earlier smiles of victory faded from their faces. With some relief they turned to investigate a fresh outbreak of excitement beyond the Sansarc circle where a large number of Sioux had surrounded a band of Indians just arrived in camp.

"Kill them! Kill them all!" some Sioux were shouting.

But others were saying, "Wait! We must be sure!"

Above the tumult a Cheyenne voice cried, "I had nothing to do with the soldiers! I am all Indian. I am Cheyenne!"

Hearing Cheyenne speech, Wooden Leg and a Southern Cheyenne elder, Yellow Horse, hurried to the Sansarc camp to find Little Wolf and his seven lodges of people in extreme danger. The most respected of the Cheyenne old-man chiefs, Little Wolf had never mingled much with the Sioux and did

176

not know their language. Now the Sioux were ready to kill him and all his band for having—so they thought—led the soldiers to the Little Big Horn.

Yellow Horse and Wooden Leg made their way through the crowd until they were at Little Wolf's side. As the chief's kinsman, young Wooden Leg was directed to do the talking. Yellow Horse called out, "Wait until this young man talks to Little Wolf. Then he will tell you what is said."

"Have you been with the soldiers?" Wooden Leg asked.

"No, foolish boy," Little Wolf answered angrily. "Do I look like a crazy man? I have seven lodges of people with me —women, children, old men. They have all their property with them, their tepees, their packs, everything. I have few warriors. Does anyone think that is the way to join up with the soldiers and help them? No part of me is or ever was white man. I am all Indian. I am willing to fight anyone who says I am not."

Wooden Leg, who spoke Sioux, explained Little Wolf's stand to the Sioux warriors gathered around. Although much grumbling followed, it was agreed that the newcomers could join their relatives in the Cheyenne camp. Good feeling all around came when Little Wolf's people doled out gifts of sugar and coffee, brought all the way from their Nebraska agency. Such commodities were scarce on the Little Big Horn. From Little Wolf the other Indian leaders first learned that the soldiers they had beaten were from the northeast and apparently were not the Gray Fox and his men, after all.

Throughout the village people were preparing hasty burials for the slain warriors, all of whom were dressed in their finest war clothing and had their faces painted in bright ceremonial colors. The remains of the Cheyennes were loaded on pony drags and taken out into the neighboring hills or gulches, away from camp sites or main travel lanes. Hidden in sheltered coves in out-of-the-way coulees, the bodies were wrapped in buffalo robes and covered with piles of rocks to keep the coyotes away. Mourners stayed close to the graves to grieve. The greatest ceremony attended the burial of Chief Lame White Man. Many people went along and the war chief's entire family stayed behind to mourn through the night.

Having a different way of disposing of their dead, the Sioux designated certain lodges as burial tepees and left them standing in the Hunkpapa circle when the move was made to the new camp site in the bottoms. Scaffolds were erected inside the lodges and the bodies laid out on them, after which the tepees were completely abandoned by the live inhabitants. Some twenty bodies, a majority of the Sioux casualties, were placed side by side in one large burial lodge on the old Hunkpapa camp site.

People in the nearby Blackfeet Sioux circle, where no deaths had occurred, were looking over a captured horse. The animal, a prancing sorrel with blazed face and white stockings, was proudly displayed by Walks-Under-the-Ground, a Santee. To all who would listen he insisted he had slain the "head man" during the fight on the ridge. After the battle had ended, the Santee claimed, he had found the horse tied by the reins to the wrist of the dead soldier-chief. Few actually believed Walks-Under-the-Ground since there were already conflicting claims as to who had killed the soldier-chief—as well as to just *which* white man had been the leader. But none could deny that the sorrel with the mincing gait was a mount worthy of any chief, Indian or white.

On a quiet hilltop beyond Battle Ridge a lonely warrior

sat and wept beside the body of a fallen comrade. After all the soldiers were dead and no more killing was to be done, Eagle Elk had returned to the place where he had left High Horse's body, remaining there until the sun hung low over the mountains off to the west. Then at last he rose and slung the body of his brother-friend across the soldier's saddle on the captured cavalry horse. Walking slowly, he led the horse back to the Minneconjou circle to deliver the body to his brother-friend's father. Back in his own lodge in the Ogalala camp he would take no food when the family gathered for the evening meal. Turning into the shadows, away from the light of the cookfire, he wept silently.

With each passing minute the soldiers on Reno Hill found the thirst more unbearable. One detail after another crept down the bluff by way of a deep gulch, then sprinted across an open space to reach the water's edge. Iron Hawk shot a soldier as he straightened up after dipping water up with a bucket. The trooper pitched forward, face down in the river. Iron Hawk waded in after him, striking him with his bow until he was dead. Then he dragged the body ashore downstream. In the man's pockets he found only worthless bits of green paper and several pieces of metal money. Iron Hawk saved the metal discs but tore up the paper and threw it away.

Inside the oval of trenches on top of the bluff three of the Crow scouts hunkered down near the pack mules, waiting for the sun to set. Only Half Yellow Face and White Swan stayed in the trenches and kept fighting for the soldiers. But, as the other scouts well knew, shooting at an all but invisible enemy out there in the growing dusk was useless indeed. Now that Captain Benteen had seen to it that they got good soldiers'

guns White-Man-Runs-Him, Goes Ahead, and Hairy Moccasin began to think of trying to get through the hostiles to
reach their own people.

"We should get away from here before the Sioux charge us,"
said White-Man-Runs-Him, although there was little chance
that the hostiles would storm the bluff before morning. The
three Crows were well aware that no warrior of the Plains
liked to fight at night, for in darkness he might go unrecog-
nized by the Great Mystery in the event of his death.

Signing agreement with White-Man-Runs-Him, the other
two Crows got up to go.

"Where d'you think you're going?" asked the head packer.

White-Man-Runs-Him cunningly answered him in signs:
"We are going to get water."

The head packer promptly handed each of them a flat,
canvas-covered canteen to fill down at the river and bring
back to the thirsty packers. Without saying anything to Half
Yellow Face the three Crows left the bluff. Instead of going
down to the river for water, they threw away the flat canteens
and cut across Ash Creek, following it upstream until they
reached the divide. Four Sioux wolves had been sent out here
to watch for more soldiers. One of these Sioux scouts was
lagging behind the others. He rode a gray horse and led a
sorrel mule that somehow had gotten away from the pack
train. Goes Ahead stalked the Sioux and killed him. The mule
broke away but the gray horse got tangled up in his trailing
jaw rope and Goes Ahead caught him. Giving the horse to
White-Man-Runs-Him, Goes Ahead bent over the dead Sioux
and took his scalp. The three Crows took turns riding the
captured horse until they reached the pine trees along the
summit of the divide. Swinging northwest, they circled wide

180

to come out on the Big Horn River, the enemy Sioux and Cheyennes far behind. They crossed the river and pushed on west toward the Crow village on Arrow Creek. Ahead of them, beyond the shining mountains, the setting sun sank slowly— looking like a great blood-red shield in the cloudless sky.

Darkness settled over the Little Big Horn valley, but the soldiers on Reno Hill did not sleep in spite of their weariness. Long hours after sundown the hostiles ringing the bluff kept up a sporadic fire, still making it hot for the troopers in the trenches. Varnum gathered the remaining scouts together to tell them that a message was to be carried through the night. Eldest of the surviving Arikaras, Forked Horn acted as their spokesman. He agreed to lead the scouts through the hostile lines. Since he was wounded, Goose was not to go. The two Crows would also stay, Half Yellow Face to look after the wounded White Swan.

"All you others will carry the same message," Varnum told the Arikaras. "You will carry word to the Grandfather in Washington, in order that everyone in the land will know what has happened here. You'll ride troop horses, they're faster than your ponies."

"The troop horses wear iron shoes," Forked Horn complained. "They will run better if the iron shoes are taken off."

"I'll get the farrier to work right away," promised Varnum. "Now each of you is to ride hard and pay no attention to any of the others. It'll be every man for himself. Maybe one of you will get through. If any of you are shot, pull out the paper message and leave it on the ground where other soldiers can find it when they come."

Then Varnum gave each of them a piece of paper with

writing on it. Goose refused to be left behind. "If my cousins are killed, I too wish to be killed."

Varnum consented. At last they were ready. In the group were Goose, Forked Horn, Red Foolish Bear, Young Hawk, and a white sergeant. Stealthily, they worked their way through the darkness down the ravine to the river. Just as escape seemed certain the hostiles opened fire. Young Hawk and Goose fired into the black night, seeing nothing. Then they all saw it was no use and clattered back up the hill. No one tried to get through.

Varnum shook his head wearily. Half Yellow Face stood at his elbow.

"Perhaps my three Crows went on to bring help," the Crow leader suggested. "Maybe that is why they have not come back."

Varnum shook his head hopelessly, saying nothing.

In the late night hours, the three Crow scouts were heard by camp sentries at the tribal village on Arrow Creek. Crow warriors were roused from sleep and sent out to meet them. In the darkness the scouts were mistaken for Sioux and the Crow warriors charged them fiercely. Goes Ahead had to shoot two of their horses before they realized their error. The proximity of the hostiles on the Little Big Horn made everybody jumpy that night.

It was not a happy homecoming. Certain that Half Yellow Face and White Swan had already been wiped out with the remaining soldiers on Reno Hill, the three scouts reported them dead. One of Goes Ahead's wives, Pretty Shield, a niece of Half Yellow Face, joined her family in mourning. Relatives of the supposedly dead scouts gave away all their horses and clothing and gashed their heads and arms and legs until they were covered with blood. All through the night the keening of the women was terrible to hear. Mingled with the names of Half Yellow Face and White Swan was that of Son-of-the-Morning-Star. One by one, the Crow people wandered off alone, chanting the dreadful mourning song and weeping.

Few slept in the great village on the Little Big Horn. In every quarter was unusual stir and activity. Acting as self-appointed heralds, old men rode through the camps singing old brave-heart songs, calling out to the warriors: "Brave up! Brave up!"

In the Ogalala circle, Kit-Fox warriors, acting as camp police, rode all around singing:

> *"I am a Fox.*
> *I am supposed to die.*
> *If there is anything difficult,*
> *If there is anything dangerous,*
> *It is mine to do."*

Big fires danced high in the darkness as each mourning family burned its lodge and the dead warriors went up in flames. The keening of the women was a continuous wail during the night, as those related to the dead hacked off their hair, gashed their heads and the calves of their legs, or lopped off their own fingers to show their sorrow. Male relatives dressed in rags. Sioux men in mourning cropped their hair at the jaw line, while Cheyenne males let their normally braided hair hang loose.

A few agency Indians, mostly Santees and Yanktons, got drunk on the whisky found in the soldiers' canteens and fired volleys of captured bullets at the stars. Distant firing could be heard upstream from the bluff where a night guard kept the entrenched soldiers surrounded. The Indians there did not hope to hit anything in the dark, but kept shooting long after sundown to keep the soldiers from trying to escape. All through the long night hours warriors kept coming and going from the bluff as the guard was frequently changed.

Nowhere in the village were scalp or victory dances held this night, for the success over the soldiers could not be celebrated until all mourners had given formal consent—normally after a waiting period of four days. But here and there were spontaneous paeans of triumph. Proudly, the people were saying over and over to one another:

"Wicunkasotapelo! We killed them all!"

Once during the dark hours sudden terror again gripped the camp. "Soldiers are coming!" went the cry. Looking from their lodges, the people saw troops in uniform bearing down on the village. A bugle blared a raucous charge. A wild scramble began to save belongings and get away. Women shrieked and old men shouted advice to the warriors. Dogs barked in a frenzied renewal of the afternoon's excitement. Just as pandemonium reached a peak, those in the camp got a closer look at the soldiers. They were all laughing, grinning Indians! A large band of mischievous young warriors had dressed themselves in captured uniforms to "attack" the camp—all in fun.

After that, everybody relaxed but sleep was now out of the question. People gathered in little groups to recite the events of the long day. It seemed a long time since the death of Four Horns's aged wife in the Hunkpapa camp had foreshadowed a day of victory.

Some of the warriors started making up kill-songs. Soon

the people picked up the words and their shrill voices echoed up and down the valley, singing the new kill-songs all through the night:

> *"Long Hair has never returned,*
> *So his woman is crying, crying.*
> *Looking over this way, she cries.*
>
> *"Long Hair, horses I had none.*
> *You brought me many and I thank you.*
> *You make me laugh!*
>
> *"Long Hair, guns I had none.*
> *You brought me many and I thank you.*
> *You make me laugh!*
>
> *"Long Hair, let go your guns.*
> *You are not man enough to do us harm.*
> *You make us laugh!*
>
> *"Long Hair—where he lies nobody knows.*
> *Crying, they seek him everywhere.*
> *He lies right over here."*

The spoils of battle

Aftermath

NEXT MORNING before dawn—the watches of the soldiers on Reno Hill read two o'clock—the Indians resumed the fight around the bluff. At daylight a fresh band of warriors took over, and the men who had been watching the soldiers through the night went back to camp. A number of people came out from the village to look on. Among them was young Black Elk and his mother from the Ogalala camp. The woman was mounted on a mare with a small colt. Every so often the colt wandered out ahead, then came scurrying back each time a shot was fired.

There was little to see. The soldiers were now dug in securely and only the horses and mules in the center of the oval entrenchments were visible. Most of the animals were dead.

Across the river were thick berry bushes. Round Fool, an Ogalala youth, kept running around the bushes. Black Elk asked him what he was doing.

"A white soldier is in those bushes," said Round Fool.

Peering closer, Black Elk saw a man trying to hide in the thick brush. He had apparently been there all night, unable to reach the soldiers on the bluff. Black Elk and some other boys began shooting arrows at him. He crawled around in the undergrowth, trying to dodge the swift arrows. Once he cried out in pain, indicating that an arrow had found its mark.

Presently the boys set fire to the dry grass around the bushes and the soldier came rushing out. A warrior shot him dead.

From his lookout on a nearby hilltop, White Cow Bull looked down into the trenches on the bluff and watched the soldiers crouching there. A good shot, the Ogalala warrior was among many marksmen harassing the troops with long-range fire. During the night it had rained a little and the troops were huddled together against the morning chill. Then, as the sun climbed high and the dry heat of the day settled over the bluff, the soldiers moved around more and White Cow Bull was able to pick off his share of the enemy. Using a buffalo

White Cow Bull sniping at Reno's besieged command.

skull to rest his rifle on, he killed one soldier, Trooper Jones of H Company, as he tried to remove his heavy overcoat. He shot another trooper in the foot—or so he thought until he saw the man hobbling about with only the heel of his boot shot away. He wounded at least two others. Several soldiers kept firing at his hilltop, but their carbines lacked sufficient range to reach him.

It soon became clear to the Ogalala that the troops had another problem on their hands, one even more urgent perhaps than Indian gunfire—water. Since yesterday the soldiers had had no chance to replenish their water supply except once, when a detail of seven men had made it down to the river and back. The rain had not helped them much. As the morning wore on the soldiers were obviously getting more and more desperate.

Finally one trooper urinated in his tin cup and drank from it. He seemed to go crazy there in the trenches. Suddenly he climbed out and ran down the hill toward the river. White Cow Bull fired at him, missed. Another Sioux marksman brought him down.

Both sides had plenty of ammunition. Reno had all of 24,000 rounds brought up by the pack train. The Indians had some 10,000 rounds taken yesterday from dead soldiers. Delighted with their captured weapons, many warriors had never before used breech-loading guns and were highly pleased with the shiny new cartridges.

But they soon grew weary of this static style of fighting. About midmorning a large party of warriors stormed the trenches from the steep south slope toward the river. Without a twig of cover they charged up the bluff. Long Robe, a Sansarc, got close enough to strike a trooper with his coup-stick. As he started back down, he was shot dead by the soldiers. His comrades were unable to recover his body. (His fall is indicated by a marker on the present battlefield.)

Had the Indians carried out a co-ordinated charge on the

bluff from all directions, there is little doubt but that the entire Seventh Cavalry would have been wiped out. The besieged troopers could not have retreated—they had no place to run. Reno, Benteen, and other survivors of the regiment owed their lives to the arrival on the scene at midday of Sitting Bull, who ordered the warriors to stop shooting.

"*Henala!* Enough!" he shouted. "Those soldiers are trying to live, so let them live. Let them go. If we kill all of them, a bigger army will march against us."

Knife Chief, an Ogalala, relayed Sitting Bull's commands to the fighting leaders. As he moved along the line passing the word, Knife Chief was shot through the body by a soldier who rose up and fired from the trenches. Taking the wounded Ogalala with them, the warriors withdrew and went back to the village. Thirsty, tired, ready for a rest, they were glad to leave off fighting for a while. The Battle of the Little Big Horn had ended.

That afternoon the women began to strike their lodges and load their belongings on pony drags for an announced move to the south. After a brief nap, White Bull rode north with Many Lice, a Sansarc, to scout the rumored approach of more soldiers from the north. These new troops had camped for the night at the mouth of the Little Big Horn, some twelve miles away. Mostly infantry, they now came marching slowly upriver. This was Gibbon's column, nearing the appointed rendezvous with Custer almost a half day behind schedule. Charging into the soldiers' herd of pack horses, the two warriors ran off seven head, then hastened back to alarm the camp.

By the time they got back the entire village had moved.

Only a few tepees were left standing. These were lodges of mourning families who had abandoned and left behind everything they owned. The warriors pushed on, following the broad trail and catching up with the people some distance to the south.

That night the great caravan stopped a few hours to rest without setting up lodges. Next day they traveled on up the Little Big Horn valley, halting during the afternoon about two miles below the mouth of Lodge Grass Creek in the shadows of the Big Horn Mountains.

Here the Indians held their great victory dance. No other warrior had a record equal to that of White Bull for bravery and daring. All told, he had counted seven coups—six of them firsts—and had killed two men in combat, captured two guns and twelve horses, was wounded in the ankle, and had had his horse shot from under him. Bursting with pride, wearing both pairs of soldiers' breeches given him by his son, Makes Room made up a special honoring song for the occasion:

> *"White Bull, whenever there is something going on*
> *You are always out in front.*
> *This makes me very proud of you."*

For the Sioux and Cheyennes it was the last such celebration for many years to come. The tribes soon learned their triumph over Long Hair Custer had indeed been hollow. By smoke signal and moccasin telegraph, word came from the agencies that an angry Government was stepping up military operations against them. Through an uneasy summer the people followed the buffalo herds, drying meat against certain famine on the reservations to which they knew they must go.

Keeping endlessly on the move, they stayed only a skip and a jump ahead of reprisal.

Early in September the first retaliatory blow fell at Slim Buttes, Dakota Territory. A large camp of Ogalalas, Brûlés, and Minneconjous, drifting back to their agencies, was taken by surprise in a dawn attack. Badly outnumbered, their leader American Horse (or Iron Shield) mortally wounded, the fighting chiefs suffered a sharp defeat at the hands of their old adversary, Gray Fox Crook. In the vanquished camp the soldiers found three Seventh Cavalry horses, a gilt-starred swallow-tailed guidon from I Company, and Captain Myles Keogh's gauntleted gloves—proof enough to the Gray Fox that his defeated foes had been in on the big kill at Little Big Horn.

In November Colonel Ronald McKenzie struck Dull Knife's village of Cheyennes on Willow Creek in Montana. Though innocent of participation in the Custer fight, these defeated Cheyennes served their tribesmen as a sharp warning of the Government's long arm of retribution. Still only a minor chief of Fox warriors, Two Moon meekly surrendered to Army authorities and overnight became—at least in the eyes of the Government—head chief of all Northern Cheyennes. When they in turn submitted, Little Wolf and Dull Knife and their bands were punished for alleged participation in the Battle of the Little Big Horn with deportation to the Southern Cheyenne agency in Indian Territory. Three years later, faced with certain extinction through disease and starvation in the south, the gallant Northern Cheyennes fought their way fifteen hundred miles northward to win at last the right to stay on unmolested in their Montana homeland.

Late in 1876 the Sioux met their share of reverses. At

Standing Rock Agency Kill Eagle, the Blackfeet Sioux chief detained on the Little Big Horn by Sitting Bull, was thrown into prison. Gall and Crow King, still the principal Hunkpapa fighting leaders, were granted amnesty for their repudiation of Sitting Bull. White Bull was forced to surrender his captured guns and horses to soldiers at Cheyenne River Agency.

Crazy Horse submitted to a life of unaccustomed inactivity at Red Cloud Agency, where, less than a year later, he met death under a soldier's bayonet. Backed by puppet chiefs and well oiled with rotgut whisky, Red Cloud sold out his people by selling the sacred Black Hills to the whites. Unscrupulous land commissioners, hungry for the mineral-rich territory, persuaded Red Cloud to "touch his pen" to the agreement without going through the usual formality of securing approval from three-fourths of all adult Sioux males.

Thoroughly disgusted with such deterioration of tribal government and tradition, Sitting Bull decided to take his immediate following to Grandmother's Land (Canada) where he hoped to find sanctuary. Accompanied by One Bull and other faithful members of his band, Sitting Bull arrived in Canada early in 1877 for a four-year sojourn, during which the United States Army never ceased in its efforts to force or persuade him to return to American soil. Once a party of Sioux-speaking Cheyennes, now serving the Government as scouts and headed by Bobtail Horse, who had held off Custer at the ford, crossed the international boundary to try to talk Sitting Bull into coming back with them. Wily as ever, the Sioux chieftain steadfastly refused, parrying countless naïve attempts to make him submit. In the end it was the threat of starvation alone that forced Sitting Bull to give in. He surrendered with one hundred eighty-seven loyal followers at Ford Buford in July, 1881, a little over five years after Little Big Horn. Confined at a Missouri River agency for two years, disillusioned and embittered at the Government's refusal to feed his people, Sitting Bull was finally rescued from life imprisonment by perennial showman Buffalo Bill Cody, then running a Wild West Show. With Rain-in-the-Face and other warriors who had fought at Little Big Horn, the chief became a national celebrity as the Indian who had wiped out Custer.

Meanwhile, white hide hunters were finishing off the last of the great buffalo herds that once roamed the northern plains. Vast ranges in Montana and Dakota were filling up with Texas longhorns as the buffalo gradually disappeared. In the turmoil and excitement of an expanding empire, the once hostile red men were all but forgotten. Their game herds gone, their rations of Government beef sadly inadequate, the tribes languished and starved.

Then, in 1890, the Sioux again felt a little of the old power and glory they had known that far-off day on the Little Big Horn. Indian holy men preached a strange doctrine which advocated a return to the free life of the past. An obscure Paiute soothsayer, Wovoka, from distant Nevada, had taught them the rudiments of a new religion—half-Christian, half-pagan. Once again, they promised, the plains would be black with buffalo. Those beyond the grave would return to instruct the living in a tremendous revival of ancient customs. Great cracks would open across the face of the earth to swallow up the white men and their hated brand of civilization. All this would surely come to pass if the people would dance with ghosts and sing the eerie drumless chants.

And so the Ghost Dance flourished briefly. A chief to his

fingertips, always a vehement champion of self-determination for the Sioux, Sitting Bull became nominal leader of the cult. Although there is some question as to whether or not he subscribed entirely to the new belief, he forcefully insisted that the Indians be left alone to live and believe as they wished. During his wide travels with Buffalo Bill, he had discovered such basic liberty to be universally enjoyed by other Americans. It seemed simple justice to extend it to established wards of the Government, the Indians.

Frightened whites in Nebraska and the Dakotas felt otherwise. The Army was called in to occupy the Sioux reservations. A vindictive agent conspired with Indian police to have Sitting Bull murdered and fourteen years after Little Big Horn the aging chief was killed in a short pitched battle with his assassins. Two hundred miles away on Wounded Knee Creek, South Dakota, the reorganized Seventh Cavalry waylaid Big Foot's peaceful band of Minneconjous and exacted fearful vengeance for Little Big Horn in a blood bath in which two hundred and twenty men, women, and children perished.

In numb bewilderment the Sioux turned lamely to follow the white man's road. The old way had vanished sharply soon after Little Big Horn. Now even the dream of the old life was ended. The power of the sacred hoop of the universe—which had always bound the people together with earth and sky—was broken forever.

A seventeen-year-old warrior at Little Big Horn, Iron Hail (Dewey Beard), a Minneconjou, paid full price for the Sioux victory when the Seventh Cavalry came charging again at Wounded Knee. Under the soldiers' rifles and Gatling guns, he was twice wounded, saw his father, mother, two brothers, sister, wife, and child killed. Notwithstanding such reverses, he eventually married again and found a fine life of peace for himself and his new family. In later years he became prominent as a leader among a dwindling, aging group of warriors who had fought on the Little Big Horn. With the death of Sitting Bull's deaf-mute son, John, in May, 1955, Iron Hail became the last survivor—Indian or white—of Custer's Last Stand. He died that November.

Portrait sketch of Iron Hail (Dewey Beard), last survivor of the Battle of the Little Big Horn.

The Legend

CUSTER'S LAST STAND assumed legendary proportions almost as soon as news of it reached the white man's world. A myth nearly as imaginative as Homer's *Odyssey* was in the making as fiction swiftly intertwined with fact. An adulatory press had already built Custer into such a heroic figure that earliest reports of his death were not generally believed. Only a few seasoned military campaigners read the truth in the ugly message.

In some mysterious way Crow and Shoshoni scouts serving General Crook in northern Wyoming—a full hundred miles south of the Little Big Horn—got wind of the tragedy the very afternoon it occurred. Puzzled by the scout's sullen manner, Crook took advantage of his honorary membership in one of their warrior societies to quiz them in detail. Acting as spokesman, Plain Bull, a Crow, made the startling statement:

"Long Hair Custer, Son-of-the-Morning-Star, and all his soldiers, every one, were killed this morning on the Little Big Horn!"

Crook knew that Plain Bull would not deceive him, and that he had somehow known what had happened on Little Big Horn. But neither Plain Bull nor any of his tribesmen ever divulged how word had reached them.

Miles away in the opposite direction, traveling north from

the Little Big Horn, the young Crow scout Curley followed
down Tullock's Creek to the Yellowstone River the night of
June 25. Seeing a friend across the river next morning, he
waved and talked sign to Tom Leforge, a squaw man living
with the Crows and serving General Terry as a guide through
the region. Reading Curley's gestures, Leforge was the first
white man to get a direct "eyewitness" account of Custer's
defeat.

Moving on, Curley reached the mouth of the Little Big
Horn the following afternoon, June 27. He was spotted by
three crewmen from the *Far West,* fishing a mile upriver from

Curley bringing news of Custer's defeat to the steamer *Far West.*

where Terry's supply ship rode at anchor. Unable to understand Crow or sign talk, the men waved the scout on toward
the steamer. Minutes later he appeared opposite the boat on
the Little Big Horn's east bank, wearing a black white man's
shirt, a cloth about his head, and moccasins.

197

His manner seemed dejected as he strode manfully up the gangplank, but white men on the boat soon discovered his harrowing adventures, as interpreted by squaw man George Morgan, had not impaired his appetite. That Curley told a straightforward account of the battle as he saw it or guessed it to have happened cannot be questioned. At seventeen the simple Crow youth was far too naïve to have imagined many embellishments. He made it clear from the beginning that he had done nothing himself—that he had not actually taken part in the fight and had seen only enough of the battle to realize what the inevitable outcome must be.

That very day, perhaps, on the deck of the *Far West,* Curley unwittingly became a "survivor" of the Last Stand. In the retelling, his simple repetition of Bouyer's message to Terry made him not only an active participant in the fight, but one who had narrowly escaped with his life to bring news of it to the outside world. Overnight the modest Crow youth became a hero. Muggins Taylor, a scout, left in a flurry of excitement on a hard three-day ride to carry Curley's story to Bozeman and Fort Ellis.

Meanwhile, after fencing with the hostiles' rear guard through most of the afternoon and night of June 26, Gibbons and his infantry column arrived at the scene of the battle. Next day Reno, Benteen, and the other survivors of the Seventh Cavalry were rescued from Reno Hill and the dead of Custer's and Reno's commands were given a hasty slipshod burial in the flinty soil of Battle Ridge. Custer's body was carried, with the wounded soldiers of Reno's and Benteen's commands, by two-horse litters back down-river to the *Far West.* No cavalryman lived to report on the destruction of Custer and his command, so Curley's story remained the standard accepted account of the battle.

His words distorted by white interpreters who put trite pseudo-Indian phrases in his mouth, Curley was finally quoted as saying that Custer was the *last* man to be slain on Battle Ridge where "he stood like a sheaf of corn with the ears fallen all around him."

The other three Crow scouts who had ridden with Custer could have refuted Curley's story, for they had been far closer to the action, had seen Custer fall, and had stayed a while longer near the doomed command. Now, however, Goes Ahead, White-Man-Runs-Him, and Hairy Moccasin were in disfavor with Seventh Cavalry survivors for having "deserted" Reno Hill the evening of June 25, although their duty to the soldiers had ended with their location of the enemy village that morning. They were a long time getting back in the Army's good graces. Hero of the hour, Curley was whisked off to Washington to be wined and dined and feted as the "sole survivor of Custer's Last Stand." Significantly, as the Army's guest he was given no chance to return to his people before leaving for the nation's capital. The authorities were taking no chances on having their growing legend watered down by more authentic accounts.

Two Crow scouts other than Curley also carried word of the Custer battle to the whites. Neither was attached to Custer's command. They had been guiding Gibbon's column upriver from the *Far West*'s anchorage. Their garbled accounts contributed to one of the many dark mysteries surrounding Little Big Horn—the question of Custer's suicide. Arriving at Fort Rice, Montana, a day or so after the fight, Speckled Cock told members of the garrison:

"Big battle lost. Son-of-the-Morning-Star shot himself."

Horned Toad rode on with Speckled Cock to Fort Abraham Lincoln, where he was heard by several officers' wives nearly a week before the return of the *Far West*.

"Speckled Cock and me, Indian scouts. Just come. Rode ponies many miles. Ponies tired, scouts tired. Custer shoot himself at end. All dead. Speckled Cock and me good Indians. No lie!"

When Custer's widow screamed and fled the room, the scouts said no more. Army authorities never permitted publication of the story.

Later, a report was issued by Lieutenant James Bradley, Seventh U.S. Infantry, who discovered Custer's body. With a bullet hole in the left temple, and a similar wound in the left breast or side, the corpse had not been mutilated according to Indian custom. Bradley reported that the wounds, either of which might have been fatal, had been next to impossible to locate. Custer's face had, in death, a calm, untroubled expression, like that of a man asleep, the report read. Various officials privately feared that this was a calculated attempt to spare the feelings of Mrs. Custer.

Significantly, the General's remains were never opened to view after removal from Battle Ridge. Seasoned frontiersmen read between the lines of local accounts and sensed possible suicide in the fact that Custer had not been mutilated—at least according to the report. For it was common knowledge throughout the West that Plains warriors inflicted considerable posthumous mutilation on the body of an enemy—*save only when the enemy was seen to have taken his own life.* After Custer's death by his own hand, they reasoned, any of his subordinates, or Bradley himself, might have wiped away black powder burns or other traces. Needless to say, any such opinions on the part of Indian scouts or other Army personnel were squelched immediately before the press or the public might learn of them.

In spite of James Gordon Bennett's elaborate nationwide preparations to cover Custer's operations in the field, newspapers across the country were scooped by Montana's tiny *Helena Herald* in a fabulous Fourth of July Extra. Outraged citizens turned from a long-awaited centennial celebration to read in horror of the defeat and partial destruction of the nation's crack military unit. Even more shocking was the death of Custer, pumped by the press into demigod proportions. As fast as limited means of communication would permit, news of the tragedy spread across the land.

Advised by telegraph from Bozeman, the Virginia City (Montana) *Madisonian* brought out a Little Big Horn Extra on July 6. That same morning, the *Tribune* and Associated Press correspondent in Bismarck roused from bed to get firsthand accounts from survivors on the newly arrived *Far West*. Next day every newspaper in the land flashed broadside editions covering all aspects of the tragedy. Legend has it— unreliably—that the Sioux City (Iowa) *Journal* actually had news of the event some four days earlier, having picked it up from distant smoke signals deciphered for the night editor by friendly members of the nearby Omaha tribe. The saddened night editor thereupon proceeded to get roaring drunk with his Indian comrades, while the account of the fight, so the story goes, got buried in a stick of local news where it remained unseen until months later.

All along the line, various editors added fantastic embellishments to the original account until fact became indistinguishable from fiction. Curley was quoted as saying that hundreds of hostiles had been killed by Custer and his men before they finally went down. One story had Curley wrapped up to his eyebrows in a captured Sioux blanket and skulking around the battlefield trying to persuade Custer to grab another Sioux blanket and escape with the scout. On that hot day of June 25, any blanket—Sioux or otherwise—would have been as conspicuous as a suit of armor!

One remarkable variation of the story line had Curley holed up in the carcass of a dead horse until the fighting was over, at which time he made a stealthy getaway.

In the light of the Army's anti-Indian policy, it was not surprising that the Battle of the Little Big Horn should sooner or later be referred to as "The Custer Massacre," though in no way did the facts qualify it as a slaughter of unarmed noncombatants. Nevertheless, the designation, with its implied bias against Indians, was found useful by whites throughout the country and quickly came into common usage.

Custer quickly became a revered martyr, mourned across the nation by a hero-worshiping public. Frustrated in life as a power-hungry opportunist, Custer in death personified an almost sacred memory. His remains were taken to West Point, where they were buried with full honors. Throughout the land the legend flourished. Artists and poets turned their talents to the dedicated task of eulogizing Custer and preserving for posterity the high drama of the Little Big Horn.

Although it was indeed unpopular to dispute such a patriotic myth, particularly in a centennial year, a few men in high office had the courage to convey their convictions to the public. Still titular commander of the Seventh Cavalry, old Colonel Sturgis announced that "Custer's luck has backfired"—actually a mild criticism in light of his natural bitterness over the fact that his son, a lieutenant, had died on Little Big Horn.

President Grant went further in castigating Custer in an interview with *New York Herald* representatives at Long Branch in September, published that month in the *Army and Navy Journal*. In part he said: "I regard Custer's massacre as an unnecessary sacrifice of troops brought on by Custer himself."

While Grant's statement only added to his own unpopularity, the Army was forced to admit that some confusion regarding Terry's orders to Custer had existed and that Custer had failed to wait for Gibbon to join him in the planned attack on the hostile village. Overnight a fierce and prolonged controversy began to rage. The public violently took sides and the slaying of General Custer became a *cause célèbre*.

Badly needing a scapegoat to keep Custer's name clear, high-ranking Army officials led by General Phil Sheridan carelessly allowed Major Reno to bear the onus of having failed to come to Custer's rescue. The fact was conveniently overlooked that Reno could hardly have done better than he did in getting the remnant of his command to a defensible position on the bluff. Adding to Reno's difficulties were widely circulated reports, mainly from disgruntled civilian packers, that he had been drunk the afternoon and night of June 25. Threatened with disgrace, Reno demanded an official investigation of the facts. In the spring of 1879 a Court of Inquiry sat in lengthy session in Chicago's old Palmer House, reviewing the battle from testimony presented by all available survivors of the Seventh Cavalry. Reno was eventually cleared of willful disobedience of orders, but the taint of cowardice and dishonor clung to his name until his death several years later in a Washington hospital.

One aspect of the battle which most disturbed the hero-worshipers who concocted the legend was the breakdown of Seventh Cavalry strategy at Little Big Horn. Custer was known to have been an excellent tactician by all existing standards. An excuse for his defeat at the hands of mere savages must somehow be devised. Among the propounders of the legend, certain graduates of West Point between 1846 and 1850 recalled a cadet of unusual appearance nicknamed Bison. Supposedly from the western borders of Missouri, Bison's age and description—even his sallow skin—came close to matching that of Custer's archfoe, Sitting Bull. At once the authorities circulated a rumor to the effect that Sitting Bull had acquired a superior knowledge of strategy at West Point! Grist for the mill of legend, nothing could have been further from the truth. Until long after Little Big Horn, Sitting Bull did not set foot east of Dakota Territory and would have had little to do with a military academy if he had. Still the story persisted that the chief of the Hunkpapas must have had formal military training in order to out-general Custer.

An outgrowth of this popular idea was a common belief that Sitting Bull had been advised throughout the battle by a number of half-breeds and former Confederate officers, still set as ever on whipping the Federal Army. Seeing distant Indians in uniforms taken from dead soldiers, several troopers on Reno Hill had been fooled into thinking the hostiles had made allies of deserters from the ranks of the Army. Such tales were, of course, utterly preposterous. No white man fought on the side of the Indians at Little Big Horn and none were staying in the great village. Not even squaw men and mixed-bloods who belonged to the tribes had ventured there that season in light of the unusually strong anti-Indian sentiment among whites. Participation by whites in Indian affairs at that time of year was further unlikely because of rigid religious taboos among the Indians themselves. Their sun dance had just been held and whites could have no part in it, for it served each tribe of the Plains as an annual renewal of fertility and productivity.

Some writers suggested that Sitting Bull himself was a French half-breed, thus accounting for his unusual capability as a strategist as well as for his skin tone which to many observers seemed light for an Indian. Here again were pure fabrications. Sitting Bull was a full-blood Sioux who spoke only his native tongue.

Released from confinement at his agency in Dakota, Sitting Bull was taken East in 1884 by Colonel Alvaren Allen who exhibited the chief among the waxworks at the Eden Musée in New York. Next season, Buffalo Bill Cody made Sitting Bull an important part of his Wild West Show and began touring the country. Though billed as "Custer's killer," the aging chief was too affable by nature to be convincing as the villain of the Custer legend. Doing his best to exploit the situation, Cody had his picture taken with Sitting Bull and sold thousands of souvenir photographs captioned, "Enemies in '76, Friends in '85."

Touring with Buffalo Bill, Sitting Bull was not invited to join Seventh Cavalry survivors in observing the tenth anniversary of the battle at Little Big Horn. Already an unofficial national shrine, the Custer Battlefield had been visited a number of times during the intervening years by various military men, including several burial and reburial expeditions. However, no accurate reconstruction of the fight had yet been possible since much of the action had been seen only by Sioux and Cheyenne participants. The Army prevailed upon the Indian Department to allow one of the former hostile leaders to come to the Little Big Horn on June 25, 1886.

Constantly seeking to destroy what remained of Sitting Bull's power and prestige among his own people, Agent James McLaughlin at Standing Rock Agency, Dakota Territory, sent Gall to represent the Sioux. In many ways it was an unfair choice. Gall was still a bitter rival of Sitting Bull and a tool of the Government's policy of breaking down the traditional forms of tribal authority by setting up puppet chiefs. McLaughlin was touting him as the true leader of the Northern Sioux.

At the Little Big Horn reunion Gall did his best not to disappoint his backers. Although no competent interpreter was on hand to translate his words, Gall managed to convey in signs and a few words of English the distinct impression that he, himself, had actually been master strategist as well as commander in chief of the Indian forces. His own military genius had whipped Custer, he stated, not that of Sitting Bull or Crazy Horse or any of the other leaders. His listeners failed to realize that it was then bad form for any warrior to discuss the exploits of another. With complete disregard for the established customs of his people, Gall went on to deride Sitting Bull, claiming that the chief, who was then too old to lead fighting men, had skulked in his tepee, "making medicine," and had run away in terror as the battle progressed.

Further significant inaccuracies grew out of Gall's statements. He claimed that Custer had never brought his troops down Medicine Tail Coulee to attack the village by way of the ford. Instead, he said, Custer's command had kept well to the east, following the high ground all the way to Battle Ridge. Completely misled, Benteen, Godfrey, and other Seventh Cavalry officers present assumed that their earlier and more accurate ideas of Custer's movements had been entirely wrong. Not until years later, when other Indian informants told their versions of the battle, were the facts made straight. But this was long after Gall's erroneous testimony and an analysis based upon it by Godfrey had been accepted as final authority by the general public.

Of the Crow scouts, only White Swan was present at Custer Battlefield that day in 1886. Bitter over his wounds, for which the Government had never compensated him, he contributed little to what was already known.

For ten years an intense controversy had raged within the Crow tribe over the stories newspapermen had put into Curley's mouth when the Army had taken him to far-off Washington. Upon his return, the other scouts—knowing how untrue his stories were—called him a liar and made him a laughing stock in the tribe. Yet to the whites, Curley was still a hero. Few outside the Crow tribe dared refute the statements attributed to him. It was years later, after the turn of the century, before historians decided to consult Goes Ahead, White-Man-Runs-Him, or Hairy Moccasin. By that time they had drifted into outspoken feuding with Curley and his faction, a rift that never healed until Curley and White-Man-Runs-Him, last of the scouts, died in the 1920's.

Uncertain how the truth might be received after so many years of erroneous belief, White-Man-Runs-Him, Hairy Moccasin, and Goes Ahead never told their entire story to a white man. After the death of White-Man-Runs-Him in 1929, Goes Ahead's widow, Pretty Shield, did what she could to set the record straight. She knew the scouts' story nearly as well as they, for on many occasions she had covered every inch of Custer Battlefield with her husband. In light of other Indian testimony, her convincing arguments now help to explode much of the Custer myth.

Among the Sioux and Cheyennes, White Cow Bull, Bobtail Horse, and other defenders of the ford agreed in later years that the soldiers halted in mid-charge, halfway across the river, when a white leader in buckskins was shot from a sorrel horse. Had this been any officer other than Custer he would have been left behind in the ford. *Only Custer's body would have been carried by the troops as they fell back.*

The fact that they fell back at that point was in itself conclusive. The sharp switch from offensive to defensive tactics indicated something had gone drastically wrong. Indians at the ford insisted that the soldiers' charge down Medicine Tail Coulee could have swept on into the village and might have won the battle for the whites. Only one solution is clear: when the troops halted in midstream, *Custer was no longer in command!*

Aside from the confusion arising from Gall's testimony, early attempts to get accurate stories on the battle from the Sioux and Cheyennes were beset with numerous difficulties. After their surrender to the Government most of the former hostiles were reluctant to say too much about their part in the Custer battle for fear of added reprisal. Out of a sense of enforced diplomacy, many Indians answered leading questions in a way calculated to satisfy their interrogators—at times regardless of the truth. A few, like Gall, went out of their way to deceive the whites. Claiming to have been head chief of *all* Cheyennes at Little Big Horn, Two Moon later made light of the fact that he had not told the truth.

"I do not think it wrong," he said to fellow tribesmen, "to lie to the white men."

The disparity among various Indian versions of the battle made it all the easier for the hero-worshipers to perpetuate the Custer legend. A substitute for Sitting Bull as Custer's slayer turned up unexpectedly at an exhibit of "wild Indians" at Coney Island in the late eighties. Delving into a sullen Sioux warrior's arrest and imprisonment by Tom Custer some fourteen years earlier, writer Kent Thomas got Rain-in-the-Face drunk and with him concocted a cheap publicity story in which the warrior said he had cut out Tom Custer's heart and eaten it. It made fine copy. Henry Wadsworth Longfellow used it as the basis of his epic poem, "The Revenge of Rain-in-the-Face." Taking full dramatic license, Longfellow wrote in part:

> " 'Revenge!' cried Rain-in-the-Face,
> 'Revenge upon all the race
> Of the White Chief with yellow hair!' "

But in the popular concept of the affair, it was Long Hair Custer, rather than his less colorful brother, who was cast as the object of the warrior's vengeance. People across the land accepted Longfellow's verse as historical fact. Later Rain-in-the-Face vigorously denied having killed either of the Custers or having performed such mutilations on their bodies as the poem described. In the dust and turmoil of the battle, he explained emphatically, it had been impossible to distinguish one soldier from another and, like most of the hostiles, he had not known until days later that it was Custer they had been fighting. Nevertheless, the public largely accepted Rain-in-the-Face as Custer's killer.

In self-defense Rain-in-the-Face himself finally laid the onus of having killed Custer on Hawk, a young Cheyenne who later accompanied Sitting Bull to Canada and never returned. Few people were convinced, and on his deathbed in 1905 Rain-in-the-Face "confessed" to a missionary, Mary C. Collins, that he thought he had killed Custer, having been "so close to him that the powder from my gun blackened his face."

During early kill-talks soon after the Custer battle, various warriors claimed credit for having killed Long Hair. One of them was Red Horse, a Minneconjou. Another was Flat Hip, a Hunkpapa. Another of the same tribe, Little Knife, announced that young Brown Back, brother of the slain boy Deeds, had shot the soldier-chief. The two sons of Inkpaduta (Scarlet Top), chief of the Santees, also asserted they had been in on the kill. Among the Santees, however, the claim of Walks-Under-the-Ground, parading around on Custer's horse, carried more weight. Fast Eagle, an Ogalala, said that he and another warrior had pinioned Custer's arms at the end of the fight while the girl warrior, Walking Blanket Woman (later known as Mary Crawler), stabbed Long Hair in the back. Since Custer's body bore no visible stab wounds, few Indians believed her victim had been the soldier-chief. However, she was afterward permitted to take a man's part in all war dances.

Although White Bull of the Minneconjous never made formal claim to the slaying of Custer, he was convinced until his dying day in 1947 that he had killed Long Hair after the soldier-chief had fired twice at him and missed. Because of his deep misgivings as to what might happen to him, he divulged his belief to only one or two trustworthy whites who kept his secret as long as he lived.

The Cheyennes had conflicting ideas on which of their warriors might have slain Custer. Far from being conclusive as to who did the killing, Two Moon, Harshay Wolf, and Medicine Bear each claimed to have counted coup on his body though none of them remembered seeing him fall.

For years Indian claimants to the distinction were considerably inhibited by fear. They never knew when rumor alone might bring the Army's swift vengeance. And so, many participants in the battle kept silent, not daring to share secrets with younger, more civilized members of the tribe. Through a confusion of claims, the mysterious identity of Custer's slayer became more obscure than ever. Strangely enough, none of the five warriors who faced Custer at the ford—one of whom almost certainly fired the fatal shot—ever came forward to say he was the slayer of Long Hair.

Long after the Sioux and Cheyennes learned of the remarkable esteem in which Custer had been held by the whites, several warriors insisted they had planned to capture him. Flat Iron, a Cheyenne, stated that such a plot was foiled by Two Moon who had an old grudge against Custer and so killed the soldier-chief before he could be "rescued." Flat Iron blamed the failure on Two Moon's greediness for battle honors. Spotted Rabbit, a Minneconjou, claimed that he had dashed unarmed into the thick of the fighting, hoping to capture Long Hair alive, when his horse had suddenly been shot from under him. Such tales rate little credence since no Indian, as far as is known, recognized Custer or knew he was on the field until *after* the battle.

Portrait sketch of Brave Bear, honorary slayer of Long Hair Custer (from Rodman Wanamaker photograph).

The tribes eventually found the question of "Who killed Custer?" as perplexing as it had long been to the whites. With characteristic wisdom, the Indians settled the matter once and for all in September, 1909, when wealthy Rodman Wanamaker of Philadelphia gathered chiefs and warriors from eleven tribes to take part in a last great Indian Council on the Little Big Horn. Confident such an inducement would bring out the truth at last, the prominent Philadelphian offered a sizable cash reward to be prorated among those present provided some warrior could prove himself the slayer of Custer.

For days the chiefs deliberated in secret council. None of them *knew for sure* which warrior had done the killing. And yet a generous reward for all of them was now at hand. The tribes were starving and the need of the people was too desperate to be overlooked. Simple prudence dictated a solution.

After lengthy palaver, the record of one elderly war chief was brought up for discussion. It seemed made to order for the purpose. He had been on the Washita when Custer had destroyed Black Kettle's village; he had spilled pipe ashes on Custer's boots during the Panhandle peace conference; he had taken an active part in the great fight on the Little Big Horn.

At council's end, the sturdy old chief mustered all his courage and came forward to accept Wanamaker's tempting largesse to his people—after which he expected to be shot by the whites. For, having found him eminently qualified, the council had unanimously *elected* Chief Brave Bear of the Southern Cheyennes to bear the honorary distinction of having slain Long Hair Custer. To the tribes the matter of the Little Big Horn was closed.

Sources

I have been over the battlefield many times with various Indians who were veterans of the battle. Among these old-timers were One Bull, White Cow Bull, High Eagle, and Dewey Beard, all Sioux; and Turkey Legs, Limpy, Bobtail Horse, Young Two Moon, and Young Little Wolf, all Cheyennes.

Sunup

The story of the killing of Deeds by Sergeant Curtis and his detail was told to me by Drags-the-Rope in 1939, when the old warrior was eighty-one years old. Additional data concerning the death of Four Horns's aged wife was given me by One Bull, Kills Alive, White Bird, and other old-time Hunkpapas.

The story of the Crow scouts throughout this book is derived from interviews with the following members of the Crow tribe in south-central Montana:

Bad Man (aged 105 in 1939 when interviewed) ... Cousin of Scout Hairy Moccasin

Bull-Over-the-Hill Son of Scout White-Man-Runs-Him

Bird Horse ..... Cousin of Scout White Swan
White Bear ..... Kinsman of Scout Curley
Little Nest ...... Brother-in-law of Mitch Bouyer
Pretty Shield .... Widow of Scout Goes Ahead
Plain Bull ...... Scout with Crook in 1876
Mountain Sheep . Scout with Crook in 1876
Yellow Brow .... Scout with Gibbon in 1876

The Crows called themselves *Upsaroka* or *Absaroka*, after a fork-tailed bird similar to a magpie. Early mountain men translated the tribal name as Crow People and so they have been known ever since. Two main tribal divisions existed: River Crows and Mountain Crows. All the above informants belonged to the latter group, who lived mostly in the Big Horn Mountains.

The story of the Arikara scouts came largely from Jerome Good Elk of Fort Berthold, North Dakota. He was a member of Varnum's Arikara detachment at Little Big Horn. Additional data was found in O. G. Libby's "The Arikara Narrative of the Campaign Against the Hostile Dakotas," published by the North Dakota Historical Commission. Like their kinsmen the Pawnees, the Arikaras were mortal enemies of the Sioux and Cheyennes, who called them Corn Indians because of their habit of living in semi-permanent earth-mound villages and following agricultural pursuits. They were particularly despised by the Sioux who considered farming an especially degrading occupation. A small tribe like the Crows, the Arikaras were among the first Indian groups to provide scouts for the United States Army operations in the upper Missouri River region.

Long hair was sacred to most Indians. A warrior took great

pride in its cultivation and length and protested if anyone tried to touch it. During religious ceremonies, priests and other participants wore their hair loose and unbraided in order to derive greater spiritual power from the ritual. Hair culture reached a peak among the Crows, some of whom let their hair grow to the astonishing length of fifteen feet! Those who lacked long locks often spliced hair taken from dead enemies onto their own. To all tribes—friendly and hostile—Custer's Indian name and normally shoulder-length tresses conjured up more than usual respect.

The men of all Plains tribes were warriors by profession. War was considered the noblest of pursuits, the only one an adult male might follow. From earliest youth, boys were taught that no pleasure equaled that of the joy of battle. Success in war brought universal respect and admiration. Far from being a bitter fate, death in combat was regarded as a glorious end. No higher reward existed than the wholehearted applause of the tribe for a victorious warrior.

Among other occurrences which the Arikaras found disturbing was an unseasonal snowstorm on June 1, while the expedition was marching west through Dakota Territory. Drifts a foot deep delayed the column's progress for nearly two days. The blizzard was regarded by the scouts as an unfavorable omen. Even more upsetting was the dismantlement of a Sioux scaffold grave in an abandoned hostile village at the mouth of Tongue River. Isaiah Dorman, Negro interpreter, was ordered by Custer to strip the Indian corpse and dispose of it as best he could. Isaiah threw the body in the river. Since he was later seen fishing there, the superstitious Arikara whispered that he was using bits of the Sioux corpse for bait!

The killing of enemies brought a large measure of comfort

and consolation to those whose kin had been killed by members of the hostile tribe. A warrior who had thus lost a relative might "carry the pipe" and ask other fighting men to help him assuage his grief by raiding the enemy. If his friends smoked the pipe with him, they committed themselves to assist him and temporarily acknowledged his leadership. Often the basis for a war party, this was the manner in which Half Yellow Face enlisted Crow scouts for the Little Big Horn campaign. Among the Crows the carrier of the pipe always wore a magpie tail in his hair to show that until the mission was accomplished he had the status of chief and would perform no menial tasks. Those who led a number of successful war parties often became fighting leaders for the tribe.

White Man's World

The year 1876 is remembered by the Sioux as *Pehin Hanska ktepi*—when "they killed Long Hair (Custer)." Spanning an unbroken period of 147 years, the Sioux winter count recorded in picture writing on buckskin the outstanding event of each year, beginning in 1759, ending in 1906. Years were divided into "moons," corresponding to the months of the white man. Each year began in August, "the time the berries ripen." Since Plains tribes lacked a method of reckoning specific dates, June 25 is simply remembered as having occurred at "the time the ponies are fat."

Among the foremost tribes to welcome whites to the upper Missouri, the Crows first called the white man *Beta-awka-wahcha*—"Sits-on-the-water," owing to the fact that early trappers traveled by canoe up the big rivers. Years later, the

Crows adopted the Cheyenne term, "yellow eyes"—*Masta-chuda* in Crow, *Vebo* in Cheyenne. To the Sioux the white men were always *Wasicun*—meaning literally, "You can't get rid of them."

Among the Sioux and Cheyennes, women usually ruled the camps. They owned the tepees and furnishings, and many of the horses as well. The men generally did pretty much as the women wanted. Since men were normally more conservative, the women acted as a spur. The rank of a family depended as much upon the sensibility and morality of its womenfolk as it did upon the generosity and bravery of its men. Adding to the influence of Indian women was the fact they outnumbered the men nearly two to one. Leading a violent existence, the average warrior's life expectancy was short. Polygamy was logical and practical. The sorority of wives was usually desirable and harmonious. Often sisters by blood, a man's wives provided a close-knit family life dominated by the eldest or first-married wife, called "the sits-beside-him-wife" because of her place of honor in the lodge. Never a chattel, an eligible girl was considered a gift to a prospective husband, who naturally felt obligated to return the favor—usually in ponies—to the girl's father. Only rarely were marriage pacts concluded without the wholehearted consent of the bride. Although young men were expected to philander, young women were watched closely by their elders. Feminine chastity was highly prized and absolutely required for most religious ceremonies, such as the annual sun dance. Buffalo hunting would inevitably be poor if the maidens of the tribe were not virtuous. From puberty until marriage, a small protective rope, knotted around the waist and passed down between the legs with each end wrapped around a thigh, was worn by a young woman.

Though confining, the rope permitted the wearer to walk freely, even to ride horseback. It was always worn at night and when the girl went abroad alone. Almost never violated, the protective rope's removal by a man made him subject to death at the hands of the girl's relatives.

A grandmother held an honored position in the family. Since the wife or wives were often busy with tasks about the camp, small children were gently disciplined and watched over by the grandmother. Even after death her spirit was believed to help them always, and, as they grew older, they might pray to her for guidance or aid in recovering lost objects.

Nose bobbing or nose splitting was extreme measures in punishing adulterous women. After such punishment, however, a woman might resume married life. I knew one such ancient woman—a Blackfoot—who had outlived six husbands *after* losing her nose! Seldom resorted to, the Sioux and Cheyennes had a simple method of divorcing faithless wives. At a dance or other public gathering, the cuckolded husband threw a small stick in the air and shouted, "There goes my wife! I throw her away! Whoever gets that stick can have her!" Sometimes he might add, "A horse and my wife go with that stick!" If the stick happened to hit a bystander, he might be kidded for wanting the disloyal woman. The "throw-away" ceremony was usually a keen disgrace to the wife and her paramour, who sometimes sought to save face by paying the injured husband the original price of the wife in ponies.

Carlisle Indian School was established in the fall of 1879 by Captain R. H. Pratt in a converted cavalry barracks. Around a nucleus of sixty Sioux boys and twenty-four Sioux girls, mostly from families that had been at Little Big Horn in 1876, Pratt managed to build an institution of learning for Indians that later was world-famous for its unbeatable football teams and All-American athletes.

The tribes at Little Big Horn enjoyed a wide variety of amusements and games. A favorite pastime among men and boys was sham fighting, using moist clay, thrown from the ends of four-foot switches, for weapons. At night, burning coals were added to the clay and hurled as balls of bright fire. "Arrow mark" consisted of throwing rather than shooting arrows, the first arrow thrown setting the mark for the contest. Kicking matches were somewhat like sham fights and were sometimes intertribal or between various warrior societies. A player could sit down suddenly if he wanted to avoid being kicked. Wrestling, a favorite of the Cheyennes, was an attempt between two players to swing the other off his feet. The stick-and-hoop game was similar to hockey. The hoop was made of slender willow rod. (Cheyennes named the white man's wagon after the hoop used in this game which greatly resembled the wagon's wheels.) Both men and women loved the hand game, moccasin game, or hide-a-stick game—all similar guessing contests upon which the Indians bet heavily. Gambling frequently assumed tremendous importance during any of these games and some men even gambled away their wives. Women particularly enjoyed a sort of football game in which they used only their feet to keep a deerskin ball filled with antelope hair off the ground as long as possible. This was occasionally modified by the women throwing the ball at each other and using sticks to keep the ball from hitting them. Another women's game was throwing sticks. Played on a course of smooth ground, willow sticks six feet long and tipped with elkhorn were hurled underhanded and made to slide a long distance.

220

While scouting for the Fifth Cavalry on July 17, 1876, Buffalo Bill Cody helped the soldiers turn back some eight hundred Cheyennes from Red Cloud Agency who were seeking to join Sitting Bull in Montana. In a famous duel at Warbonnet Creek in northwest Nebraska, Cody sought out and killed *Hay-o-wai*—Yellow Hair, popularly known as Yellow Hand, young fighting chief of the band. Having just gotten news of the Little Big Horn disaster, Cody scalped the young chief with the cry, "First scalp for Custer!" Demoralized at the death of their leader, the Cheyennes fled back to their reservation. The regiment hotly pursued them, but failed to catch or kill any more of them. So widely publicized were Cody's heroics that he later re-enacted the duel regularly in his world-famed Wild West Show.

Data on the white man's world of 1876 was gathered largely from periodicals of that era. Among other sources I consulted the *New York Herald, Harper's Weekly, Leslies', Godey's,* and *Scribner's* Magazines, *The Century Magazine,* and various small-town newspapers. Certain quotes pertaining to social highlights in the 1870's are from *Life.* Material on President Grant was taken from his *Memoirs* and various biographies. Much information on Custer and his activities at Fort Abraham Lincoln was given me by the late First Sergeant Charles Windolph, formerly of the United States Seventh Cavalry and the last *white* survivor of the Battle of Little Big Horn. At my urging, he joined in several unofficial reunions with Indian survivors of the battle. He died in Lead, South Dakota, in 1950, aged 98.

Another natural feature which attracted the tribes to Little Big Horn was the large cottonwood growth native to the valley. These trees not only provided unlimited firewood but also furnished "cottonwood ice cream," a frothy gelatinous sap obtained by peeling away the outer bark of a tree and scraping the exposed surface. It was considered a great delicacy by Plains Indians.

According to the greatest Indian estimates, fewer than half of all warriors at Little Big Horn had or were able to get possession of any sort of firearm during the battle. Since the armament carried into the fight by the Seventh Cavalry was considerable—a repeating carbine and a pistol for every trooper, a revolver or two for every officer—there is little doubt the soldiers *began* the battle with superior fire power.

In the upper Missouri country between 1850 and 1860, a quarter of a million buffalo were slaughtered annually by whites. J. A. Allen, author of *The American Bisons, Living and Extinct,* says: "The total killed between 1870 and 1875 cannot have been less than 2,500,000 annually!" By 1889 only 541 animals remained alive. Although the buffalo has since made a comeback under Federal care, the destruction of a remnant band of two bulls, a cow and a calf at Lost Park, Colorado, in 1897 marked the killing of the last original wild stock in the United States.

On the night of June 24, Sitting Bull was singing the *heyokan lowan,* or thunder song, and saying the *hanbleoklake,* a prayer for advance knowledge. The words were given to me by One Bull to whom Sitting Bull himself had later repeated them. The chief was heard that night in the Sansarc camp across the river from the lonely ridge where Sitting Bull kept his vigil. Gathered in Elk Head's lodge were Crazy Horse, Horned Antelope, Bear Ribs, Four Bears, and Elk Head. Young Elk Head and Two Runs told me in 1939 that they had heard both Sitting Bull's song in the distance and the talk of the men discussing the solitary ritual. An Indian believed that to smoke was to pray. A portable altar, the pipe was a combination of important symbols. The pipestone bowl represented the Mother Earth. The wooden stem represented all growing things. Red porcupine quillwork was a symbol of magic power. By mingling his breath with sacred tobacco and divine fire, the smoker (i.e., the worshiper) put himself in tune with the universe.

The story of Elizabeth Custer's nightmare came from an account by Walter David Coburn as told to him by Major Will A. Logan, onetime staff officer with Gibbon and a member of the regular garrison at Fort Abraham Lincoln in 1876.

A favorite pastime among officers and their ladies at Fort Abraham Lincoln was the playing of charades. The General and his wife were particularly avid fans of the game, and, while the Custers were in garrison, musicales placed a lame second in popularity.

Midmorning

As Plains Indians generally did not count above a thousand and felt no honest person needed higher figures, it is difficult to get accurate Indian estimates of the number of people camped at Little Big Horn the day of the Custer fight. My informants all agreed, however, that the following divisions and tribes were represented, in part or entirely:

TETON-DAKOTA—main western division of the Sioux Nation:
Hunkpapas or Cutthroats

Sihasapas or Blackfeet (not to be confused with the
  Blackfeet tribe of Montana and Alberta)
Minneconjous or Those-Who-Plant-by-the-Water
Itazipchos or Sansarcs, sometimes called No-Bows
Sichangus or Brûlés, sometimes called Burnt-Thighs
Oohenonpas or Two Kettles
Ogalalas or Those-Who-Stand-in-the-Middle

(Common usage has mixed Sioux, French, and English
names in designating the tribes throughout this book.)

SANTEE-DAKOTA—southeastern division of the Sioux Nation:
Mdewakantons
Wahpekutes

YANKTON-ASSINIBOIN—northern division of the Sioux Nation:
Yanktonnais
Yanktons
Assiniboins

(All Sioux call themselves Allies, which in their speech is
Lakota among the Teton tribes, *Dakota* among the Santees,
Nakota among the Assiniboins and Yanktonnais. *Sioux* is a
French contraction of the Chippewa word *Nadowessioux*—
meaning "enemy." The name has stuck, however, and the
Allies have long been known to the whites as the Sioux.)

CHEYENNE NATION:
Northern Cheyennes
Southern Cheyennes

(Cheyennes call themselves *Tsististas*—"the people"—but
have long been known by their common name which was

given them by the Sioux: *Sha-hi-ye-na*—"red talkers," i.e., people of alien speech.)

ARAPAHO NATION:
 Northern Arapahoes
GROS VENTRES NATION:
 Atsinas or Big-Bellies-of-the-Prairie.

In addition, families and individuals from various other Plains tribes were present. No record of them exists, as most of them hurried back to their respective agencies after the battle.

Loose political units, the tribes were divided into clans, phratries or bands, *tiyospaye*—a Sioux word for "extended family groups"—and families. The usual unit for traveling and camping was the band.

Indian life at Little Big Horn was well ordered but complex. People lived in the public eye and there were few secrets. What concerned one, concerned all. Polygamy was common, but few men had more than four wives and the usual number was two. Multiple wives were generally sisters. A husband had first claim on his first wife's younger sisters. Occasionally, extra wives were captives but no stigma was attached to them. Marriages could be dissolved without ceremony. Young men married at twenty-five or as soon as they had distinguished themselves in war. Girls sometimes married at puberty. A young girl at puberty had her whole body painted red by her grandmother. Naked, covered only with a buffalo robe, she stood over a low smudge fire made from sage and juniper needles, letting the purifying smoke bathe her painted body. She stayed in a separate lodge for four days during which she ate no meat. If the camp moved, she rode a mare. Young people from childhood up were advised by their grandparents, who also gave them their original names. There was an effective overlapping of generations which bound the tribes closer together than would otherwise have been possible.

Courting lasted anywhere from one to five years. It was done under a blanket. A couple usually walked long distances, talking not of love, but of camp news and tribal affairs, and the man wrapped his blanket around the girl. He did not propose to the girl himself, but asked for her hand in marriage through an intermediary—usually an older man mutually respected by the families involved. Sometimes the couple exchanged rings made of metal or bone after the manner of whites. Medicine men were consulted to provide love potions or aphrodisiacs with which the youth might tempt the girl. Spruce gum was a favorite. A white-tailed deer's tail, carried on the windward side of the girl's lodge so she could catch the scent, was also highly rated. Flashing a looking glass in the girl's eyes often had good effect. Flageolets or cedarwood flutes produced dulcet tones known to have considerable influence on girls—particularly at night, when the eager suitor stayed up long after dark, inspiring the girl with his music. The favorite courting time was when a girl performed her regular tasks of fetching water or firewood and could be encountered along some quiet camp trail.

Once married, there was no set rule on where the couple should live, although the tribes were basically matrilocal. In-law taboos protected everybody from possible friction or disharmony within the family. Modesty prevailed throughout most Indian lodges. A man might strip down to his breech-clout for sleep or battle, but a woman stayed covered from shoulder to shin save during her morning bath with other women at the river. The first part of a camp to be set up was a tripod in front of the lodge from which was hung the shield of the owner. A favorite wife or daughter was given the honor of carrying this shield and placing it on the tripod except when she was menstruating. At such times the women stayed completely away from all sacred objects. If a menstruating woman happened to visit the lodge of a shield owner, he was forced to arrange an immediate purification ceremony with his medicine man, who permeated the shield and holy objects with sage smoke. Sometimes "medicine bundles" of sacred objects were also hung on the tripod. Great care was taken in arranging such bundles, as it was thought the power of the medicine would be impaired if it touched the ground.

The size of a lodge was governed by the number of horses a family had to haul it. The larger the lodge, the larger the poles had to be. Two horses were required to drag large poles, another to haul the buffalo-cow-hide cover. The poles were arranged in a rough cone, twenty-two poles in a large tepee, sixteen in a small one. Poles on the windward side were slightly shorter than the others, so that the floor space of the lodge was not a true circle. Two poles controlled the wings or the smoke flaps. The covers varied, but usually consisted of eighteen cowskins for a large tepee, eleven for a small one. The fireplace was a rectangle, longer east to west than north to south, or a crude half-moon with stones ringing its edge. It was dug in the center of the oval floor. Furniture in the lodge consisted of decorated dew cloths, hung from the poles around the tepee, behind which was handy storage space; backrests of willow sticks hung from tripods; mattresses of willow rods; and mats of bulrushes or loosely woven tule. Painted rawhide *parfleches* were used for storage, as well as

227

soft deerskin bags for small objects. No pottery was made by these tribes, and the only basket was a tiny one of split strands of yucca or buffalo grass used in the Cheyenne seed game. The woman of the lodge always lighted the fire. Smoldering ashes were often carried long distances packed in buffalo dung. Mountain mahogany leaves were scattered on the floor to keep away lice and bedbugs. They had a pleasant aroma.

The man of the family had the place of honor at the rear or west side of the lodge, the entrance always facing east. Youths and boys shared the space to his left. Women and girls kept to his right. If the family had an old woman, she stayed in her place as keeper of the entrance. No one, male or female, crossed the space between the man of the family and the fireplace. A visitor, entering the lodge, kept to his right and took the space just to the owner's left. It was not etiquette for an outsider to go to that part of the lodge occupied by his host's womenfolk.

If a small boy were in the family, it was his job to cut tobacco, light pipes, carry messages, and tend the livestock. When an Indian smoked, he prayed and meditated. Smoking was always an important ceremony in which the host smoked first, then passed the pipe to the first visitor on his left, who in turn passed it until it reached all adult males present. The man farthest left then handed it back all the way around to the host. The men felt it was unlucky to touch anything with the stem of the pipe and held it straight up and down with the bowl toward the ground. The pipe had great power and if thrust between disputers would stop any argument.

The disciplining of children was mild. The usual way of securing obedience from a child was to frighten him or splash him with water. Ridicule was often the most effective deterrent to misbehavior. Beating, or even slapping, was rare. Indians considered it wrong to resort to corporal punishment and thought white parents treated their offspring like enemies when they struck them. Children were allowed to learn their own lessons without parental restraint. A crawling baby learned by experience how to get warm beside a fire without getting burned. A six-week-old child often learned how to swim before he had his ears pierced and could handle himself in water before he could walk. All babies were taught never to cry. No lesson in tribal life was more important, for Indians lived by the axiom that no single person should endanger the people, that no individual should lure an enemy or drive away game by unnecessary sound.

In adult life crime was rare. Since most property was communally owned, theft was almost unknown. Stealing horses from an enemy tribe was, of course, honorable, but stealing from one's own people was almost unthinkable. Murder was seldom committed. The only motive for it was to get another man's wife, and this could usually be accomplished with far less risk. One guilty of murdering a tribesman was banished from the tribe for four years or forever, according to circumstances. The tribes recognized four cardinal virtues:

Generosity—Bravery—Moral Integrity—Fortitude

Four sins were regarded as unpardonable:

1. To permit anyone to go hungry;
2. To lose one's eldest son in battle;
3. To permit the baby of a dead mother to cry from hunger;
4. To return alone from war after one's comrades have all been slain.

229

In his dream of soldiers coming, Box Elder claimed, the word was brought to him from the *maiyun* (spirits) by wolf messengers whose language he fully understood. Box Elder got his power from his father, Blind Bull, who told him he would not die in battle but from old age. He always seemed to know far in advance what important events were going to take place. After predicting the occurrence, he took part in a raid against the Pawnees and captured four of their women. True to his father's prognostication, he died of old age in 1885. Box Elder's story was told to me by Black Wolf, a Cheyenne medicine man, whose own exploits appear elsewhere in this book. The principal medicine man in the Cheyenne tribe at the time of the Custer fight was Charcoal Bear. He was not, however, a prophet like Box Elder. Cheyenne medicine men had developed an elaborate pharmaceutical system to cure various ailments. Among many other items they used alum root for treating diarrhea; niggerhead root for toothache; wallflower tea for cramps and stomach trouble; daisy tea for stomach pains and rheumatism; blazing-star root for heart trouble and lameness; umbrella wart for swellings and broken bones (used externally only); and horsemeat for colds and fevers. A certain root which grew only in the southern Black Hills was well known to all the tribes as a love medicine and aphrodisiac. Wars were fought in earlier times to control the area in which this root was known to flourish.

Crazy Horse's chieftainship may have been held up by his tribesmen for moral reasons. Having entered into a loveless marriage pact arranged in 1865 by his parents with Black Robe Woman, Crazy Horse stole away the wife of Subchief No Water the following fall. No Water tracked down the illicit lovers, shot at Crazy Horse, the bullet grazing the great warrior's cheek. Only the prompt intervention of Crazy Horse's friend, Touch-the-Cloud, saved his life. No Water's wife returned to her husband, but numerous other affairs followed. Shortly before the death of Black Robe Woman from tuberculosis, Crazy Horse took a second wife, a half-breed French girl named Nellie Laravie. (These little-known facts were told me by relatives of Crazy Horse now living at Pine Ridge Reservation, South Dakota.)

The buffalo seemed to serve no end of purposes to the Indian. While performing the *hanblecheyapi,* i.e., "crying for a vision," young men stood barefooted on the skull of a buffalo and faced the sun constantly from sunrise to sunset, without food or drink, and with only four brief rest periods all during the day. If by nightfall no vision had come, the seeker was compelled to take the heavy skull to a nearby river, plant it on the bottom, and stand on it in chest-deep water all through the night.

According to Eagle Elk, scouts generally smeared themselves with white clay and wore animal skins to make them look like wolves. Yellow Brow told me that the Crows and Cheyennes often wore white cloths with feathers attached to serve the same purpose. In winter, deerhides smeared with clay or white trade blankets were worn by scouts with separate cloths around their heads. Weapons could be cunningly concealed under such covering so that no telltale glints of sunlight on gun barrels would betray their owners.

The description of Sitting Bull was given to me by his nephews, One Bull and White Bull.

Individual exploits told throughout this book were given to me by the warriors themselves in various interviews between 1935 and 1955. (See master list of Indian informants.)

The Sioux winter count is complete only for a period of 147 years, from 1759 to 1906. However, earlier records in picture writing exist. One such document, according to the American Museum of Natural History, indicates that the year of the arrival of the Buffalo Calf Maiden was 1540. Among other things, the Maiden predicted the coming of horses to the Sioux people. Oddly enough, 1540 was the year in which the Spanish conquistador Coronado brought the first horses across the Plains.

Later a famous medicine man in his own right, Black Elk told me of a number of methods used in the art of healing. Each medicine man had his own unique procedure. Some used rattles to drive out evil influence. Some fanned away the illness with eagle wings. Others sucked out stones, feathers, live lizards, or colored field mice—all believed to have caused sickness or injury. Buffalo hair was universally accepted as having great healing properties, its use dating back to the arrival of the Buffalo Calf Maiden. Gourd rattles were thought necessary when much blood was lost. Although few healers knew how to cure a rattlesnake bite, Black Elk told me of a Cheyenne medicine man named Bull Head who cured snake bite by eating rattlesnake meat. This was also said to be successful in treating bullet wounds. No medicine man who tried to cure a horse ever ate horseflesh or shot at a horse, tame or wild.

The sweat lodge was universally used in healing ceremonies. Any illness might be cured by bathing the patient in the purifying smoke of a fire made from sweet grass, sweet pine, juniper needles, pulverized mushroom or toadstool, and powdered bitterroot. Purification was always a preliminary to healing. If a boy happened to throw an earth clod against the lodge of a medicine man, he had to be purified immediately

232

to avoid bad luck all around. There was usually much wiping with sagebrush all over the boy's hands and arms, lest the lad be struck by lightning.

Although amputation was never practiced—death was considered preferable—Indian healers were good bone setters, using rawhide splints and parfleche casts which provided traction. One month was usually sufficient to allow for a broken bone to mend.

Sacred stones were sometimes rolled around on a sick person's body to locate the exact nature of the ailment. Such stones were called *tunkan*—short for *Tunkasila,* meaning "Grandfather," as the Sioux sometimes called God. They were carried in pouches made of antelope ears and were otherwise used to predict events or locate distant objects. (They were small polished fragments of native brown sandstone.)

Both the bear and the wolf were thought to have strong curative powers, hence many medicine men used the heads and hides of these animals in their ritual. Some medicine men had the power to kill merely by looking at a person. Others used a flicker's tail as a dart and threw it deep inside the body of an enemy. If nothing was done at once to "remove" the tail, severe illness would result. Usually the enemy begged for immediate treatment.

Medicine men preached certain stringent taboos among the people: all were forbidden to point at a wolf with a knife blade (the wolf was considered supernatural and friendly); the loss of a finger might result from pointing at the sun, moon, or an individual star; women were forbidden to handle the body of a golden eagle, lest they get patches of pale skin (one transgressor, Pipe Woman, a Southern Cheyenne, became spotted all over when she touched a golden eagle); women were for-

233

bidden to burn owl feathers, lest they become deaf (the only remedy for which was the difficult feat of removing owl feathers from the sufferer's ears by the medicine men).

Before a battle, warriors often came to the medicine man to be painted and have sacred songs chanted over them while special painting was done. Blue clay was frequently used to daub a fighting man's body and face with protective symbols.

The story of Jack Red Cloud's humiliating experience during the Rosebud fight was told to me by two of Crook's Crow scouts. Plain Bull and Mountain Sheep, who had been among the lad's attackers. Various Ogalala Sioux informants grudgingly admitted that such an incident had occurred. Although it was 1940 when I learned the facts and sixty-four years had passed since the event took place, the old-timers still got a lot of satisfaction out of having bested the son of Red Cloud. The ancient hostility between Sioux and Crow has disappeared only recently with the passing of the last old warriors who once engaged so fiercely in intertribal warfare.

The Arapahoes' story was told to me in 1939 by Sherman Sage, one of the five stray warriors. Black Wolf, a Cheyenne, later corroborated his part in the incident, although like several other Cheyennes he was under the impression that there had been six Arapaho visitors rather than five.

The Buffalo Head or Buffalo Hat (*Issiwun*) was kept in a painted lodge, colored red above—representing day, black below—representing night. Other Cheyenne and Sioux lodges were occasionally painted, but generally only if they belonged to a chief or war leader, or were used for some special purpose. Sometimes a chief put his name on the outside of his tepee in picture writing or indicated a dream symbol from which he hoped to derive greater power.

The famous "medicine arrows"—*mahuts*—were not at Little Big Horn, as they belonged to the Southern Cheyennes. The two tribes were actually one people, having split into two sections about 1830. Frequent intercourse was maintained between them. In 1876 Southern Cheyennes were on their way north to fight beside their kinsmen when soldiers met them in the upper Powder River basin in central Wyoming and turned them back.

Only three of the seven Cheyenne warrior societies fought at Little Big Horn. One, the Bull Soldiers (or Red Shields), consisted largely of elderly men who were past fighting age and stayed out of the Custer battle. Absent altogether were the famous *Hotamitanio,* "Dog Soldiers," primarily a Southern Cheyenne organization. Many of the Crazy Dogs, one of which was the warrior Calf, were closely associated with the Sioux and intermarried with them.

The Sioux had an even more elaborate system of warrior societies. Scattered through all tribes of the Teton-Dakota were the *akicita* or "soldiers," such as the Kit Foxes, Crow Owners (referring to a special type of dance bustle), Badgers, White Marks, Bare Lance Owners, Owl Feathers, White Horse Riders, and Strong Hearts (famous for their unique ermine-skin horned bonnets worn only in battle). The Silent Eaters, of which Sitting Bull was a member, were more or less confined to the Hunkpapa tribe. Designed primarily as a fighting group, each society fought as a unit whenever possible. Each had its own chiefs, heralds, or criers, and coterie of four virtuous young women.

A certain society was selected every spring by the tribal chiefs to act as camp police until fall. It was their function to preserve order during camp moves, to see that rules of the buffalo hunt were obeyed, and to punish all offenders or law-breakers. The fighting leaders of the tribes, Sioux and Cheyenne alike, were usually chiefs of the warrior societies.

Another type of organization, completely mystical in character, was the dream society, made up of men who shared the same or similar dream of one animal from which they derived power. Principal of these were the elk and buffalo. The elk provided sexual power and long life. Elk dreamers usually carried a small rawhide circle representing the universe and went around giving elk teeth to newborn babies as tokens of good luck. Buffalo dreamers believed their totem provided great protective power. Bits of shed buffalo hair were used as charms. One such charm, dyed a deep red, was used in later years—after Little Big Horn—by Sitting Bull. As dreams of either animal were always desirable, men studied their favorite of the two, hoping to induce a dream and thus become eligible for membership in the society of their choice. A dream imposed certain obligations on the dreamer. Failure to fulfill them usually resulted in the dreamer being struck by lightning. He first had to announce his dream to the tribe, then secure whatever supernatural aid was indicated, finally arrange his life so as to be completely in accord with the vision.

The greatest possible supernatural power was acquired from dreams of thunderbirds. Although no Thunderbird dream society existed, the dreamer was under heavier obligation. The least infraction of the conditions of the dream exposed him to extreme ridicule by the lowest element in the tribe, the *heyoka*—"joker" or "contrary." Pseudo-sacred, often an assistant or apprentice to a medicine man, the *heyoka* expressed joy by sighs and groans, sorrow and pain by laughter, had

236

to wear the poorest of garments and suffer public humiliation as a professional buffoon.

The story of Monahseetah and Custer's son, Yellow Bird, was told to me by several Cheyenne informants including Black Wolf, Little Chief, Rising Sun, and Dives Backward of the Northern Cheyennes; and Eagle Nest and Yellow Eyes, both Southern Cheyennes. Additional data concerning the Washita campaign and Brave Bear's peace conference was given me by Hunting Horse, Kiowa Indian scout who served Custer. (Hunting Horse died in 1956, aged 107.) In his *My Life on the Plains: Or Personal Experiences with Indians,* published in 1874, Custer recalled the pipe ceremony with the Southern Cheyennes as "an amusing experience." He added that when he bound himself in smoking the pipe never again to take up arms against the Cheyennes, he was certain "the Cheyennes would never have surrendered to him *had they any idea how I really felt.*"

Midday

The material on Mark Kellogg appeared in *AP—the Story of News,* by Oliver Gramling. The Arikara reaction to Man-Who-Makes-the-Paper-Talk was provided by Jerome Good Elk, one of the Arikara scouts.

Custer, who fancied himself as something of a correspondent, wrote an article for the magazine *Galaxy* at the base camp two miles below the mouth of the Tongue.

The question of the actual time of the fight has long been a source of considerable disparity between white and Indian accounts of the Battle of the Little Big Horn. Nearly all

Indian informants agreed that the heavy fighting against Custer's command ended shortly after noon, although they had no exact method of determining the hour. Survivors from Reno's and Benteen's commands insisted it was somewhat after 4 P.M. according to their watches. Happily, it seems both sides were correct. The fact that the soldiers' watches indicated it was after 9 P.M. at sundown proves that the Seventh Cavalry was still operating on Chicago time, although they were then nearly *three modern time belts* away from the Windy City.

The story of Little Wolf's cautious maneuvering was told to me by his son, young Little Wolf, an old man when I interviewed him in 1946. Many details were substantiated by Two Birds, another ancient member of the old Little Wolf band.

According to Old Eagle (also known as Amos Clown), who told me about the death and burial of Old She-Bear, only a chief or chief's relative was left in a lodge when he died. Any ordinary dead person was dressed in his or her finest, then removed through the side of the lodge, never through the entrance. Sometimes if a dead chief already lay in a tepee, other warriors might be placed on scaffolds within the same lodge, as later happened at Little Big Horn. People in mourning had a choice: they could go into prolonged mourning, or they could get it over with in a hurry by gashing their heads and legs and whacking off their hair (among Sioux and Crows) or unbraiding it and rubbing dirt and ashes into it (among the Cheyennes). Prolonged mourning usually involved "keeping the spirit" of the dead for several months or a year, then "letting the spirit go" at a formal ceremony. During this time the mourners could not hunt, go to war, or share in social activities, but they dressed in their plainest clothing and

238

stayed as much as possible out of the public eye. They often kept a "spirit bundle" or a cottonwood "spirit post" dressed in the clothing of the deceased with a face painted on it. A child's spirit bundle was more often kept than that of an adult, and usually bits of the youngster's hair, purified with sweet grass and shed buffalo wool, was the basis of the bundle. The spirit post of a child was generally much smaller than that of an adult.

Old Eagle told me the story of Old She-Bear and Two Bears seeing their reflections in badger blood. Few warriors had the courage to use this hair-raising method of looking into the future. Old Eagle assured me that he had been most careful to look in another direction while this was going on.

Buffalo Calf Road Woman was not the only woman fighting in the Rosebud battle. Plain Bull, Mountain Sheep, Pretty Shield, and other Crows told me that one hundred fifty members of their tribe fought under Chief Plenty Coups on the side of the Gray Fox, and that one was a woman and another was a hermaphrodite. (Among all Plains tribes, hermaphrodites were thought of as a source of good luck around a camp or, occasionally, in a war party.) The Crow girl warrior was The Other Magpie, whose brother had been killed by the Sioux. Courageous as well as pretty, she wore a woodpecker skin on her head, painted her forehead yellow, and rode a black horse. The hermaphrodite, Finds-Them-and-Kills-Them, normally wore woman's dress, but changed to warrior's clothing before riding into battle. During the fighting, Bull Snake, a Crow warrior, was badly wounded and shot from his horse. Finds-Them-and-Kills-Them and The Other Magpie dashed in and managed with a coupstick to bring down the Sioux warrior who was threatening Bull Snake's life. Singing a shrill war song, Finds-Them-and-Kills-Them killed the Sioux. The Other Magpie took his scalp, which she cut up into many pieces. Later, the pieces were passed out among women of the tribe to be tied to willow poles and waved during the scalp dance.

According to Jerome Good Elk, Lieutenant Varnum's detachment of scouts included four Sioux married to Arikara women, who had come out from Fort Abraham Lincoln to guide the expedition and interpret should the need arise. They played a negligible part in the battle, and nothing is known of their individual exploits at Little Big Horn. They were: White Cloud, Buffalo Ancestor, Red Bear (not to be confused with the Arikara scout of that name), and Caroo.

Afternoon: Reno

The fishing incident was related to me by Dives Backward and Little Chief. White Shield's account appears in George Bird Grinnell's *Fighting Cheyennes*. It is interesting to note that in Cheyenne the word for fish line is *no-nun-o,* meaning a trap or device for catching something. It also means rainbow, for in the poetic Cheyenne mind the appearance of a rainbow at the end of a storm meant the rainbow had *trapped* the thunder and rain.

Cheyennes were the only Plains Indians who normally ate fish, due, perhaps, to the fact that they had once lived in permanent riverside villages. Each tribe had certain food taboos. No Indian would eat mice, rats, moles, muskrats, owls, or frogs. The Crows would not eat snakes or dogs, although dogs

240

were sometimes eaten ceremonially by the Sioux. Most tribes would not eat turtles.

There is some evidence that several Sioux women out digging turnips were killed by the Arikara scouts. Gall, a Hunkpapa, later said that his two wives and three children were slain by the Arikaras during their attempt to capture the hostile pony herd; but Red Horse, a Minneconjou chief, claimed to have been out with the women and reported no casualties among them. In the light of various misstatements made by Gall, this part of his story may well be in error. George Herendeen, white scout with Reno, was quoted in a Bismarck communiqué published July 8, 1876, in the *New York Herald*, as saying, "Our men did not kill any squaws, but the Ree [Arikara] Indian scouts did. The bodies of six squaws were found in the little ravine. . . ." None of my Indian informants ever mentioned any casualties among the women at Little Big Horn and it is doubtful whether any were killed.

Usher L. Burdick's short biography of Rain-in-the-Face states that the warrior had *not* been harshly treated during his confinement at Fort Abraham Lincoln, that he and the Custer family became good friends, that he was visited almost daily by the General and Mrs. Custer. In later years, Rain-in-the-Face was said to make frequent inquiries about the health of Mrs. Custer and "whether or not she had a new chief." Although he may have taken a solicitous interest in Mrs. Custer long after the battle, there is every indication that, in 1876, he was intensely bitter about what he felt was an entirely unjust punishment.

This council was described to me by One Bull, Kills Alive, and several other Hunkpapas. Kill Eagle, who was anxious to convey to the whites the impression that he and his band had

241

been kept unwilling prisoners in the hostile camp, later denied having even seen Sitting Bull the day of the battle. His account was the first one gotten from any Indian who had been in the village at Little Big Horn and was included in a story datelined Bismarck, D.T., September 23, 1876, which appeared the next day in the *New York Herald*.

Like Kill Eagle, a number of Indians were undecided about joining Sitting Bull. Less uncertain was Black Bull, a Blackfeet Sioux medicine man and a sworn enemy of Sitting Bull since the day when at a council meeting he had made light of the whites' attempts to take Indian lands and had facetiously suggested that the Sioux get a big scale and sell earth to the white men by the pound. While the tribes were streaming out of the agencies to join Sitting Bull, Black Bull remained in Dakota Territory to help protect the lives and property of his white friends who lived along the Cannonball Trail leading west to the Little Big Horn. A ranch belonging to the Tuttle family, parents of a newly born son, lay directly in the path of the restless hostiles. In desperation the Tuttles turned to Black Bull whom the hostiles thought to be "bad medicine" and shunned like the plague. Unable to be everywhere at once, Black Bull acted fast. In spite of his firm belief that having his picture taken would deprive him of his soul, the medicine man galloped into Bismarck, had his tintype taken, and hastened back to give the Tuttles his tiny photograph to hang in their cabin window. From that time on, the hostiles, seeing Black Bull's likeness staring at them, hurried on their way without further delay.

Drags-the-Rope reached camp after Brown Back's arrival, having made a wide circle along the divide as far as the headwaters of Tullock's Creek, then cross-country to Medicine Tail

Coulee, which he followed down to the ford and across into the village. He told me that, since he could report having seen only three white soldiers, no one in the Ogalala camp seemed at all worried until the alarm went up a few minutes later. He joined Crazy Horse at that time, fighting near the Ogalala leader through most of the battle.

Sitting Bull's attempt to arrange a parley with the soldiers through his nephew was related to me by One Bull himself. Other informants substantiate the little-known fact that the warriors were to fight back only if the soldiers forced them into it. In 1941 Feather Earring told me, "If Long Hair had wanted to come up and talk with us, we had all agreed ahead of time we would have surrendered and gone back to our agencies with him."

The mother-in-law taboo was the most stringent of several behavior customs designed to prevent possible friction within the family. Men, the warriors particularly, were forbidden to look at or speak to their in-laws save for sisters-in-law, with whom the Indian males had a unique relationship. Regarding her as a potential wife, a man often made semi-obscene jokes with his sister-in-law, might even raise her dress and expose her in public. She was encouraged to retaliate in kind. Conversation with other in-laws was strictly prohibited and messages had to be relayed through a third person or, if none was around, an inanimate object. Sioux babies were delivered by the prospective mother's mother-in-law but no direct communication could pass between the two women. Brothers and sisters seldom spoke directly to each other after reaching puberty. In all aspects of tribal life, Indians believed that close living demanded a lack of overfamiliarity.

Lieutenant McIntosh's father was said to have been a store-keeper in Washington State at the time of his son's death.

Red Bear's story was passed on to me by Jerome Good Elk. Much of it also appears in the Arikara Narrative.

Black Elk always said he was thirteen years old that summer of 1876. However, he was slight and sickly, and Plains Indians usually reckoned age by development and accomplishment rather than years. Accomplishment alone would have rated him much older than thirteen, for he had already had an important vision and had performed feats of valor prior to that time.

Isaiah Dorman was among the few Negroes known to the Sioux. The Crows had long had a mulatto squaw man, Jim Beckwourth, living among them, but he was unknown to the hostiles.

Afternoon: Custer

For whatever it is worth, Custer once made the following immodest estimate of himself: "I am not impetuous or impulsive. I resent that. Everything that I have ever done has been the result of the study that I have made of imaginary military situations that might arise. When I become engaged in a campaign or battle and a great emergency arises, everything that I ever heard or studied focuses in my mind as if the situation were under a magnifying glass and my decision was the instantaneous result. My mind works instantaneously but always as the result of everything I have ever studied being brought to bear on the situation."

Roan Bear eloped with another man's wife the year after

the Custer fight, then sent the cuckolded husband a pipe by a respectable old man. The husband sent back word to Roan Bear that he wanted to eat a woolly dog, thus expressing his contempt for his faithless wife and amiably settling the matter. Had the husband been a chief, according to Black Wolf, he would have been compelled to overlook the offense altogether.

The fight at the ford was described to me by White Cow Bull and Bobtail Horse, both of whom lived to be quite old. Custer's fall at mid-river was witnessed simultaneously by White Cow Bull and the three Crow scouts, although White Cow Bull did not know Custer's identity at the time. The account of the Crows was passed on to me by Pretty Shield, widow of Goes Ahead, with whom I had my first interview in 1940 when she was almost eighty-two years of age. Publicized earlier, Pretty Shield's accurate account could make little dent in the Custer myth until corroborated here by the hostiles' side of the story.

Yellow Nose and his mother were both captured by the Cheyennes in 1858. The story was told to me by Dives Backward, whose father (of the same name) had been a member of the war party making the capture. No stigma was attached to captives, and female prisoners were often taken as wives by their captors. The mother of Yellow Nose was not content in her new situation, however, and, leaving her son behind, finally escaped.

The various companies or troops engaged in the battle are referred to in some accounts according to the names of their commanding officers. C Company was Tom Custer's command; F Company, George Yates'; I Company, Myles Keogh's; and L Company, Calhoun's. E Company, Smith's command, was the famous gray-horse troop which gallops ghostlike through nearly all Indian accounts of the fight. These large handsome band horses were easier for the hostiles to follow through an action than the more nondescript bays and sorrels of other troops. "Company," incidentally, was the official designation of the unit until 1883 when the terms "troop" and "squadron" replaced "company" and "battalion." The word "troop," however, had been in common use for some years prior to that time, even before 1876. Officers generally rode horses the same color as the mounts of their men. Trumpeters rode grays. Adjutant Cooke's mount was almost white.

Brilliant planning played little part in Indian warfare. Staff level operations, or any type of high strategy, brought no honors. All any Indian leader could do was to set the pace for his followers.

In spite of oppressive heat, no Cheyennes fought naked at Little Big Horn, although a dozen or more Sioux were stripped down to the breechclout. Among all Plains tribes the breechclout was a symbol of manhood. Even more important to Indian males was the "G string," a slender cord tied around the waist and never removed after puberty. (It could be adjusted to fit an expanding waistline.) Buckskin leggings had a "fork" cut in the side, a flap from the calf to the ankle, the use of which is unknown. War shirts were decorated with colored porcupine quillwork or beaded strips and were usually heavily fringed. In accord with an age-old custom of dressing in one's finest clothing when faced with possible death, no warrior rode into the fight until he felt he looked his best. Some of them believed much advance preparation was necessary, but this did not affect their fighting courage once they were in the battle. About fifteen Cheyennes wore eagle-feather war bonnets, of which ten had long trails, while some forty Sioux wore similar feathered headgear. In every war bonnet worn, each feather represented a brave deed performed in battle. (Crown bonnets consisted of about thirty such feathers, but trail bonnets, which might have as many as a hundred, never had fewer than seventy.) Unless all feathers were earned by the wearer, other warriors might snatch the bonnet off his head. Several Sioux and one Cheyenne wore headdresses made from the mane and horns of buffalo bulls. One Sioux had a bearskin headdress, and Sun Bear, a Cheyenne, wore a war bonnet with a single buffalo horn projecting from its center.

Pine's experience with his father was related to me by Pine himself in 1940.

Part of this Cheyenne's immunity to lead can be explained by the fact that nearly 20 per cent of the regiment's total strength was made up of recruits, divided among the troops. These green soldiers were new to any sort of warfare, let alone the specialized training that went into Indian fighting. They, as well as more seasoned troopers, did not even get target practice before leaving Fort Abraham Lincoln!

Left Hand's mistake was described to me by Sherman Sage, one of the Arapaho's warrior companions.

The story of Walking Blanket Woman was told to me by Black Elk. Also known as Mary Crawler, she died in 1936.

The mass suicide of C Company was described to me by Black Wolf, Pine, Limpy, Bobtail Horse, Rising Sun, Red Fox, and Dives Backward—all Northern Cheyennes. Wooden Leg, also a Cheyenne, described the same incident to his friend, Dr. Thomas B. Marquis.

Aged thirty-eight, Chief Lame White Man was therefore

close to the forty-year mark at which warriors among the Sioux and Cheyennes were compelled by custom to retire. Other tribes, such as the Crow, had no such age limit, and Washakie, chief of the Wind River Shoshonis, once went on the warpath at the age of seventy-five. Any man who had a son in the battle was not expected to fight, but each family in the village was required to furnish at least one warrior in the common defense.

The suicide of the escaping officer led some Sioux and Cheyennes into believing later that he might have been Long Hair Custer. The story of Custer's suicide, however, seems to have sprung from other sources.

"Brother-friends" were invariably closer than blood brothers, who often stayed somewhat aloof from each other because of age differences. The brother-friend relationship called for unlimited loyalty and was the normal pattern of Indian friendship.

"Counting coup" or striking the enemy was the basis of all Plains Indian warfare. It was far more important for a warrior thus to prove his courage than to kill the enemy outright. For the last there was no reward unless he also struck him. Weapons used in counting coup were lances, war clubs, bows, quirts, or gun barrels. Sometimes a warrior carried a special coupstick for the purpose. Bent at one end somewhat like a shepherd's crook, it carried no sharpened point or blade. If he had no weapons, a man might strike his enemy with the flat of his hand. Fists were seldom used. Among the Cheyennes, as many as three warriors might strike the same enemy and earn battle honors. The first warrior usually shouted, *"Ah haih!* I am first!"* so there could be no argument about his having been first to touch the enemy. The Sioux and the

Arapahoes allowed four coups on one enemy. Coup claims were carefully ironed out during kill-talks after a fight.

The word "coup," meaning blow in French, was applied to the Indian custom of striking an enemy by early French-Canadian trappers. A warrior who had counted a first coup was entitled to paint his face black with buffalo blood mixed with cottonwood buds or rye-grass ashes. Black was the color of victory. Signifying the end of hostilities, it meant that revenge was accomplished on the enemy and that the war spirit now lay dead like burned-out coals. One who had counted a second coup might unbraid his hair and wear it loose for a while, but he could not paint his face black. A warrior who had killed an enemy after striking him could wear an erect eagle feather in his hair. One who had struck the enemy without killing him wore the feather in a horizontal position but with equal honor. A wounded warrior often painted his "honor" feathers bright red or notched them according to the number of wounds received.

At one time the Sioux took enemy heads. Prior to the arrival of whites on the Plains, they and the Cheyennes had learned the more refined art of scalping from Indians farther east who had been taught how to do it by the British during the French and Indian Wars. Scalps, however, were mere trophies and did not represent battle honors. Normally they were kept only a short time, until the scalp dance had been held to celebrate a victory or successful raid. It was customary for warriors upon their return from battle to give scalps to their women-folk, who would sew them to small willow hoops which they tied to long poles. After drying them properly in the sun, the women would wave them proudly during the scalp dance. Sometimes bits of enemy hairs were saved to fasten onto war shirts or to braid into a person's own locks to make them seem longer.

Sitting Bull's warning to his warriors against looting was told to me by his nephew, White Bull, who nevertheless took two pairs of soldiers' breeches which he later gave to his father, Makes Room.

Woman-Who-Walks-with-the-Stars actually did better at Little Big Horn than her husband, Crow Dog, who succeeded only in capturing three badly shot-up cavalry horses. Her story was told to me in 1941 by Hollow Horn Eagle and Brave Bird, both Brûlé survivors.

Mitch Bouyer may also have been killed down by the river toward the end of the battle. Sherman Sage, Arapaho warrior in the fight, told me in 1939 that a man in a calfskin vest and a soldier with a bugle and a carbine escaped from the ridge and got down to the river, reaching the west bank before the Sioux and Cheyennes found them. Bouyer, it was said, begged the Indians to kill him, which they eventually did. His body was thrown into the river along with that of the bugler. The story rings true, for the Arikara scouts knew Bouyer as Man-with-a-Calfskin-Vest rather than as Two Bodies, and it is probable he was wearing such a garment the day of the fight.

My Indian informants have agreed unanimously that no man of Custer's command escaped them. Nevertheless, stories of Custer survivors have been legion. As recently as the early 1950's, grizzled old characters have been brought out of obscurity to tell hair-raising tales of escape—even on television. Such claims have been supported by extremely thin evidence, if any. However, it is true that the bodies of at least six members of Custer's command were never recovered. They were Lieutenants Sturgis, Porter, and Harrington, Dr. Lord, and two enlisted men. Captain Benteen described, in a letter to his wife dated July 4, 1876, the finding of Porter's and Sturgis's clothes in the deserted village, implying that these men were taken captive and tortured to death. Scout Herendeen's statement, made on July 7, 1876, reads: "The heads of four white soldiers were found in the Sioux camp that had been severed from their trunks, but the bodies could not be found on the battlefield or in the village." All Indian accounts deny categorically taking prisoners or inflicting torture on living enemies at Little Big Horn. The Sioux recall that one trooper on a runaway horse galloped quite a distance through the village before he was brought down, but he was one of Reno's command. If any of Custer's men got away, the Indians never admitted it, and no authentic "survivors" ever returned to the white man's world.

In August of 1876, General (then Captain) E. S. Godfrey discovered the carcass of a Seventh Cavalry horse at the mouth of the Rosebud River, some miles from Little Big Horn. Shot in the head, the animal had apparently been killed for meat. Its saddle leather had been cut away, possibly to be used in fashioning a crude raft. A carbine had been found near the carcass, indicating a white man had ridden the animal, for no Indian would have abandoned such a valuable weapon. No trace of the rider was ever found. Willis Rowland told me in 1940 that, some years after the battle, he and another Cheyenne had found human bones fifteen miles east of the battlefield. He concluded they were those of a trooper who had been clubbed and stripped and left for dead by the Sioux but had regained consciousness and wandered away into the badlands to die of exposure. In 1926, a week before the fiftieth

251

anniversary of the Custer fight, a Crow Indian named High Medicine Rock came across a man's skeleton a mile and a half southeast of the battlefield. Buttons, bits of rotted cloth, and an old Seventh Cavalry carbine saddle boot identified the bones as those of a stray trooper, while a Sioux arrowhead imbedded in the neck vertebrae showed how one of Custer's soldiers had met his end.

Sundown

The story of Sitting Bull asking his people to mourn for the dead soldiers was told to me by One Bull, the chief's younger nephew. White Bull was more the vigorous man of action, while One Bull, no less courageous, seemed to have deeper insight into matters pertaining to tribal government. Both nephews later became chiefs in their own right—One Bull of the Hunkpapas, White Bull of the Minneconjous.

Among other charges later leveled against him, Reno was accused of having slapped a civilian teamster, of having been drunk during the afternoon and night of the siege, and of proposing that all able-bodied survivors make a run for safety, leaving the wounded behind on Reno Hill. None of these charges was substantiated during the Reno Court of Inquiry in 1879. (See "The Legend," p. 196.)

Had Reno chosen to leave the bluff and take his command back the way they had come, no Indian would have stood in his way, according to all Indian informants who fought around Reno Hill. By that time, the warriors felt they had won a sufficient victory to convince the soldiers of their foolishness in attacking the village and most of them felt the survivors should be allowed to warn other troops out of the area.

In later years White Bull became convinced that he had killed Long Hair. He told me in 1939 that he was the warrior who had slain the soldier-chief and that I was the *first* white man to whom he had confessed. Although the facts of his story were well known to other Sioux, many of whom substantiated his claim, I felt compelled at the time to follow the wishes of his son, James, who feared that publication of the story might result in harm coming to the old man.

Within Army circles and in the press, the horse Comanche enjoyed lasting fame until his death in 1891. Widely known as "the only living thing found on the battlefield of the Little Big Horn," the claybank gelding was actually one of several badly wounded animals discovered by First Lieutenant Henry Nolan of the Seventh Cavalry, acting quartermaster on General Terry's staff. Nolan was a member of an advance party led by First Lieutenant Bradley, who was scouting the Custer battlefield three days after the fight and discovered the dead bodies of Custer's command. Unable to move under his own power, Comanche was taken down-river to the steamer *Far West* and was returned to Fort Abraham Lincoln where he finally recovered from his wounds. Never ridden again, draped in black and with boots set backward in the stirrups of his saddle, the little horse was an important part of all regimental ceremonies. After his death at Fort Riley, Kansas, Comanche's body was mounted and exhibited at the Columbian Exposition in Chicago, in 1893. It is now in a glass case in the rotunda of the natural science building on the campus of Kansas University.

Bloody Knife, who was half Sioux, was not the only tie the

hostiles had with the Arikara tribe. The father of Two Moon, Cheyenne fighting leader, was a full-blooded Arikara.

Plains Indians have had a long-standing belief, probably inspired by missionaries, that whisky is the root of all the white man's evil. For many years Indians were prohibited by Federal law from buying and drinking alcoholic beverages. This law was derived from early treaties in which, at the request of the signing chiefs, stipulation was made that no liquor was to be brought into Indian territories by whites. Oddly enough, this was long one of the few provisions of the treaties which the white man's Government kept. Considered discriminatory, the anti-liquor law for Indians was repealed in 1953. Although now free to drink outside their reservations, many Indians still attribute Custer's downfall to the effects of alcohol. It is true that until noon of June 23, 1876, sutler James Coleman sold whisky and grog to Seventh Cavalry troopers on the deck of the *Far West*, and that they all presumably rode up the Rosebud with full canteens bubbling with liquor. It is doubtful, however, that much remained by the afternoon of the 25th or that even a canteenful would have gotten a hard-drinking trooper drunk.

As far as is known, a complete list of Indian casualties at Little Big Horn has never before been published. Sioux names were provided by White Bull, One Bull, Kills Alive, Feather Earring, Black Elk, Iron Hawk, High Eagle, Iron Hail (Dewey Beard), Eagle Bear, and White Cow Bull. Cheyenne names were given to me by Black Wolf, Rising Sun, Pine, Red Fox, Limpy, Bobtail Horse, Eagle Nest, Little Chief, Dives Backward, and Willis Rowland. A breakdown of the casualties is as follows:

Indians killed in bottoms fighting Reno's command:

3	Hunkpapas:	Swift Bear, White Buffalo, Long Road
1	Two Kettle:	Chased-by-Owls
2	Sansarcs:	Two Bears, Standing Elk
1	Ogalala:	White Eagle
1	Cheyenne:	Whirlwind

8 Total

*   *   *

Indians killed at the bluff fighting Reno's command:

1	Sansarc:	Long Robe
1	Hunkpapa:	Hawk Man

2 Total

*   *   *

Indians killed on the ridge fighting Custer's command:

2	Hunkpapas:	Rectum (Guts), Red Face
3	Sansarcs:	Long Dog, Elk Bear, Cloud Man, Kills-Him
4	Ogalalas:	Many Lice, Bad-Light-Hair, Young Skunk, Black White Man
2	Minneconjous:	High Horse, Long Elk
11	Cheyennes:	Left Hand, Owns-Red-Horse, Black Cloud, Flying By, Bearded Man (Mustache), Swift Cloud, Noisy Walking, Limber Bones, Hump Nose, Black Bear, Lame White Man

22 Total

32 Grand Total Indians killed

That night of June 25, 1876, was particularly harrowing for four men of Reno's command. Cut off during Reno's retreat to the bluff, they were left surrounded in dense brush. Sergeant O'Neill of G Company had attempted to escape with his troop commander, Lieutenant McIntosh, but had dashed back into the brush after his horse was shot from under him. Presently, he had found Lieutenant DeRudio of A Company. Later the two men located Billy Jackson, one of the mixed-blood Piegan scouts, and Fred Girard, interpreter for the Arikara scouts. All four lay breathless under a scattering of leaves and sticks while Sioux women poked through the underbrush, picking up their dead and wounded. Tense moments passed as the women stripped and mutilated the bodies of fallen soldiers. Tortured by intense thirst, O'Neill's discomfort was increased by a bloody nose. Only after dark were they able to crawl through the thicket and make their way to the riverbank. One by one, they drank hastily from Jackson's slouch hat. Jackson and Girard, who had ponies tethered in the brush, went to find them. They finally abandoned the animals when an Indian war party rode near. Moving upstream in the darkness, the scout and the interpreter rejoined Reno on the bluff without further incident. DeRudio and O'Neill, however, ran headlong into the war party. DeRudio fired twice, O'Neill once, before they turned and ran several hundred yards downstream. The desperate men plunged through neck-deep water to reach a tiny island, only to discover themselves in the middle of a shallow ford. Soon a column of troops rode up in the darkness, led by a rider in a buckskin jacket. Thinking they must be Custer's command, DeRudio shouted, "Hey, Tom Custer!" The troops whirled and answered with shrill war cries. To their horror, the two soldiers saw that the "troops" were Indian warriors in captured uniforms. From their uneven ranks a raucous bugle sounded, blaring out a savage challenge no trooper ever heard before, as the hostiles charged. DeRudio and O'Neill poured eight shots into the massed chargers, heard splashes as two Indians fell or jumped into the water. The uniformed Indians answered with a volley, then swirled away in the darkness. Taking what cover they could, the two soldiers waited grimly for them to return to the attack. It never came. By five o'clock on the afternoon of the next day, the twenty-sixth, after an agonizing day and a half of terror, the two exhausted men crawled out of hiding and stumbled upstream until they reached Reno Hill and comparative safety.

This kill-song, celebrating the victory over Long Hair, was taught to me by Black Elk, Iron Hawk, and High Eagle in 1947.

Aftermath

Sergeant Charles Windolph was lying beside Trooper Jones when he was killed in the trenches on Reno Hill. The soldier, the heel of his boot shot away, was within a few yards of Windolph's own position. Benteen highly regarded Windolph's talent with firearms, and had placed him with other sharp-shooters at the outer perimeter of Reno's defenses. By a quirk of fate, he happened to be opposite White Cow Bull's position. Although Windolph and White Cow Bull never met, so far as I know, both men told me their separate stories which I have here correlated.

The story of the wounding of Knife Chief was told to me

by his son, Andrew Knife, who is still living at Pine Ridge Agency, South Dakota.

After 1876, the Sioux and Cheyennes held no victory dance until Armistice Day, November 11, 1918.

Plains Indians enjoyed an almost pure democracy. The will of the people controlled the chiefs, and every adult male had a voice in the affairs of the tribe. No council was held in secret and all within earshot might hear everything that was said. For those who were not present, mounted criers later announced all important decisions of council. Land cession was one of several tribal matters in which a three-fourths majority vote was required. Red Cloud's signing of the nefarious Treaty of 1877 without the consent of his people was indicative of the growing deterioration of old tribal forms and customs.

After years of fierce struggle to win for his people the right to live in their native Montana, Little Wolf suffered deep personal tragedy. When one of his wives was seduced by a warrior named Starving Elk, Little Wolf shot him dead. Under Cheyenne tribal law, a chief was not permitted to take offense at such an injury, and no Cheyenne could take the life of another lest the sacred arrows be blooded. Before the council could take action, Little Wolf voluntarily accepted his punishment—permanent banishment from his people. Renouncing all rights as a chief, he was "thrown away" and never again ate or smoked with his tribesmen. In 1892, the Northern Cheyennes named Sun Road as Little Wolf's successor.

When the Hunkpapas crossed into Canada in 1877, old Four Horns went on ahead of Sitting Bull and became known as the actual leader of the tribe. According to One Bull, however, Four Horns's capacity was strictly that of a *civil* leader, whereas Sitting Bull was still *fighting* leader and head chief of the Hunkpapas as long as he lived. Not all of Sitting Bull's band returned with him in 1881. On November 12, 1956, Julia Lethbridge died at Fort Qu'Appelle, Saskatchewan, at the age of ninety. She was believed to be the last direct follower of Sitting Bull in Canada.

Black Elk became a high priest of the Ghost Dance in 1890-91. Along with Kicking Bear and Short Bull, he was a foremost leader of the movement. In later years he traveled with Buffalo Bill Cody and finally became a lay reader in the Catholic Mission near Pine Ridge Agency. A haranguer during the Ghost Dances, Iron Hawk never fully accepted any of the white man's ways. Both men took the spirit trail in 1950.

Among those slain at Wounded Knee on December 29, 1890, was a small group of Sitting Bull's Hunkpapas who had fled their reservation, Standing Rock, after the murder of their chief. They joined Big Foot and his Minneconjous in time to be slaughtered by a vindictive Seventh Cavalry.

The Legend

Curley never told his complete story to a white man. In 1913, while going over the Custer Battlefield with E. A. Brininstool and an agency employee named Squires, the former scout seemed ready at last to tell his tale. Squires unaccountably began to tease Curley about his trip to Washington right after the Custer fight. Curley set his jaw and no amount of coaxing could ever get him to tell his story to a white man after that. What is known of Curley's own version comes largely from Russell White Bear, a Crow Indian and Curley's kinsman. Curley died in 1923.

One prominent proponent of the theory that Custer committed suicide was Colonel Richard Irving Dodge. In his book, *Our Wild Indians,* published in 1883, he wrote: "Custer's body was found unscalped and unmutilated. My knowledge of Indians convinces me that he died by his own hand."

The Sioux City *Journal* incident has been preserved for posterity by John Edward Hicks in his *Adventures of a Tramp Printer.*

Variants of the Curley story have him cowering in the carcass of a buffalo instead of that of a horse.

Contributing to Reno's final downfall was his seduction of a fellow officer's wife in the early 1880's, an incident which resulted in his being cashiered out of the Army for "conduct unbecoming to an officer and a gentleman."

The story of Bison, the curious West Point cadet, was found in W. Fletcher Johnson's *Red Record of the Sioux,* published in 1891.

A number of whites and mixbloods, largely of French-Canadian descent, lived among the hostile tribes as squaw men and traders. William Rowland, according to his half-Cheyenne son Willis, had run away from home as a youngster to join the Cheyenne tribe. Nick Genneiss and Baptiste (Big Bat) Poirier were old fixtures in the Sioux Nation by 1876. Frank Grouard, a Sandwich Islander thought by the Indians to be a mixblood, had long association with the Sioux. Frank Huston, a former Confederate officer and "unreconstructed Reb" as he called himself, had lived among the hostiles since the end of the Civil War. Although Huston later admitted to having been on his way to Little Big Horn and was fifty miles away at the time of the Custer battle, none of these men were actually in the hostile village the day of the fight. Indians have insisted no whites or mixbloods were then with them.

Buffalo Bill Cody made an effort to "rescue" Sitting Bull before McLaughlin's Indian police could assassinate the aging chief. The agent was wise to Cody's failing and saw to it that the showman-scout was drunk under the table with the help of a relay of co-operative Army officers from the nearby garrison at Fort Yates. In his cups, Cody never made it to Sitting Bull's camp and the chief was killed according to plan.

Several burials and reburials of dead soldiers at Custer Battlefield make the location of many of the present markers all but meaningless. There is still some question as to the place where Custer's body was found. Bradley's report indicates that it was lying on top of other soldiers' bodies somewhat down the *west* slope of the hogback ridge. White Bull's account substantiates this location. The Cheyennes, on the other hand, were in disagreement. Only Weasel Bear remembered seeing Custer's body on the west slope. Other Cheyennes, including Two Moon, Harshay Wolf, and Medicine Bear, all of whom claimed to have counted coup on the body, insisted it had been lying on the *east* slope, a hundred paces or so from the present monument. A story of questionable authenticity has been told for years among the Cheyennes about how a number of them, having recognized Custer's body, moved it all the way upstream to Reno Hill, then sought to open communication with Reno by means of a white flag. At Reno's refusal to parley, the Indians had then carried the body all the way back to where they had discovered it! Although the tale otherwise defies credence, it might explain two possible locations for Custer's body if the warriors who had moved it back and forth forgot its exact placement.

Goes Ahead's three wives, all sisters, were Standing Medicine Rock, Pretty Shield, and Two Scalps. Pretty Shield, though the second to marry the scout, considered herself his great favorite and was the only one of the three to bear him children. At all tribal functions she rode his war horse and carried his shield, among the Crows the privilege of the favorite wife.

After Little Big Horn the hostiles had good reason not to trust the white man's sense of justice. Like Sitting Bull, Inkpaduta led his Santees across the border into Canada, for he well remembered the public hanging of thirty-eight of his tribesmen at Mankato, Minnesota, on December 26, 1862, after the abortive Little Crow uprising.

Among the nobler attempts to immortalize Custer was John Greenleaf Whittier's "On the Little Big Horn."

Bradley's report on the finding of the dead at Custer Battlefield mentions that "Tom Custer's belly had been cut open and entrails were protruding." Although "no examination was made to determine if his vitals had been removed," this cursory look at a decomposing corpse was considered enough evidence upon which to base the myth that his heart had been cut out and eaten.

The amount of Wanamaker's reward to the "Indian Who Killed Custer" was never publicly disclosed, but the Cheyennes say it was a thousand dollars in cash and enough fresh beef to feed all the bands represented at the Last Great Indian Council.

Until his death in 1932, at the age of eighty-seven, Brave Bear never had much to say about his honorary distinction as the Slayer of Custer. His one and only statement on the Custer fight was: "I was in the Battle of the Little Big Horn. The Indians called the General 'Long Hair.' It is a fight I do not like to talk about."

INDIAN INFORMANTS

(all are now deceased)

ARAPAHOES
  NORTHERN ARAPAHO (enrolled at Wind River Agency, Wyoming)
    Sherman Sage

ARIKARA
  ARIKARA (enrolled at Fort Berthold, North Dakota)
    Jerome Good Elk

CHEYENNES
  NORTHERN CHEYENNES (enrolled at Lame Deer, Montana)
    Bear Comes Out
    Black Wolf
    Blind Man
    Bobtail Horse
    Dives Backward
    Limpy
    Little Chief
    Little Head
    Pine
    Rising Sun
    Strange Owl
    Turkey Legs
    Two Birds
    Walking Bear
    Weasel Bear
    Wolf Road
    Young Little Wolf
    Young Two Moon

SOUTHERN CHEYENNES (enrolled at El Reno, Oklahoma)
  Eagle Nest
  Yellow Eyes

SIOUX

  BLACKFEET (enrolled at Standing Rock Agency, North Dakota)
    Standing Bear
  BRÛLÉS (enrolled at Rosebud Agency, South Dakota)
    Brave Bird
    Coffee
    Crazy Bull
    Elk Thunder
    Grass Rope (enrolled at Lower Brûlé Agency, South Dakota)
    High Bald Eagle
    Hollow Horn Eagle
  HUNKPAPAS (enrolled at Standing Rock Agency, North Dakota)
    Bear Soldier
    Belt
    Black Bear
    Callous Leg
    Care Moccasin
    Feather Earring
    Iron Hawk   ⎱ enrolled at Pine Ridge Agency,
    John Sitting Bull ⎰ South Dakota
    Kills Alive
    Kills Pretty Enemy
    Looking Horse
    Male Bear
    One Bull—hereditary chief
    One Elk
    White Bird
    White Horse
    Walking Hunter

MINNECONJOUS (enrolled at Cheyenne River Agency, South Dakota)
  Bear Stop
  Bull Eagle
  Ghost Dog
  Iron Hail (Dewey Beard) [enrolled at Pine Ridge Agency, South Dakota]
  Little Skunk
  White Bull—hereditary chief
OGALALAS (enrolled at Pine Ridge Agency, South Dakota)
  Black Elk
  Blue Horse
  Comes Again
  Drags-the-Rope
  Eagle Bear
  Eagle Elk
  Fools Crow
  High Eagle
  Holy Rock
  Kills-a-Hundred
  Little Warrior
  Long Commander (Fast Hawk)
  Moves Camp
  One Feather
  Pemmican
  Red Paint
  Sitting Eagle
  Straight Forehead
  White Cow Bull
  White Eagle
SANSARCS (enrolled at Cheyenne River Agency, South Dakota)
  Butcher (Afraid-of-Him)
  Did-Not-Go-Home
  Elk Head
  Old Eagle (Amos Clown)
  Two Runs

INDIANS *OTHER* THAN INFORMANTS
MENTIONED IN BOOK

ARIKARA INDIAN SCOUTS
>Bear's Eyes
>Black Fox
>Bloody Knife
>Bob-tailed Bull—chief
>Bull-in-the-Water
>Bush
>Crooked Horn
>Forked Horn
>Good Face
>Goose
>Horns-in-Front
>Little Sioux
>Long Bear
>One Horn
>Owl
>Red Bear
>Red Foolish Bear
>Red Star
>Running Wolf
>Scabby Face
>Soldier
>Stab (Stabbed)
>Two Strikes
>Young Hawk

CROW INDIAN SCOUTS
>Curley
>Goes Ahead
>Hairy Moccasin
>Half Yellow Face—leader
>White-Man-Runs-Him
>White Swan

HOSTILES
>ARAPAHOES
>Left Hand

266

Waterman
Yellow Eagle
Yellow Fly
BLACKFEET SIOUX
  Kill Eagle
  Scabby Face
CHEYENNES
  Brave Bear—chief
  Buffalo Calf Road Woman
  Calf
  Lame White Man—chief
  Mad Wolf
  Mahwissa
  Monahseetah (Meotzi)
  Roan Bear
  Two Moon—chief
HUNKPAPAS
  Black Moon
  Brown Back
  Crow King
  Deeds
  Gall
  Rain-in-the-Face
  Sitting Bull—chief
MINNECONJOUS
  Fast Bull
  High Backbone
  Hump
OGALALAS
  Big Road
  Crazy Horse
  Jack Red Cloud
  Walking Blanket Woman (Mary Crawler)
SANTEES
  Inkpaduta (Red-on-Top)
  Walks-Under-the-Ground

ORGANIZATION AND STRENGTH TABLE OF
GENERAL CUSTER'S SEVENTH U.S. CAVALRY, JUNE 25, 1876

On June 25, 1876, about 12:00 noon, on the slopes of the low divide between the valleys of the Rosebud and Little Big Horn Rivers, in the State of Montana, the Seventh U.S. Cavalry, Lieutenant Colonel George A. Custer commanding, was halted while Custer split his regiment temporarily into three combat groups and a pack train, in furtherance of his reconnaissance-in-force mission, to locate and pin down the Indians reported to be assembling in unknown strength.

The four separate elements of the command, with the names, rank, and unit assignments of the officers; the fate in store for each; and the strength of each troop as represented on the pre-battle rosters † of the regiment, are shown in the following table.

NAME	RANK	BATTLE ASSIGNMENT	FATE OF OFFICER	BATTLE STRENGTH PRESENT June 25, 1876		June 25-26 NUMBER		
				Officer	Enlisted	KILLED Officer	KILLED Enlisted	WOUNDED All Enlisted Ranks
HEADQUARTERS and HQ. DETACHMENT								
*George A. Custer (Brevet Major General)	Lieut. Colonel	Comdg. Officer	K	2	30	2	16	..
*William W. Cooke (Brevet Lieut. Colonel)	1st Lieut.	Adjutant	K	..	..	..	..	..
THE CUSTER BATTALION								
*Thomas W. Custer	Captain	Troop "C"	K	2	60	2	36	4
*Henry M. Harrington	2d Lieut.	Troop "C"	M	..	..	..	..	..
*Algernon E. Smith	1st Lieut.	Troop "E" 1	K	2	53	2	37	2
*James G. Sturgis	2d Lieut.	Troop "E" 2	M	..	..	..	..	..

* George W. Yates	Captain	Troop "F"	K	1	61	1	36	None
* Myles W. Keogh (Brevet Lieut. Colonel)	Captain	Troop "I"	K	2	49	2	36	2
* James E. Porter	1st Lieut.	Troop "I"	M	:	:	:	:	:
* James Calhoun	1st Lieut.	Troop "L" [3]	K	2	57	2	44	2
John J. Crittenden	2d Lieut.	Troop "L" [4]	K	:	:	:	:	:
Dr. G. E. Lord	Asst. Surgeon—	attached	K	:	:	1	:	:
William Van W. Reily	2d Lieut.	Unassigned	K	:	:	1	:	:
TOTAL BATTALION				9	280 [5]	11	189	10
THE BENTEEN BATTALION								
* Thomas B. Weir (Brevet Lieut. Colonel)	Captain	Troop "D"	S	2	49	:	3	3
* Winfield S. Edgerly	2d Lieut.	Troop "D"	S	:	:	:	:	:
* Frederick W. Benteen (Brevet Colonel)	Capt. Comdg.	Troop "H"	S	2	46	:	3	20
Frank M. Gibson	1st Lieut.	Troop "H"	S	:	:	:	:	:
* Edward S. Godfrey	Captain	Troop "K"	S	1	41	:	5	6
TOTAL BATTALION				5	136 [6]	:	11	29
THE RENO BATTALION								
* Marcus A. Reno (Brevet Colonel)	Maj. Comdg.	Troops "A," "G," "M"	S	2	:	1	:	:
* Benjamin H. Hodgson	2d Lieut.	Adjutant [7]	K	:	:	:	:	:
* Myles Moylan	Captain	Troop "A"	S	2	47	:	8	14
Chas. C. DeRudio	1st Lieut.	Troop "A"	S	:	:	1	:	:
Donald McIntosh	1st Lieut.	Troop "G"	K	2	44	:	13	2
George D. Wallace	1st Lieut.	Troop "G" [8]	S	:	:	:	:	:
* Thomas B. French	Captain	Troop "M"	S	1	55	:	12	10
H. R. Porter	Surgeon		S	1	:	:	:	:

NAME	RANK	BATTLE ASSIGNMENT	FATE OF OFFICER	BATTLE STRENGTH PRESENT June 25, 1876		June 25-26 NUMBER		
				Officer	Enlisted	KILLED Officer	KILLED Enlisted	WOUNDED All Ranks
J. M. DeWolf	Acting Surgeon		K	1	‥	1	‥	‥
*Chas. A. Varnum	2d Lieut.	Comdg. Indian Scouts[9]	S	1	‥	‥	‥	‥
*Luther R. Hare	2d Lieut.	Comdg. Indian Scouts[10]	S	1	‥	‥	‥	‥
Attached								
*George Herendeen	Civilian	Courier	S	‥	19 Indian Scouts[11]	‥	‥	‥
*Charley Reynolds	Civilian	White Scout	K	‥	‥	‥	‥	‥
*Fred Girard	Civilian	Interpreter	S	‥	‥	‥	‥	‥
*Isaiah Dorman	Civilian	Interpreter	K	‥	‥	‥	‥	‥
*Billy Jackson	Civilian	Scout	S	‥	‥	‥	‥	‥
*Bobby Jackson	Civilian	Scout	S	‥	‥	‥	‥	‥
TOTAL BATTALION				11	146[12]	3	33	26
THE PACK TRAIN								
*Thos. M. McDougall	Captain	Comdg.[13]	S	2	45[15]	None	‥	‥
Edward G. Mathey	1st Lieut.	2d in command[14]	S	‥	(84)[16]	‥	‥	‥
TOTAL TRAIN				2	(129)	‥	‥	‥
TOTAL STRENGTH OF REGIMENT				29 officers and	637 enlisted men[17]	14	233	65

† Custer may have made oral transfers and reassignments at the divide; if so, no record exists.

K—Killed

M—Missing and unidentified, presumed killed

S—Survived

Normally assigned to: [1] Troop "A"   [2] Troop "M"   [3] Troop "C"

[4] Attached from 20th Infantry

[5] Strength of 280 men was reduced to approximately 214 before reaching Custer Field, by details to pack train, messengers, and losses en route.

[6] Reduced to approximately 120 officers and men by details to pack train.

Normally assigned to: [7] Troop "B"

[8] Acting Engineer officer, normally assigned to Troop "G"

Normally assigned to: [9] Troop "A"   [10] Troop "K"

[11] 6 Scouts left to forage for Indian ponies

[12] Actual strength, about 112 after details to pack train and other losses.

Normally assigned to: [13] Troop "B"   [14] Troop "M"

[15] Troop "B"

[16] Men in charge of troop packs, 1 NCO and 6 privates from each of 12 troops, 6 civilian packers

[17] Exclusive of scouts and civilians

* Mentioned in this book

m647

DATE DUE

FE 14 '89			
MY 12 '89			
JE 23 '89			
JY 13 '89			
AUG 1 4 1989			
DEC 8 1989			
JAN 2 4 1990			
FEB 7 1990			
OC 17 '90			
AG 19 '91			
MAY 2 9 1995			
JUN 2 1 1995			
JUL 5 1995			

DEMCO 38-297